Globalization or Regionalization of the American and Asian Car Industry?

Robert Boyer, Elsie Charron, Ulrich Jürgens and Steven Tolliday (eds)
BETWEEN IMITATION AND INNOVATION: The Transfer and Hybridization of
Productive Models in the International Automobile Industry

Robert Boyer and Michel Freyssenet
THE PRODUCTIVE MODELS: The Conditions of Profitability

Jorge Carrillo, Yannick Lung and Rob van Tulder (eds)
CARS, CARRIERS OF REGIONALISM

Elsie Charron and Paul Stewart (eds)
WORK AND EMPLOYMENT RELATIONS IN THE AUTOMOBILE INDUSTRY

Jean-Pierre Durand, Paul Stewart and Juan-José Castillo (eds)
TEAMWORK IN THE AUTOMOBILE INDUSTRY: Radical Change or Passing Fashion?

Michel Freyssenet, Andrew Mair, Koichi Shimizu and Giuseppe Volpato (eds)
ONE BEST WAY? Trajectories and Industrial Models of the World's Automobile
Producers

Michel Freyssenet, Koichi Shimizu and Giuseppe Volpato (eds)
GLOBALIZATION OR REGIONALIZATION OF THE EUROPEAN CAR INDUSTRY?

John Humphrey, Yveline Lecler and Mario Sergio Salerno (eds)
GLOBAL STRATEGIES AND LOCAL REALITIES: The Auto Industry in Emerging
Markets

Yannick Lung M. (ed.)
THE CHANGING GEOGRAPHY OF THE AUTOMOBILE INDUSTRY

Yannick Lung, Jean-Jacques Chanaron, Takahiro Fujimoto and Daniel Raff (eds)
COPING WITH VARIETY: Flexible Productive Systems for Product Variety in the
Auto Industry

Yannick Lung and Giuseppe Volpato (eds)
RECONFIGURING THE AUTO INDUSTRY

Karel Williams (ed.)
THE TYRANNY OF FINANCE? New Agendas for Auto Research

Globalization or Regionalization of the American and Asian Car Industry?

Edited by

Michel Freyssenet
Department of Sociology, National Scientific Research Centre (CNRS), Paris

Koichi Shimizu
Faculty of Economics, University of Okayama

Giuseppe Volpato
Faculty of Economics, University Ca'Foscari, Venice

in association with

GERPISA

Réseau International
International Network
Groupe d'Étude et de Recherche Permanent sur l'Industrie et les Salariés de l'Automobile
Permanent Group for the Study of the Automobile Industry and its Employees
École des Hautes Etudes en Sciences Sociales, Paris, Université d'Évry-Val d'Essonne

Selection, editorial matter and Chapters 1 and 9 © Michel Freyssenet,
Koichi Shimizu and Giuseppe Volpato 2003

Foreword © Michel Freyssenet and Yannick Lung 2003

Individual chapters (in order) © Bruno Jetin, Gérard Bordenave and Yannick Lung,
Bernard Jullien, Koichi Shimizu, Hiroshi Kumon, Koichi Shimokawa, Myeong-Kee
Chung 2003

First published 2003 by
PALGRAVE MACMILLAN
Houndmills, Basingstoke, Hampshire RG21 6XS and
175 Fifth Avenue, New York, N.Y. 10010
Companies and representatives throughout the world

PALGRAVE MACMILLAN is the global academic imprint of the Palgrave
Macmillan division of St. Martin's Press, LLC and of Palgrave Macmillan Ltd.
Macmillan® is a registered trademark in the United States, United Kingdom
and other countries. Palgrave is a registered trademark in the European
Union and other countries.

ISBN 1–4039–0582–7

This book is printed on paper suitable for recycling and made from fully
managed and sustained forest sources.

A catalogue record for this book is available from the British Library.

Library of Congress Cataloging-in-Publication Data
Globalization or regionalization of the American and Asian car industry?/edited
by Michel Freyssenet, Koichi Shimizu, Giuseppe Volpato.
        p. cm.
    Includes bibliographical references and index.
    ISBN 1–4039–0582–7
      1. Automobile industry and trade—United States. 2. Automobile industry and
trade—Asia. 3. Globalization—Economic aspects. I. Freyssenet, Michel. II. Shimizu,
Koichi. III. Volpato, Giuseppe.
HD9710.U52 G54 2003
338.4'7629222'095—dc21   2002030787

10   9   8   7   6   5   4   3   2   1
12 11 10 09 08 07 06 05 04 03

Printed and bound in Great Britain by
Antony Rowe Ltd, Chippenham and Eastbourne

Contents

List of Tables

List of Figures

List of Statistical Appendix Tables

List of Abbreviations

AEU	Amalgamated Engineering Union
AMC	American Motor Company
AMI	Australian Motor Industries
ASEAN	Association of South East Asian Nations
BBC	brand to brand complementation
CAW	Canadian auto workers
CBU	completely built up
CEO	chief executive officer
CKD	completely knocked down
CNUCED	Conférence des Nations Unies sur le Commerce et le Développement (UNCTAD: United Nations Conference on Trade and Developement)
COO	chief operational officer
DFIs	direct foreign investments
EAC	Executive Automotive Committee
EC	European Commission
EEC	European Economic Communities
EFTA	European Free Trade Association
EU	European Union
FDI	foreign direct investment
FT	*Financial Times*
4WD	four-wheel drive
GATT	General Agreement on Tariffs and Trade
GAAP	General Accepted Accounting Principles
GERPISA	Groupe d'Études et de Recherche sur l'Industrie et les Salariés de l'Automobile (Permanent group for the study of the automobile industry and its employees)
GM	General Motors
HAOS	Hyundai Assan Otomotiv Sanayi
ILO	International Labour Organization
IMF	International Monetary Fund
IPO	Initial Public Offering
JAMA	Japan Automobile Manufacturing Association
KD	knocked down
Mercosur/ Mercosul	Common Market of South American countries
MIT	Massachusetts Institute of Technology
MITI	Ministry of International Trade and Industry
MVMA	Motor Vehicle Manufacturing Association

n.a.	not available
NADA	National Automobile Dealers Association
NAFTA	North America Free Trade Agreement
NICs	newly industrialized countries
NIEs	newly industrializing economics
NNA	Nissan North America, Inc.
NUMMI	New United Motor Manufacturing
OEM	original equipment manufacturing
OICA	Organisation Internationale des Constructeurs d'Automobiles
OJT	on-the-job-training
PLC	public limited company
QC	quality control
R&D	research and development
ROCE	return on capital employment
RVs	recreational vehicles
SJPVM	Shenyang Jimbei Passenger Vehicle Manufacturing Co.
SKD	semi-knocked down
SUVs	sport utility vehicles
TKM	Toyota Kirloskar Motor
TMA	Toyota Manufacturing Australia
TMAB	Toyota Members Advisory Board
TMC	Toyota Motor Corporation
TMCA	Toyota Motor Corporation Australia
TMMC	Toyota Motor Manufacturing Canada
TMMF	Toyota Motor Manufacturing France
TMMI	Toyota Motor Manufacturing Indiana
TMMK	Toyota Motor Manufacturing Kentucky
TMNA	Toyota Motor North America
TMS	Toyota Motor Sales
TMSA	Toyota Motor Sales Australia
TMT	Toyota Motor Thailand
TMUK	Toyota Motor Manufacturing in UK
TPM	total production maintenance
TPS	Toyota Production System
TSAM	Toyota South Africa Motors
TSMT	Toyota Sabanci Motor Manufacturing Turkey Inc.
UAAI	United Australian Automotive Industries (Australian version of NUMMI)
UAE	United Arab Emirates
UAG	United Auto Group
UAW	United Automobile Workers
UNCTAD	United Nations Conference on Trade and Development
USA	United States of America

USSR	Union of Soviet Socialist Republics
USTR	United States Trade Representative
UV	utility vehicles
VP	vice-president
WTO	World Trade Organization

Foreword

Over the next few decades, will 'lean production' and a generalized deregulation of trade have become the norms for the international environment in which firms and political and economic spaces will be operating? The GERPISA Group, a French-based permanent research network devoted to the study of the automobile industry and its labour force, has been transformed into an international network of researchers whose backgrounds cover a wide range of social sciences (economics, business, history, sociology, geography and political science). From 1993 to 1996, the Group carried out an initial international programme entitled 'The Emergence of New Industrial Models', a project in which it examined whether existing industrial models were effectively starting to converge towards the principles of 'lean production' – as had been theorized by MIT's IMVP (International Motor Vehicle Program) team. By focusing on what was happening in the automobile industry, the GERPISA Group's work was able to demonstrate the great diversity, and divergence, of the trajectories that firms have been following in recent times. Examples have been the wide spectrum of product policies; of productive organizations and labour relations; and the hybridization of production systems in the new areas towards which firms have been expanding. At the time of writing, there is no 'one best way' – there never has been, and there probably never will be. In fact, the first GERPISA research project made it possible to identify and characterize not one, but three industrial models, all of which have been in operation since the 1970s: the Toyotaist model; the Hondian model; and the Sloanian model (epitomized today by Volkswagen, not GM). The reasoning behind this conclusion is presented and discussed in the four collective books produced by the four working groups, which represent different elements of the integrated project: Freyssenet, M., Mair, A., Shimizu, K. and Volpato, G. (eds) *One Best Way? Trajectories and Industrial Models of the World's Automobile Producers*, Oxford/New York: Oxford University Press, 1998; Boyer, R., Charron, E., Jürgens, U. and Tolliday, S. (eds) *Between Imitation and Innovation: The Transfer and Hybridization of Productive Models in the International Automobile Industry*, Oxford/New York: Oxford University Press, 1998; Durand, J. P., Stewart, P. and Castillo, J. J. (eds) *Teamwork in the Automobile Industry: Radical Change or Passing Fashion*, London: Macmillan, 1999; Lung, Y., Chanaron, J. J., Fujimoto, T. and Raff, D. (eds) *Coping with Variety: Flexible Productive Systems for Product Variety in the Auto Industry*, Aldershot: Ashgate, 1999.

This made it possible to construct theories to explain the processes that had led to this multiplicity of models. Companies follow different profit strategies – their attempts to increase their profitability cause them to favour certain policy combinations over others (for example, volume and diversity, quality, innovation and flexibility, the permanent reduction of costs, volumes and so on). However, in order to be efficient, all these strategies have to fit in with the environments in which they are to be applied – especially with respect to the modes of income growth and distribution that are being practised in the areas under consideration. Moreover, to form a 'productive model', developed from an 'enterprise–government compromise' between the main parties (the shareholders, management, unions, workforce and suppliers), the strategies need to be implemented coherently. This analytical framework is presented in Boyer, R. and Freyssenet, M., *The Productive Models: The Conditions of Profitability*, London/New York: Palgrave, 2002.

From 1997 to 1999, GERPISA realized a second international programme, entitled 'The Automobile Industry between Globalization and Regionalization'. This project tested the thesis that globalization is an imperative for corporate profitability; and that it is the inevitable consequence of the deregulation of trade in the aforementioned 'new' areas. This was a logical extension to the first programme, given that 'lean production' was considered to be the most suitable model for markets that are variable and diversified, and ostensibly moving towards a single global standard. Firms are establishing themselves across the whole world; new industrialized nations are emerging, as a result of their having opened up to international trade; and more recently, certain automakers have been at the heart of some mega-mergers. All these events have supported the thesis of globalization, a process supposedly galvanized by the fact that companies, in their efforts to benefit from economies of scale, and from improved costs structures, are continually increasing their organizational integration, and are doing this on an ever greater geographical scale. The commercial opening of the new areas, which some expect to create a homogenization of demand, is also deemed to contribute to this process.

A previous study (Humphrey, J., Leclerc, Y. and Salerno, M. S. (eds) *Global Strategies and Local Realities: The Auto Industry in Emerging Markets*, London: Macmillan/New York: St. Martin's Press, 2000) constituted a first attempt to put this hypothesis to the test, and it did so by focusing on the situation in the emerging countries. The main objective was to scrutinize a concept that is being presented now as if it were self-explanatory: economic globalization. The authors who collaborated had all emphasized the diversity of the productive and spatial configurations that can be observed in the emerging countries.

This book aims to carry out a systematic description and analysis of the trajectories of internationalization that are being followed by the various types of firms involved in the automobile industry in America and Asia (manufacturers, suppliers and dealers). A companion book looks at the European car industry from a similar perpective (Freyssenet, M., Shimizu, K. and Volpato, G. (eds) *Globalization or Regionalization of the European*

Car Industry?, London/New York: Palgrave, 2003). Another book (Carillo, J., Lung, Y. and van Tulder, R. (eds) *Cars, Carriers of Regionalism*) analyses the process of regionalization of the auto industry in different areas of the world (industrialized and developing countries) considering the geographical level at which supply and demand in the auto industry get coupled, such 'automotives spaces' could be national (Japan) regional (EU or MERCOSUR) or still in balance (Russia/CIS). These studies identify and characterize the different processes of periodic re-heterogenization, and the conditions that are necessary if firms, and areas, are to be successful. Moreover, within this perspective, they will be particularly keen to analyse the steps being taken to allow firms' and areas' trajectories to be adjusted and hybridized – actions which in all probability will require considerable strategic and organizational inventiveness. A recent book from the second GERPISA programme particularly examines the form and the character of the internationalization of employment relationships in the automobile industry (Charron, E. and Stewart, P. (eds) *Work and Employment Relations in the Automobile Industry*, London/New York: Palgrave, 2003).

GERPISA's books are not only the result of the work done by their contributors, and by the editors who have assembled and organized them. Through their participation in international meetings, and in annual symposiums, the members of the programme's international steering committee, and the other members of the network, have contributed in varying degrees to the discussions, and to the general thought process. In addition, the books would have never seen the light of day had it not been for GERPISA's administrative staff, who take care of the tasks that are part of the daily life of an international network. We thank them all.

MICHEL FREYSSENET AND YANNICK LUNG
Scientific co-ordinators of the GERPISA programme entitled
'The Automobile Industry between Globalization and Regionalization'

Notes on the Contributors

Gérard Bordenave is a Lecturer in Economics at the University of Bordeaux IV, France. His research topics are industrial economics and the automobile industry. He has published 'Globalization at the Heart of Organizational Change: Crisis and Recovery at the Ford Motor Company', in Freyssenet, M., Mair, A., Shimizu, K. and Volpato, G. (eds) *One Best Way? Trajectories and Industrial Models of the World's Automobile Producers*, Oxford/New York: Oxford University Press, 1998.

Myeong-Kee Chung, with a PhD from Marburg University, Germany, is Professor of Economics at Hannam University, Korea. His work has focused mainly on production systems and industrial relations in the Korean automobile industry. A recent research paper is 'The Expanding Buyer–Supplier Partnership for Product and Process Technology Development in the Korean Automobile Industry', *International Journal of Automotive Technology and Management*, vol. 1, nos 2/3, 2001.

Michel Freyssenet is Research Director in Sociology at the National Scientific Research Centre (CNRS), in Paris. He is co-founder and co-director of the GERPISA international network. He is working on the division of labour, productive models, employment relationships and the concept of work. His most recent book in English is Boyer, R. and Freyssenet, M., *The Productive Models: The Conditions of Profitability*, London/New York: Palgrave, 2002.

Bruno Jetin is Associate Professor in Economics at the 'Economics Centre of the University of Paris Nord', Paris, where he specializes in International Finance topics such as currency transaction taxes and capital controls. He is a member of the Steering Committee of the GERPISA. His most recent publications are: 'The Historical Evolution of Product Variety in the Automobile Industry: An International Comparative Study', in Lung, Y. *et al.* (eds) *Coping with Variety*, Aldershot: Ashgate, 1999; and, with Suzanne de Brunhoff, 'The Tobin Tax and the Regulation of Capital Movements', in Bello, W. *et al.* (eds) *Global Finance*, London: Zed Books, 2000.

Bernard Jullien is a Professor at the University of Bordeaux (Université Montesquieu-Bordeaux IV). He is Assistant Director of the E3i group (Industries–Innovation–Institutions) within the IFREDE Research Centre. He is interested in technological and regulatory changes that have an impact on industrial organization. He has published numerous articles concerning distribution and utilization systems in the automobile industry and has acted as Scientific Adviser for Group ESSCA, a French business school that has developed an educational programme specific to the management of car distribution channels. His most recent publication in English is: 'Consumer v. Manufacturer or Consumer v. Consumer? The Implications of a Usage Analysis of Automobile Systems', *Competititon and Change*, 2002.

Hiroshi Kumon is a Professor at Hosei University, Japan, in the Faculty of Social Sciences. His main research fields are: the automobile industry, multinational enterprise, and technology transfer. His most recent publication in English is: 'Experiences of Japanese Companies in the Netherlands: Hybridization at Work', in Benders, J., Kumon, H. *et al.* (eds) *Mirroring Consensus: Decision-Making in Japanese–Dutch Business*, Utrecht: Lemma, 2000.

Yannick Lung is Professor of Economics at Université Montesquieu, Bordeaux, France. He is Director of the Institut Fédératif de Recherches sur les Dynamiques Economiques (IFReDE, Université Montesquieu, Bordeaux IV) and co-director of the GERPISA international network (Université d'Evry, et CRH-EHESS, Paris). He co-ordinates the GERPISA scientific programme 'Co-ordination of Knowledge and Competencies in the Regional Automotive Systems', and the thematic network CoCKEAS supported by the European Union. His main areas of research are the dynamics of technological and institutional changes, with a specific interest in their geographical impact (dynamics of proximity, regional development policy) and on the automobile industry. His most recent publication in English is: Lung, Y. (ed.) 'The Changing Geography of the Automobile Industry, Symposium', *International Journal of Urban and Regional Research*, 2002.

Koichi Shimizu, Doctor of Economics (Paris IX), is a Professor at the Faculty of Economics, the University of Okayama, Japan. He is a member of the Steering Committee of the GERPISA. His research topics are: studies on the evolutionary theory of the firm, labour relations in the Japanese and French automobile industry, and Toyota. His most recent publication in English is: Freyssenet, M., Mair, A., Shimizu, K. and Volpato, G. (eds) *One Best Way? Trajectories and Industrial Models of the World's Automobile Producers*, Oxford/New York: Oxford University Press, 1998.

Koichi Shimokawa is a Professor at the Tokai Gakuen University and Professor Emeritus of Hosei University, Japan. He is a member of the Steering Committee of the GERPISA. His research field is the globalization of the automobile industry. His most recent book in English is: Shimokawa, K., Jürgens, U. and Fujimoto, T. (eds) *Transforming Automobile Assembly*, Berlin: Springer Verlag, 1995.

Giuseppe Volpato is Dean of the Faculty of Economics at the Ca'Foscari University, Venice, Italy, and Professor of Management and Business Strategy. He is a member of the Steering Committee of the GERPISA. His main research interests include: industrial economics, strategic management, management of innovation, and the theory of the firm. A number of theoretical and empirical studies have been carried out in these fields, resulting in the publication of a large number of national and international contributions. His most recent publication in English is: Lung, Y. and Volpato, G. (eds), 'Reconfiguring the Auto Industry', *International Journal of Automotive Technology and Management*, vol. 2, no. 1, 2002.

1

Introduction: The Diversity of Internationalization Strategies and Trajectories of Automobile Sector Firms

Michel Freyssenet, Koichi Shimizu and Giuseppe Volpato

For most observers, the globalization of firms is under way and irreversible. In accordance with their descriptive and analytical orientation, GERPISA contributors to this book question this common affirmation, describing the internationalization trajectories of automobile sector companies: builders, suppliers and distributors over forty years. They show the diversity of ways and forms of internationalization, the reversibility of these processes observed in the past, the restrictive conditions of profitability in overseas operations, and the prevalence of regionalization in spite of globalization attempts since the early 1990s. For this reason, the automobile firms' trajectories are grouped and analysed by their region of origin. This book considers North America and Asia. A companion book deals with the European automobile industry (Freyssenet *et al.*, 2002). In the conclusion we propose to consider the diversity of the forms of internationalization, their successes and their failures, examining differences in the companies' profit strategies and the variable relevance of these strategies according to the evolutionary regional context. To facilitate the understanding of the rest of the book, we explain in this introduction the different forms of internationalization observed in the automobile industry since its beginning.

The relevance of the internationalization process in the automobile industry

The internationalization of the automotive industry is a typical feature of the establishment of the first automakers who, as soon as they were able to offer products with enough competitiveness and reliability to domestic customers, tested their luck in foreign markets, searching for the scale economies that were necessary to gain a position in an industry in which manufacturing investments were undoubtedly high (Bardou *et al.*, 1977; Bonnafos *et al.*, 1983; Volpato, 1983; Laux, 1992; Chanaron and Lung,

1

1995). But a quick thought about the history of the industry and a glimpse at the current structure of the automobile supply chain show clearly how past forms of internationalization differ from those currently being developed.

To a certain extent we could say that the history of internationalization of the automotive industry is the history of the automotive industry *tout court*, given the extraordinary role that such a phenomenon has always played, both in defining the types of competitive confrontation between automakers, and in the evolution of growth and consolidation strategies by automakers and by their suppliers.

Such a statement aims at underlining the two-edged nature of the phenomenon of internationalization in the automotive industry – on the one hand always present, but on the other hand always different, compared to that which had developed over previous years, because of the changes in automobile demand in the various markets, to the degree of maturity of the competitive challenge among industry players, to the evolution of product and manufacturing process technologies, and to the opening of the various national economies to exchanges and multilateral agreements.[1] Hence, if one chooses that internationalization, as a concept both descriptive and interpretative of some of the most relevant aspects of the automotive supply chain, has some hermeneutic meaning, it must be storicized – in other words, applied to a given historical time and described in the aspects that derive from it, with respect to any automaker.

The multiplicity of forms of internationalization

It is commonly agreed to divide the internationalization process into many stages, representing the stages of progress in the manufacturing and marketing organization of the industry's firms on a multinational scale. Given the aims of introduction here, compared to the contributions that follow, it is worth listing (albeit briefly) the various roles of the internationalization process which at the beginning was measured by the amount of direct foreign investment. It was therefore referred to as:

- The export of completely-built-up vehicles (CBU). It is important to note that, contrary to popular belief, such a first stage represents an important international involvement as well, since it implies the establishment of a decentralized marketing organization, a network of dealers and service agents, a system of parts warehouses, a logistics organization for their shipment to end customers, and finally marketing and promotion activities, with a multi-year time-frame. All this implies relevant investments, often higher than those required by small manufacturing and assembly plants. The failure of some European automakers entering the North American market, as well as of some North American firms entering Europe through various historical stages, including the most recent ones, stems from the complexity of problems that arise even during the first steps of the internationalization process, and from the difficulties shown by firms in adapting marketing and product strategies, carried out successfully in the domestic market, to the needs of foreign markets.

• Assembly abroad of semi-knocked-down vehicles (SKD); that is, vehicles partially assembled which require further operations, mainly with respect to the coupling of internal parts to the external body. It is a fairly frequent solution in the first stages of the internationalization process, but currently seldom applied outside the manufacturing of vehicles in small volumes.

• Assembly abroad of completely-knocked-down vehicles (CKD); that is, complete assembly of vehicles whose individual parts are imported from abroad.

• Assembly of CKD vehicles through component parts partially manufactured in the same country and partially imported.

• Assembly of CKD vehicles starting from components wholly manufactured in the country where assembly takes place. A further development of this stage can consist in the organization of product export flows by the foreign country where assembly takes place towards other export markets (or even return exports to the country where the automobile company is based).

New forms of internationalization

However, at the beginning of the 1990s it became evident that these forms of internationalization, believed to be the most typical and relevant within the strategies adopted by automakers, while being important, were not exhaustive, since they all revolved around a single parameter: the one based on the degree of manufacturing integration achieved by automakers in the country to which the end product was directed. Such integration was minimal when there was export of complete vehicles, but maximum with local manufacturing of parts and final assembly. With the change in industry equilibria that took place mainly in the 1990s, it became evident that internationalization is a fact that presents a range of forms which cannot in the main be related to the degree of manufacturing integration. It encompasses a growing set of features which tend to play a higher role relating mainly to organizational, financial and decision-making aspects (Boyer *et al.*, 1998; Carrillo *et al.*, forthcoming; Freyssenet and Lung, forthcoming).

The forms of internationalization referring to organizational aspects can be defined by an automaker within a continuum between two extremes: at one end an internationalization based on a high standardization of the various organizational and decision-making forms of activity located abroad, with a replication of procedures adopted in the mother company, and at the other end an eclectic organization inspired by localism, where in each individual market the organizational criteria are driven by the specific traits of the foreign situation.

Financial aspects are manifold. They range from less invasive forms of financial internationalization characterized by the forms of acquisition and the source of borrowed capital, to stronger forms that can affect the degree of international dispersion of capital, mainly in cases in which foreign placements of stocks are not acquired by individual investors, who are only interested in returns on specific investments, but by other companies in the industry which swap stocks in order to strengthen a range of agreements mainly on the industrial front. Then comes the most relevant form of financial internationalization, in which an automobile company holds such a relevant stake in a foreign automaker as to become the economic subject of reference, which inspires manufacturing and marketing strategies.

Also, decision-making aspects can be framed according to the various forms of internationalization. With the growth in forms of internationalization that has already been described, the possibility of co-ordinating on a tight basis the policies adopted by individual makes controlled by an automobile company acquires a specific meaning.[2] In the past, both because of the complexity of the phenomena and the absence of communication media that were adequate to deal with and solve the problems, the decision-making internationalization was limited. But now, thanks also to the innovation potential offered by the most recent information and communication technology (ICT) systems, the possibility of developing competitive strategies on a world-wide scale appears as hard a goal as it is a necessary one (at least as a final objective) for all its implications, and it is currently being pursued more and more firmly by all automakers, albeit with different paths and priorities. In this case as well, the forms of globalization of decision-making choices can develop on a set of areas of application. By limiting ourselves to the analysis of the forms that currently involve automakers to any great extent, we must mention at least two specific areas: the design of shared platforms, and system integration and modularization.

The search for economies of scale and scope by suppliers can be exploited adequately only with forms of further product standardization by automakers. However, it is now evident that the 'simple' forms of internationalization based on the offer of a similar model for a range of markets (the world car) turned out to be a failure. This has emerged with the difficulties encountered in transferring products within the most advanced markets – in the Triad of the USA, Western Europe and Japan, but the inadequate standardization of models will be exacerbated as emerging markets consolidate (Eastern Europe, South America, China, India and so on).[3] Therefore automakers are experimenting with new forms of standardization, more refined and complex, yet these are only partial, as they aim to use common parts without the standardization of models, which must maintain margins of customization related to both the various national markets, and the specific needs of individual end customers.[4] Such a process moves along the design of 'common platforms' capable of using a relevant number of common sub-systems, but leaves the freedom to develop the body and other elements more readily visible to the customer according to forms that are differentiated for the individual markets. It is a key move, in order to obtain considerable cost advantages, which is also hard and complex. No automaker can declare having achieved it in a satisfactory way, but all of them, without exception, are moving towards it, aware that only in such way will they solve the current contradiction between the advantage of expendable variety on the marketing side, and standardization linked to low-cost and high-quality manufacturing.

Another key element of the strategic reorganization of the automotive supply chain is the design of the vehicle in parts or systems, and the modularization of assembly. These are different features, which must be considered separately, but they share some common aspects. Vehicle design by systems that are integrated internally stems from the fact that the vehicle can be described as a set of functional groups, each of which is responsible for carrying out different tasks: the production of moving energy and its transmission to the wheels (engine and powertrain), the braking system, the vehicle driving system, the control system, and the exhaust system. In the past, such systems had, from the design standpoint, a low degree of internal integration, since they were made of single mechanical elements which could be designed with modest levels of interdependence. At the time of writing, all these functional systems have a very high degree of integration because their operation is governed by electronics. In substance, each functional system is no longer the mechanical sum of many different parts, but represents an integrated complex which can be designed in an optimal way only in a single direction, carried out by a supplier acting as system integrator.[5] On the other hand, the phenomenon of modularization does not refer to the design of individual component parts of a functional system, but focuses on its assembly and on the testing activities to be carried out in the stage which comes immediately before the transfer on to the vehicle assembly line. The module is therefore a macro-component, made up of many parts, which it is possible and economically attractive to assemble and test outside the vehicle final assembly line, in order to increase the line's simplicity and speed. In some cases, therefore, it can happen that a functional system is a module, as in the case of the powertrain of the exhaust emission system, but in other cases this may not be so. For example, the vehicle lighting system or the driving system clearly represent functional systems, but their complexity and their extension over a set of vehicle parts prevent their pre-assembly as modules (Sako and Warburton, 1999).

All these new forms of design and co-ordination of activities are linked intrinsically to the phenomenon of internationalization, since on the one hand the possibility of fully exploiting the synergies deriving from these strategies lies in the development of a wide-ranging internationalization process, and on the other because the continuing tension between the acquisition of the competences necessary to develop these highly complex projects and the constant compression of costs implies the selection both of partners with highly sophisticated technologies in the most advanced industrial areas, and partners featuring low manufacturing costs in the emerging areas.

The destabilizing aspect of the globalization process

The globalization process under way is a sign of a response to a situation of strong competitive tension, but it has become in turn a case of further destabilization depending on the variety of strategies adopted by some automakers, which are obviously characterized by different evolutionary trajectories (path dependency) and by different profit strategies.[6] In such a sense the policy of globalization, which had acted initially as a 'response' strategy to the tensions triggered by the competitive challenge is becoming, within the complex system of interdependencies of the international automotive supply chain, the triggering factor for further initiatives by companies which see themselves as being threatened by recent transformations.

The contributions in this volume describe in a rich and detailed way the variety of internationalization models developed by the main automakers in the different markets. While directing the reader to them for a full appreciation of the pros and cons of the various strategies, it is, however, worth underlining here two phenomena that are both relevant and general: on the one hand, the fast and to some extent astonishing exchange of competitive positions which marks once more a strong, diverging trend for the individual automakers, hence the sustainability of different profit strategies, and on the other hand a sort of convergence by individual automakers towards a strong attempt to reduce their vertical integration.[7]

With respect to the exchange of competitive positions, it is very significant that a considerable number of automakers who, over recent years, did show a marked level of activity, mainly through policies of acquisitions, mergers and equity alliances – such as DaimlerChrysler, Ford and GM-Fiat – are at the time of writing undergoing a difficult stage, whereas many observers, and financial consulting companies in particular, expected them to be in a stage of strong recovery. An exception in this picture is the Renault-Nissan group – the one that was credited with the hardest and most complex task. On the other hand, the highest-profitability spot is held by the PSA Group, which in the recent past was criticized for an excessively static attitude linked to the refusal to pursue a more marked policy of internationalization.

Instead, the traits of relative uniformity in the strategies of automakers relate to the forms of division of labour with the supply chain. All the main players in the industry are developing a further programme of reduction of their manufacturing borders, in order to transfer to first-tier suppliers not only the responsibility of the development of product and process innovations, but also final assembly activities. Even Toyota, notably the automaker least inclined towards this, seems to have adopted a more open position.[8]

Clearly, such a policy is based on the belief that automakers are capable of maintaining (in such a way of different sharing of activities and responsibilities) the necessary know-how in order to integrate the contributions of suppliers into a product that meets consumer needs, and featuring a brand image strong enough to sustain an adequate premium price compared to the policies of direct market entry by component manufacturers. Once again the automotive industry appears due to produce considerable novelties and surprises.

Notes

1 On the reorganization of the automobile industry that took place after the oil shocks of the 1970s, see Freyssenet *et al.* (1998).
2 We hereby refer to the concept of globalization in the meaning defined by Porter (1986) according to whom, an industry can be defined as global if there are competitive advantages deriving from the integration of activities on a world-wide scale.
3 On the NICs' (newly industrialized countries') automotive industry see, in particular, Humphrey *et al.* (2000).
4 For an analysis of the evolution of the variety of strategies developed over time by automobile companies, see the set of essays in Lung *et al.* (1999). On the concept of the world car and of common platforms, see Camuffo and Volpato (1997); and Volpato and Stocchetti (2000).
5 The key characteristic of a system integrator is the undertaking of the responsibility for the execution of most relevant technical tasks in the product/system chain, and the co-ordination of the chain's technical and operational performance over time.
6 The original instability appears to be generated mainly by the fact that the development of the motorization process for the NICs is still not enough to fully utilize the excess of production capacity accumulated by all automakers.
7 On the singularity of 'productive models' pursued by the various automobile companies, and on the links between their 'profit strategies', see the analysis in Boyer and Freyssenet (2000, 2002) and the Conclusion to the present volume.
8 On Toyota's trajectory and its recent changes, see in particular, Shimizu (1999).

References

Bardou, J.-P., Chanaron, J.-J. and Fridenson, P. (1977) *La révolution automobile*, Paris: Albin Michel.

Bonnafos, G., Chanaron, J.-J. and Mautort, L. (1983) *L'industrie automobile*, Paris: La Découverte.

Boyer, R. and Freyssenet, M. (2000, 2002) *Les modèles productifs*, Paris: La Découverte, 2000; English revised edition: *The Productive Models: The Conditions of Profitability*, London/New York: Palgrave, 2002.

Boyer, R., Charron, E., Jürgens, U. and Tolliday, S. (eds) (1998) *Between Imitation and Innovation: The Transfer and Hybridization of Productive Models in the International Automotive Industry*, Oxford/New York: Oxford University Press.

Camuffo, A. and Volpato, G. (1997) *Nuove forme di integrazione operativa: Il caso della componentistica automobilistica*, Milan: F. Angeli.

Carillo, J., Lung, Y. and van Tulder, R. (eds) (forthcoming) *Cars, Carrier of Regionalism*.

Chanaron, J.-J. and Lung, Y. (1995) *Économie de l'automobile*, Paris: La Découverte.

Freyssenet, M. and Lung, Y. (forthcoming) 'Multinational Car Firms Regional Strategies', in J. Carillo, Y. Lung and R. van Tulder (eds) *Cars, Carrier of Regionalism*.

Freyssenet, M., Mair, A., Shimizu, K. and Volpato, G. (eds) (1998) *One Best Way? Trajectories and Industrial Models of the World's Automobile Producers*, Oxford/New York: Oxford University Press.

Freyssenet, M., Shimizu, K. and Volpato, G. (eds) (2003) *Globalization or Regionalization of the European Car Industry?*, London/New York: Palgrave.

Humphrey, J., Lecler, Y. and Salerno, S. (eds) (2000) *Global Strategies and Local Realities: The Auto Industry in Emerging Markets*, London: Macmillan.

Laux, J. M. (1992) *The European Automobile Industry*, New York: Twayne.

Lung, Y., Chanaron, J.-J., Fujimoto, T. and Raff, D. (eds) (1999) *Coping with Variety: Flexible Productive Systems for Product Variety in the Auto Industry*, Aldershot: Ashgate.

Porter, M. E. (ed.) (1986) *Competition in Global Industries*, Boston, Mass.: Harvard Business School Press.

Sako, M. and Warburton, M. (1999) *Modularization and Outsourcing Project*, IMVP Annual Forum, Cambridge, Mass., MIT, Boston, 6–7 October.

Shimizu, K. (1999) *Le toyotisme*, Paris: La Découverte.

Volpato, G. (1983) *L'industria automobilistica internazionale*, Padua: Cedam.

Volpato, G. and Stocchetti, A. (2000) 'Managing Information Flows in Supplier–Customer Relationships: Issues, Methods and Emerging Problems', in M. Freyssenet and Y. Lung (eds), *The World That Changed the Machine: The Future of the Auto Industry for the 21st Century*, Proceedings of Eighth GERPISA International Colloquium, Paris (CD ROM).

2
The Internationalization of American and Asian Automobile Firms: A Statistical Comparison with the European Companies

Bruno Jetin

Introduction: internationalization, a necessary but risky adventure

The internationalization of the automobile industry is a phenomenon that goes back a long way. Most automobile firms have tried to move into the international theatre within a few years of beginning operations, first through export activities and later by establishing overseas production facilities. However, internationalization has taken on a new dimension in the context of economic globalization. The reinforcement of free trade, new rights guaranteeing the mobility of productive and financial capital, and the intensification of competition in the firms' original markets – all these factors have induced companies to try to use internationalization as a solution to the structural problems they face.

In the developed countries, the slowdown in growth, rising inequalities, the predominance of a product-replacement type of demand, and even demographic trends, have combined to make it harder to produce and sell an ever-greater volume of motor vehicles.

The profitability constraint has also become more severe. To better anticipate or adapt to demand (and to the increased number of environmental and safety-related standards), the new models that are being launched are increasingly differentiated. However, this has lead to a rise in investment outlays at a time when greater competition squeezes profit margins, causing shareholders to demand greater remuneration.

The solution to these problems can no longer be found within a national market that exists in isolation. Conversely, by making sales in as many markets as possible, some of the aforementioned constraints can be loosened.

Growth rates in the 'three poles of the Triad' (North America, Japan and the European Union) became more uncoupled during the 1990s than during the 1970s and 1980s. Renewed growth in the United States between

1991 and 2000 enabled certain Japanese and European firms to make substantial profits, which in certain cases supplemented the profits (or offset the losses) they were making in their domestic markets.

The so-called 'emerging' countries experienced rapid growth up to 1997. For the first time since the 1970s, the emerging markets' enormous potential translated into high real demand. Firms that were ready for this scenario were able to make a lot of money in these parts of the world.

To take advantage of these overseas profit opportunities without reviving protectionist tendencies (and to satisfy demand to a maximum extent while minimizing costs), most automakers were forced to manufacture in the same places as they were making their sales. This created a veritable investment race (notably in the so-called 'emerging' countries). This drive could be meaningful at the individual firm level, but at a global level it translated into a further increase in the excessive production capacities from which the automobile sector was already suffering.

According to certain estimates (PricewaterhouseCoopers, 1999), production capacities grew by 17 million units between 1990 and 1997, the equivalent of an additional North American market. This can be explained by the rapid growth of automobile demand from the 'emerging' countries up to 1997, and from the North American market until 2000. But what remained of this legacy once economic crisis struck the emerging countries (1997–8) and growth slowed down in the developed countries (2001)?

Calculated at a global level, unused production capacities were estimated to be 30% in 1990 and 39% in 1999 (PricewaterhouseCoopers, 1999; Economist Intelligence Unit, 2000). However, this average covers significant geographic variations: 40% in Asia in 1998 (PricewaterhouseCoopers, 1999); 56% in Brazil in 1999 (*Financial Times* Auto Survey, 2000); and 65% in Argentina in 1999 (*Ward's Automotive Yearbook*, 2000). At first glance, it would appear that firms that are present in all regions of the world are best able to absorb those demand shocks that can engender major financial losses. However, firms with a low level of geographic diversification can also suffer greatly in such situations, and even go bankrupt. When a fallback in growth also affects the firm's country of origin, which often remains its main market, doubts can be raised about the viability of its overseas operations. As such, the late 2000 decline in American growth led immediately to the closure of a number of American automakers' overseas plants as they tried to restore profits as soon as possible to regain shareholder confidence.

Internationalization increases firms' vulnerability to cyclical fluctuations in growth. For this reason it is at best a positive strategy for a few firms; but certainly not for all. It is from this perspective that the present chapter will try to develop a quantitative analysis of the internationalization of firms.

We shall be attempting to answer two fundamental questions:

1. What are firms' current levels of internationalization? Is there really such a thing as a 'global' firm?
2. How do international activities contribute to firms' profits (or losses)?

Although quantitative analysis cannot in and of itself answer these questions, it nevertheless constitutes a good starting point and can be supplemented by the qualitative analysis this book's other chapters offer.

At a methodological level, this quantitative analysis will exploit systematically long-term data that firms have published in their financial reports. Some will argue that this data is inconsistent because it is subject to firms' desire to publish information that is reliable within accounting and legislative frameworks which can vary over time and from one country to another. Nevertheless, and despite the difficulty of achieving total precision, we still feel that our findings correspond to the known characteristics of the firms under study, and to the events that have affected them.

In addition, this quantitative investigation will be based on the following hypotheses:

1. It will be postulated that multinational firms are not 'footloose'; rather that they are dependent upon their territory of origin, which provides them with economic and institutional support. This territory might be the firm's country of origin but it can also be the region, even if the process of regional integration varies greatly from one continent to another. Depending on the particular example, internationalization will be defined as all the activities situated outside a firm's country or region of origin.
2. Multinational automobile firms are to be considered as industrial and financial groups in addition to their car-making activities. This is indeed the relevant level of analysis for studying all of a firm's financial flows and sources of profit, rather than their physical production of passenger cars alone. Whereas, in most firms, passenger cars and commercial vehicles represent 80% to 90% of (external) revenues, there are significant exceptions. As an example, passenger cars and commercial vehicles only accounted for 55% of the Fiat Group's revenues in 1997–9; the 'motorcycle' branch accounted for 14% of Honda and Suzuki's revenues in 1995–9; and services represented 18.5% of Ford's revenues in 1996–8.

Given these hypotheses, the present chapter will be organized in the following manner: the next section is an inventory presenting the level of concentration that characterizes the world's automobile industry. We shall then measure the extent of firms' commercial internationalization, and subsequently their level of productive and financial internationalization. We shall conclude this section with a presentation of two synthetical indexes. The following section then focuses on the contributions that overseas activities make to firms' world-wide profits (or losses). In particular, we shall look at American, Japanese and French firms.[1]

The inventory

A sector's degree of internationalization is a multi-faceted phenomenon. Just using a criterion such as assets held abroad in 1998 (calculated in absolute terms), we find no less than nine automobile firms among the world's twenty-five leading multinationals (UNCTAD, 2000). Automobile firms also lead the tables in areas such as foreign sales volumes (in absolute terms) and number of overseas staff members. This is because they are among the world's largest multinational firms. If we analyse overseas business as a proportion of total activities by combining several criteria (following the UNCTAD index's transnational logic), we can see that there has been a substantial rise in the automobile industry's degree of internationalization.[2] In 1990, the transnationality index was at 35.8%, far behind the 51.1% average (all sectors combined) for the world's 100 leading multinational firms. By 1998, the automobile industry's transnationality index had risen sharply, reaching 49% and approaching the average index value of 53.9%. This was still behind the values for industries such as media (86.7%), food and drink (74.3%), pharmaceuticals (64.3%), chemicals (58.5%), and even oil (52.7%) (UNCTAD, 2000). But it is clear that the automobile industry has been experiencing a recent acceleration in its internationalization levels, thus raising questions about the existence of qualitative changes in its supply structure and forms of competition.

The constitution of a space of global competition

The automobile industry was not left untouched by the wave of mergers/acquisitions and partnerships that affected all industrial activities and services during the late 1990s. This led to a rapid rise in concentration, a development shown in Table 2.1, with its analysis of changes in the output of the world's twenty largest firms between 1985 and 1999.

Table 2.1 Changes in the level of concentration of the world automobile industry, 1985–99

Production volume (millions of units)	Number of firms		% of world output	
	1985	1999	1985	1999
4–9	3	6	42.2	65.1
2–3	2	4	11.6	17.3
1–2	8	4	27.8	9.3
< 1	7	6	9.3	4.3
Total	20	20	90.9	96.0

Sources: Calculated with data from the Comité des Constructeurs Français d'Automobiles (CCFA, 1999); and the Motor Vehicle Manufacturing Association (MVMA, 1985).

We see that, in 1985, three firms manufactured more than 4 million units, representing 42.2% of world output.[3] By 1999, six firms were producing more than 4 million units, and controlling 65.1% of global production.[4]

In 1985, two firms made between 2 million and 3 million units, representing 11.6% of world output.[5] By 1999, four firms were in this situation, representing 17.3% of world output.[6] Eight firms produced between 1 million and 2 million units, representing 27.8 % of 1985 totals.[7] By 1999, this was down to four firms, representing 9.3% of world output.[8] Finally, seven firms were producing between 400,000 and 700,000 units in 1985, representing 9.3% of world output.[9] Six firms fitted into this category fourteen years later, only accounting for 4.3% of global production.[10]

This trend towards concentration, which has accelerated with the process of globalization, raises questions about the very nature of the automobile industry. Has this sector become a 'global industry', with the meaning that M. Porter lends to this term (1986) – that is, an industry where not only are domestic markets so integrated that they form a unified market at the global level, but where firms themselves have integrated their activities world-wide, leading to the constitution of a global oligopoly? If this is the case, the six firms that produce more than 4 million units enjoy a crucial competitive advantage thanks to the economies of scale and scope they can obtain across the world – and thanks to the global integration of their innovation activities. However, the failure of the firms that have attempted to market 'world cars' and the difficulties encountered during attempts to integrate the engineering departments of the many subsidiaries located across the world's different continents demonstrates that although competition has indeed become global, the automobile firms themselves are not globally integrated companies.

As such, our six leaders do not comprise a new and definitively established global oligopoly, inasmuch as they still have to transform their relatively larger size into a real competitive advantage, notably by sharing platforms and by commonalizing components on a global scale. Yet recent experience shows that only a small percentage of mergers/acquisitions in fact succeed (*The Economist*, 1999). In the automobile industry, there have been a number of recent failures, casting doubts on the inevitability and sustainability of a global oligopoly made up of five or six automakers (Lung, 2000). The smaller firms, especially those that refuse to participate in this concentration trend, are not condemned irremediably.

The concept of a global oligopoly must therefore not be defined as a 'supply structure' that has been established once and for all. Instead, it should be defined as a 'space of industrial rivalry' (Chesnais, 1994), which 'is bordered by a type of interdependency relationship that creates linkages between the small number of large groups within a particular industry who have succeeded in acquiring and maintaining the status of someone who can compete effectively at the global level'. This is an 'area of intense competition' born out of mutual invasion strategies, 'but also out of inter-group collaboration' (Friedman, 1983). The oligopoly is global in nature because of these competition-based relationships, even if its industrial foundations are not global (in fact, they are usually regional).

This definition seems to us to be very useful for analysing automobile firms' current stage of internationalization, inasmuch as commercial internationalization is generally more advanced than productive internationalization.

This is what we shall try to verify by analysing three forms of internationalization on the basis of five quantitative criteria. The proportion of total revenues realized outside the country of origin comprise an indicator we shall call 'commercial revenues'.[11] This makes it possible to measure the degree of firms' commercial internationalization. The proportion of revenues 'produced' by subsidiaries located outside the country of origin, called 'production revenues', and the proportion of complete vehicle production carried out outside the country of origin, are factors that will help us to measure productive internationalization.[12]

Commercial internationalization is the automobile firms' most advanced form

UNCTAD (2000) studies have demonstrated that commercial internationalization has only developed in recent times. In 1993, the top 100 multinational enterprises (MNEs), all sectors of activity combined, still relied for 57% of their business on their national market. Nevertheless, commercial internationalization has been growing rapidly and represents the vanguard of the internationalization process. Foreign markets reached 52% in 1997–8. According to the same sources, the automobile sector, with 57.2%, is clearly above the average for all sectors and thus appears, at a commercial level, to be one of the world's most internationalized industries.[13]

This analysis could be enhanced by incorporating an even greater number of firms; their national origins; and the diversity of the commercial strategies they have adopted. Our own sample, comprising twenty-one firms, satisfies this objective by offering a more comprehensive vision of the automobile industry (albeit one that remains incomplete).[14] In 1995–9, the American firms analysed in Table 2.2 realized an average 51.3%[15] of their total sales outside their country of origin. Note the American firms' low level of internationalization (average 24.5%), far behind the Japanese (57%) and above all the European (72.5%), averages. For this latter subset, the domestic market is no longer the main market.

American firms' low level of commercial internationalization is surprising given that ever since the early twentieth century GM and Ford, the world's top two automakers, have been running the world's largest overseas operations (in absolute terms), primarily in Europe. It is also surprising given that Navistar is the world's second leading maker of commercial vehicles. The extremely large size of the North American market is one natural reason for this paradoxical result, but it does not explain everything. General Electric,

Table 2.2 Comparison of the degree of internationalization of automobile firms, 1995–9, and synthetical index, as percentage of total

Firms	Degree of internationalization of automobile firms, 1995–9					Synthetical index internationalization	
	Commercial revenues	Productive revenues	Production	Workforce	Total assets	Global	UNCTAD
American firms							
Chrysler (95–97)	13.1	n.d.	37.7	17.0	14.8	20.7	15.0
Ford (95–97)	34.2	n.d.	46.0	48.2	26.0	38.6	36.1
Navistar (96–98)	8.8	n.d.	27.3	11.0	8.6	13.7	9.5
GM (95–96)	30.4	n.d.	45.1	32.8	26.9	33.8	30.0
Paccar (96–99)	36.2	n.d.	33.6	n.d.	49.3	n.d.	n.d.
Average (1)	**27.4**	**n.d.**	**38.0**	**30.7**	**27.7**	**28.7**	**25.2**
Average (2)	**32.3**	**n.d.**	**45.6**	**40.5**	**26.5**	**36.2**	**33.1**
European firms							
BMW (95–99)	72.0	n.d.	49.1	41.1	61.7	56.0	58.3
Daimler-Benz (95–97)	61.1	47.5	46.7	23.4	38.0	42.3	40.8
DaimlerChrysler (95–97)	81.3	n.d.	77.0	47.5	73.4	69.8	67.4
Fiat Auto (95–99)	58.9	n.d.	41.2	34.1	41.7	44.0	44.9
Fiat Group (95–99)	62.7	38.4	41.2	39.7	45.3	47.2	49.2
PSA (95–99)	60.7	50.8	22.9	24.3	39.3	36.8	41.4
Renault (95–99)	58.2	45.7	27.2	30.8	48.5	41.2	45.8
Scania (95–99)	90.0	n.d.	74.0	50.4	n.d.	n.d.	n.d.
VW (95–99)	64.6	35.6	53.2	47.0	58.3	55.8	56.6
Volvo (95–99)	90.4	n.d.	68.1	43.5	n.d.	n.d.	n.d.
Average (3)	**72.5**	**34.1**	**51.6**	**40.5**	**54.4**	**51.1**	**53.1**
Average (4)	**62.9**	**44.0**	**45.1**	**37.5**	**53.8**	**50.6**	**52.4**

Table 2.2 continued

Firms	Degree of internationalization of automobile firms, 1995–9					Synthetical index internationalization	
	Commercial revenues	Productive revenues	Production	Workforce	Total assets	Global	UNCTAD
Japanese firms							
Honda (95–99)	69.2	64.9	46.9	73.2	53.6	60.7	65.3
Isuzu (96–99)	59.7	35.6	41.8	55.5	10.6	41.9	41.9
Mazda (95–99)	60.6	36.8	17.9	24.0	16.9	29.9	33.8
Mitsubishi (95–99)	52.5	32.9	29.8	29.7	30.4	35.6	37.5
Nissan (95–99)	56.0	51.6	39.7	71.0	37.6	51.1	54.9
Subaru (95–99)	52.1	39.2	16.6	34.7	25.9	32.3	37.6
Suzuki (95–99)	50.7	22.7	36.8	n.d.	18.1	n.d.	n.d.
Toyota (95–99)	53.5	43.3	31.0	59.8	42.9	46.8	52.1
Average (5)	**56.8**	**40.9**	**31.2**	**48.7**	**29.5**	**42.7**	**46.2**

Notes: The Global Synthetical Index is an average of the Commercial Revenues, Production, Total Assets, and Workforce Indexes. The UNCTAD's Synthetical Index is an average of the Commercial Revenues, Workforce and Total Assets Indexes. Average (1) is calculated with all American firms. Average (2) is calculated with Ford and GM only. Average (3) is calculated with all European firms except Fiat Auto and Daimler-Benz. Average (4) concerns BMW, DaimlerChrysler, Fiat Auto, PSA, Renault and VW. Chrysler's and Daimler-Benz's results are given for information. Average (5) is calculated with all Japanese firms. Italic figures are for 1995–8 only. Total assets for the Fiat and VW groups are estimations. VW's productive revenues are 1995–7 only.

which in 1998 was the world's leading multinational (in terms of total assets) makes 28.6% of its total sales overseas, a percentage comparable to GM and Ford – yet at the same time overseas sales represented 56.8% of IBM's total sales in 1998 (UNCTAD, 2000). In addition, we could have expected American firms to take greater advantage than their colleagues of their large size in order to develop their commercial presence across the world.

It remains that GM's and Ford's repeated efforts to standardize their global product range are hampered by the still highly heterogeneous nature of the preferences shown in the demand that emanates from the world's different continents, for both passenger cars and commercial vehicles. This hampers an otherwise very real chance to share components and achieve economies of scale. For example, light truck volumes in North America are higher than the volumes achieved with the infamous 'world cars'. American firms have therefore been forced to market products that are specific to each continent, thus reducing their opportunity to leverage the size advantage they have acquired in the American market in their internationalization efforts, and leaving themselves more exposed to foreign competition. This explains the highly stable geographical spread of North American firms' commercial revenues, with a predominant proportion of total sales being realized in the North American and European markets.

In 1970–9, North America accounted for 71% of Ford's commercial revenues, Europe 23%, South America and Asia/Africa/Pacific around 3% respectively.[16] By the 1990s, this breakdown had remained practically identical, despite globalization.[17] GM's experience is comparable, except for the fact that it involved an even greater initial dependency on the North American market (84.2% of the firm's commercial revenues) from 1971 to 1979. Europe only accounted for 10.3% at the time, and the rest of the world 5.5%. In 1990–9, this was rebalanced in favour of Europe (19.2%), with NAFTA's share dropping to 75.4%. The rest of the world's share of GM's total sales remained identical, with around 3% for South America and 3% for Asia/Africa/Pacific.

GM and Ford thus present a similarly bipolar geographic spread, with a strong focus on developed Western countries. The two firms have been unable to develop their market share in South America (despite the US government's very strong influence in this region), and even less so in Japan and the rest of Asia, despite the fact this latter region experienced the world's fastest rate of growth over the period of time in question.

Diametrically opposed to the American example, European firms feature a very high degree of commercial internationalization (with an Average (3) of 72.5% in Table 2.2). This can be explained partially by the smaller size of the European national markets. From the very outset local automakers have been forced to engage in export activities so as to discover the additional volumes they need abroad (and particularly in their neighbouring countries) to achieve economies of scale. This is particularly true for Swedish firms which, faced with a very narrow domestic market, realize 90% of their total sales outside Sweden, unlike American and Japanese commercial vehicle manufacturers, who feature a very low degree of internationalization.[18] Even outside this particular sub-set of firms, European generalist automakers' degree of internationalization remains high, with nearly 63% of sales being made outside the country of origin (cf. Average (4) in Table 2.2). As such, the European market has become a natural battleground for competition, much like the entity that NAFTA has created in North America. Proof lies in the European market's preponderant position (between 67% and 93%) in the geographic spread of European firms' commercial revenues (see Table 2.3). Only DaimlerChrysler is an exception to this rule, with the European market now representing only about 33% of the firm's commercial revenues (67% before the acquisition of Chrysler). Note that Europe's share has been shrinking for most firms (notably Volvo), something that is explained by the decision to increase sales in the world's other regions in order to benefit from growth in the new markets and to reduce dependency on Europe. In this respect, European firms have been pursuing highly differentiated commercial diversification strategies, as shown in Table 2.4.

Although a geographic breakdown does not enable any distinction to be made between the three poles of the Triad and the developing countries, note

Table 2.3 Europe's share (including the country of origin) in European firms' commercial revenue, as percentage of world's sales

Years	BMW	DaimlerChrysler	Fiat Group	PSA	Renault	Scania	VW	Volvo
1990–9	n.a.	66.9	79.8	92.8	86.0	71.1	76.8	60.0
1995–9	67.6	35.4	76.0	93.4	85.0	74.8	74.2	58.0
1999	64.4	33.3	79.5	93.7	83.2	82.9	74.0	55.2

Note: For DaimlerChrysler, the periods are 1990–6, 1997–9 and 1999. For Volvo, 1991–9, with passenger cars being excluded; n.a. = not available.

Source: Our own calculations with data from the firms' financial reports.

Table 2.4 Breakdown of European firms' commercial revenue outside Europe, 1995–9, as percentage of world sales

Regions	BMW	DaimlerChrysler	Fiat Group	PSA	Renault	Scania	VW	Volvo
North America	18.0	49.9	6.8	n.a.	10.0	n.a.	10.4	27.3
South America	n.a.	8.5	11.8	n.a.	n.a.	15.7	9.8	6.0
Asia/Pacific	9.2	3.7	n.a.	n.a.	3.5	4.5	4.1	5.9

Note: For DaimlerChrysler, the period is 1997–9; n.a. = not available. The total is not equal to 100% because of other countries not included in the above table.

Source: Our own calculations with data from the firms' financial reports.

that only Volvo and the three German firms have been able to build a significant commercial presence in the Triad's second pole; that is, in North America.[19] In this respect, the Japanese firms are far ahead. Fiat is an interesting example inasmuch as it owes its North American presence not to its automobile assembly activities in the strictest sense of the term but to its other group subsidiaries. Another special case is Daimler-Benz, which between 1990 and 1997 made nearly 23% of its world sales in North America, and more than doubled its sales in that continent after the creation of DaimlerChrysler. As is the case for American firms, European firms' commercial revenues in Asia (and *a fortiori* in Japan) remain less than 5% of their total sales, apart from premium brands such as BMW (9.2%) and Mercedes-Benz (9.7% over 1990–6).

Outside the Triad, European firms differ from American and Japanese firms because of their significant presence in South America, particularly in Mercosur. Fiat and Scania are the most active in this market. Mercosur represents an even greater percentage of Fiat's automobile activities, accounting for 20.7% of Fiat Auto's total world sales in 1995–8. South America provides the most accessible rapid development zone for those European firms seeking to reduce their dependency on the European market. PSA, which set itself an objective of making 25% of its total sales outside Europe by 2003, has reinforced its presence in Mercosur. Renault has announced a target of 40% of sales outside Europe by 2010, with Mercosur planned to become the firm's second largest market (after Europe) in 2005.

We should emphasize that European firms' generally high level of internationalization in fact hides a major regional phenomenon. Like GM and Ford, most European firms make around 25% of total sales outside of their region of origin (Europe or North America) because of a strong presence in a second continent. However, they are often geographically diversified to a greater extent than their American counterparts, possessing a significant presence (around 10%) in a third zone (South America or Asia).

Finally, most Japanese firms are even more geographically diversified, although the proportion of commercial revenues realized abroad is on average lower than for European firms (see Table 2.5). Japanese firms are noteworthy because they have the highest commercial presence in a second Triad pole (North America) and a significant commercial presence in a third pole (Europe). With the exception of Mitsubishi and Suzuki, all make at least a third of their total sales in North America. For Honda this percentage is 50%, higher even than its sales in Japan – the only example of such a percentage split, apart from DaimlerChrysler, which is a less straightforward situation.

The big Japanese firms realize at least 10% of their total sales in Europe. It is also the case of Toyota following its establishment of production facilities in France. As a result of this commercial diversification, Japanese firms would appear to be the least dependent on their region of origin. Although available statistics remain somewhat imprecise, we know that Suzuki alone (mainly because of its successes in Japan and India in the mini-car niche)

Table 2.5   Breakdown of Japanese firms' commercial revenues, 1997–9, as percentage of world sales

Regions	Honda	Isuzu	Mazda	Mitsubishi	Nissan	Subaru	Suzuki	Toyota
North America	50.1	35.4	31.9	21.9	33.3	43.6	12.6	36.6
Europe	12.0	n.a.	17.5	14.3	15.4	7.5	21.0	9.0
Asia/Pacific	[28.38]	46.8	[37.51]	51.1	[41.49]	[44.49]	59.9	[42.54]

Notes: n.a. = not available. Japan is included in the Asia/Pacific zone. The numbers in brackets are estimations based on the following principles: the minimum corresponds to Japan's share, the maximum to Japan's share + the share of countries from the rest of the world (Asia, South America, Pacific, etc.).

Source: Our own calculations from the firms' financial reports.

depends on the Asian market for around 60% of its business, a figure that is nevertheless lower than the region of origin's significance for American or European firms' commercial revenues.

In conclusion, the findings confirm that the automobile industry is not entirely globalized, since no firm sells a balanced proportion of its total output in all three poles of the Triad. However, if firms do reach the targets they have set, within ten years there should be an increase in the percentage of commercial revenues realized outside their region of origin.[20] American and European firms seek to reinforce their commercial presence in Asia, and specifically in Japan,[21] while Japanese firms are trying to develop sales in Europe. As competition is particularly strong in the three poles of the Triad, it is likely that only a few firms will be able to make a significant proportion (say, 20%) of total sales in each of the three continents. Hence their strong interest in emerging countries, where the potential for market growth makes it easier for a firm to gain a foothold.

The productive internationalization of the automobile industry has increased, but still remains limited in scope

Productive internationalization can first of all be analysed in physical terms by measuring the percentage of total output realized outside the country of origin, and then outside the region of origin. These first two findings will be supplemented by a value analysis that compares total sales by zone of commerce with turnover by production zone in order to evaluate the respective importance and role of commercial and productive internationalization.

Automobile firms' production outside their country of origin rose sharply during the 1990s. From an average of 27% in 1990–4, it reached 40.6% in 1995–9.[22] As such, the automobile industry has not been globalized from a production perspective, with the national framework continuing to exert a crucial influence on productive organization, employment relationships and relations with the state. But even though productive internationalization continues to rise at the same pace, most firms will be producing at least

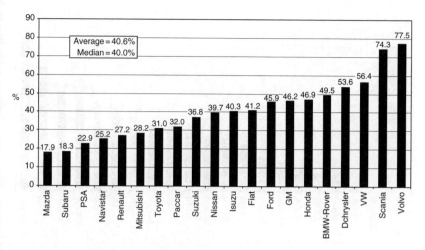

Figure 2.1 Production share outside country of origin, 1995–9
Source: Own calculations from data of CCFA.

50% of their total output overseas over the course of the first decade of the twenty-first century. Figure 2.1 shows how firms were positioned in 1995–9, with 50% of all firms realizing outside their country of origin an output that was superior or equal to 40% of their world production. Only five out of twenty firms, all European, featured an overseas production superior or equal to 50%. This category includes Volvo and Scania, who were forced to behave in this manner by the narrowness of their country of origin. There were also two firms whose presence in this leading group can be explained by their acquisition of a foreign competitor: BMW, which bought Rover in 1994 and resold it in 2000;[23] and DaimlerChrysler, after Daimler-Benz bought Chrysler in 1997. With the exception of these special cases, VW appears to be the only integrated generalist firm whose production outside its country of origin (56%) is ten points higher than Honda, Ford and GM.

This vision of an already significant yet rapidly rising productive internationalization should be fine-tuned through the incorporation of a regional dimension. As shown by Figure 2.2, which covers 1996–9, a much lower percentage of total production is being realized outside firms' region of origin.[24] This indicates that firms are more regionalized than globalized; 50% of all firms feature production outside their region of origin that is superior or equal to 19.6%, with average extra-regional output reaching 20.7%, a very low figure. Only DaimlerChrysler (54%) and Honda (43%) distinguish themselves from the pack with outcomes that are more than twice the overall average. Apart from the special case of DaimlerChrysler, Honda has gone the furthest towards productive internationalization. However, Honda's

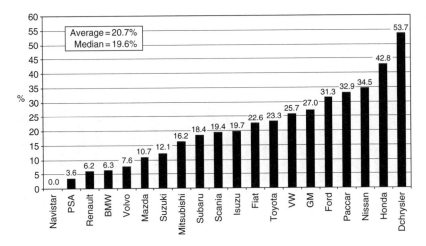

Figure 2.2   Production share outside region of origin, 1996–9
Source: Own calculations with data from the CCFA.

extra-regional production is spread very unevenly: 37.6% in NAFTA versus only 4.8% in Europe. Nissan, which manufactures 34.5% of its output outside Asia/Pacific/Africa, features a more balanced spread of productive facilities: 20.6% in NAFTA and 13.7% in Europe.

American firms' extra-regional production is just as unbalanced and concentrated in Europe: 25.2% of GM's output, out of an extra-regional production total of 27%, takes place in 'Europe and Turkey'.[25] For Ford, the percentages are 25.2% out of 31.3% (Paccar's extra-regional production being entirely located in 'Europe and Turkey'). Among the European firms, only VW (25.7%) and Fiat (22.6%) do any significant manufacturing outside Europe, mostly in South America. VW manufactures 12.8% of its world output in South America, while also producing in NAFTA (6.9%) and in Asia/Pacific/Africa (5.9%). Fiat is very dependent on South America, where it realizes 20.5% of its world output. Apart from Scania, the remaining European firms manufacture less than 10% outside Europe, although it should be said that numbers have been rising.

Apart from Toyota, most Japanese firms are characterized by extra-regional production that is inferior or equal to the overall average (20.7%). Excluding Suzuki, they all have in common the fact that basically they carry out no manufacturing in South America, and produce less than 6% in Europe. Japanese NAFTA zone output ranges from 11% (Mazda, Mitsubishi) to 19% (Toyota, Isuzu and Subaru). Production in the 'Asia/Pacific/Africa' zone can be quite significant (Mitsubishi 15%, Isuzu 22%, Suzuki 28%).

In conclusion, we are a long way from the often conjectured generalization that global firms have been carrying out manufacturing operations in all three poles of the Triad. In its current shape, international production focuses on the region of origin. At best, foreign plants have been built in a second pole of the Triad for American and Japanese firms, and some European firms; and in emerging countries for other European firms. If this concentration trend continues through the first decade of the twenty-first century, that is, if it turns out to be a durable phenomenon, we might witness the creation of firms that do manufacture in all three poles of the Triad.[26] However, given the difficulty of transforming such groupings into profitably integrated firms, it is much more likely that productive internationalization will follow a slower and more modest path involving a steady increase in existing firms' production capacities outside their continent of origin.

We have seen that productive internationalization is already significant outside firms' countries of origin, but that it remains limited to the regional framework. This in turn provides a glimpse of an incipient regional division of labour within which subsidiaries from the country of origin can play a key role as an export base destined to supplement the regional subsidiary network. A value analysis that distinguishes between commercial revenues and production revenues will help us to delve further into this phenomenon.

More specifically, the difference between commercial and production revenues, as presented in Table 2.2, helps us to calculate how important exports are to each firm's total sales.[27] When overseas sales are greater than overseas production (the sales realized by each production facility), exports coming out of a firm's country of origin automatically explains the difference.

We can then break these export flows down by main geographic zones to evaluate the regional phenomenon's significance. The results are combined in Table 2.6, which presents a geographical breakdown of exportable surpluses by firm and by era.[28] Note that the country of origin's subsidiaries almost always show an exportable surplus that can be added to the local production by foreign subsidiaries, which are generally net importers. With respect to European firms, note also that VW and Fiat, the most internationalized companies in terms of the number of vehicles produced abroad, nevertheless generate much lower revenues per overseas production facilities (35.6% and 38.4%, respectively; see Table 2.2). They must therefore be exporting a high percentage of goods and services (27.3% and 24.2% respectively; see Table 2.6). It would appear that overseas investments generate a flow of exports from a country of origin. We infer from this that overseas production is marked by a low level of local content. German and Italian subsidiaries satisfy demand from their respective countries but also serve as an export base, essentially for exports towards other European countries (and to much less an extent, to subsidiaries on other continents where firms have established operations).

In percentage terms, French firms achieve much higher revenues from overseas production facilities (45.6% for Renault, 50.1% for PSA). Above all, they are twice as high as one could expect, given the actual foreign manufacturing in which they engage (measured in physical terms). In this sense, Renault and

Table 2.6 Breakdown of exports from country of origin destined for foreign subsidiaries, as percentage of commercial revenue

Firms	Exports (+) and imports (−)				
	Country of origin	Europe	North America	Other countries	Total abroad
VW (95–97)	27.3	−19.0	−4.8	−3.5	−27.3
Fiat (95–99)	24.2	−18.7	n.a.	−5.5	−24.2
PSA (95–99)	10.6	−4.9	n.a.	−5.7	−10.6
Renault (95–98)	11.3	−5.5	n.a.	−5.8	−11.3
Honda (97–99)	3.8	−0.3	0.4	−3.8	−3.8
Nissan (97–99)	4.0	−0.2	2.5	−6.4	−4.1
Toyota (97–99)	8.6	−0.4	−2.5	−5.5	−8.4
Isuzu (97–99)	22.6	n.a.	−0.8	−21.9	−22.7
Mazda (97–99)	20.5	−7.3	−3.7	−9.4	−20.4
Mitsubishi (97–99)	17.5	−3.9	−2.4	−11.2	−17.5
Subaru (97–99)	15.0	−7.5	−3.2	−4.3	−15.0
Suzuki (98–99)	21.2	−6.5	n.a.	−14.7	−21.2

Notes: For each geographical zone, the difference between productive revenues and commercial revenues has been calculated. Whenever data are not available for individual countries (n.a.), it is included in the category 'other countries'. Fiat is the Fiat Group.

Source: Our own calculations from the firms' financial reports.

PSA are more internationalized than VW and Fiat. Unsurprisingly, their exportable surplus is two times lower (10.6% for PSA and 11.3% for Renault). It is also relatively equally balanced between their other European subsidiaries and the units they run in other continents (see Table 2.6). French firms' foreign subsidiaries are therefore much less dependent on the goods and services that their parent company subsidiaries export than is the case for VW and Fiat.[29]

The Japanese firms are divided into two groups. On one hand there is Honda and Nissan, whose revenues per production facility are very similar to their overseas commercial revenues (see Table 2.2). This explains why exports from Japanese subsidiaries only represent around 4%, the lowest figure in our sample – a confirmation that the two firms have been able to set up autonomous productive bases outside their region of origin. Honda and Nissan's Japanese exports are for the most part destined for the 'other countries' (including Asia) that also receive goods and services from North America (this latter zone features a slight trade surplus, whereas trade with Europe is more or less in equilibrium). The other firms (Isuzu, Mazda, Mitsubishi, Subaru, Suzuki) realize overseas sales of below 40% (see Table 2.2) and depend more traditionally on their Japanese subsidiaries for exports to the world's other regions (see Table 2.6). Such exports are for the most part to Asia (that is, the 'other countries' category) and to a lesser extent to Europe, where this sub-set is still running a small and sometimes non-existent productive base. Toyota is in an intermediate position, as it only exports 8.6% of the total revenues of its Japanese subsidiaries in 'other countries' and North America.

In sum, these figures confirm that commercial internationalization no longer plays anything more than a minor role for the big firms, even if it still plays a significant role for the 'small' ones. It complements productive internationalization in the region of origin, and to a lesser extent supports firms' presence in other continents.

Finally, this overview of corporate internationalization confirms that most firms remain rooted in the specific country that is crucial to their business. Although all firms have developed a commercial and productive presence in their region of origin, this is only really crucial for European firms and for certain Japanese companies (Isuzu, Mitsubishi, Suzuki). The drive to establish operations in a second region can vary greatly, accounting on average for anything between a fifth and a third of a firm's total activities (with very few exceptions; that is, Honda and DaimlerChrysler). The result is that firms' global profits continue to be highly influenced by their national context, with the international environment allowing firms to smooth out fluctuations in their national markets; and to create additional profit opportunities. This is what we shall be analysing in detail in the next section.

Internationalization, a source of profit and loss

International expansion is usually viewed as something that is indispensable for a firm's survival. Yet international activities are not always profitable, and can even be a source of substantial losses. Conversely, foreign profits can sometimes offset the losses made in a firm's country of origin, particularly when the economic situation is desynchronized from one continent to the next. In order to verify foreign profits' contribution to total profits, we have defined a contribution indicator based on the total profits realized by domestic and foreign activities. This is expressed in percentages (see the methodological appendix on page 46).[30]

Changes in American firms' international profits

Ford and GM were setting up overseas facilities from the early twentieth century onwards, first in Europe and then throughout the world. The data we have been able to gather begins after the Second World War and covers the two firms' net world profits (see Figures 2.3 and 2.4). We can see that, for GM and Ford, international profits made a positive but small contribution to world profits during the post-war boom years and up to the early 1970s. Most profits were realized from domestic activities, representing an average of 80% of the two firms' world profits – foreign activities thus only contributing an average of 20%. Then, starting with the first generalized world recession (1974–5), the two firms' paths began to diverge.

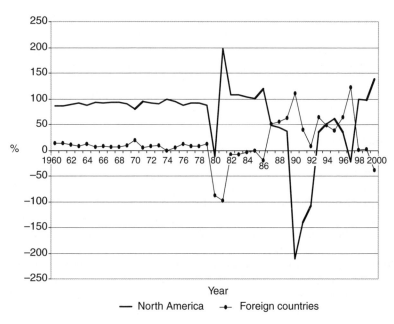

Figure 2.3 North America's and foreign countries' contribution to GM's global net profit, 1960–2000

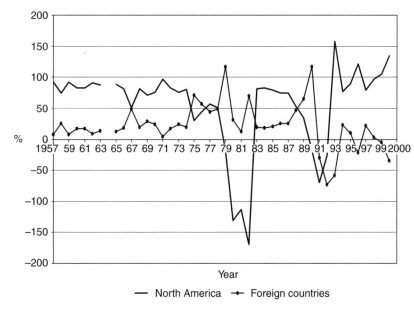

Figure 2.4 North America's and foreign countries' contribution to Ford's global net profit, 1957–2000

Ford was shaken deeply by this first recession in its domestic market, but was able to offset lower profits in North America with profits drawn from its foreign activities, which at the time represented more than half of its world profits. On the other hand, during the second global recession (1979–81), North America's preponderance in the firm's total revenues was reflected in Ford's problems in finding sufficient foreign profits (which were also in decline) to offset the losses made by its American subsidiaries. The end result was that it was no longer possible to avoid an overall loss. Renewed growth in North America from 1983 onwards re-established the hierarchy that had characterized the 1950s and 1960s (with around 80% of profits being made in North America and 20% overseas), but this was temporary. During the third global recession (1991–2 in North America; 1992–3 in Europe) overseas subsidiaries made substantial losses, exacerbating losses in North America. Subsequently, and during the entire 1990s, profits from abroad could no longer offer any significant and/or durable contribution to world profits, nearly all of which would come from North America. This change can be explained by the long duration of North American growth (March 1992–December 2000), but also by the fact that Ford was unable to adapt to a period of slow growth in Europe (1990–7). Yet it was in this latter continent that most of the firm's overseas profits were being determined, Europe accounting for 24% of Ford's total sales. From 1990 to 2000, European subsidiaries spent five years in the red, totalling US$3.5 billion of losses – against six years in the black, totalling US$639 million.

Ford's foreign profits outside Europe were nothing to write home about. The firm had been making significant profits in South America in the late 1970s, when the Brazilian market was nearing its first apex. It then lost money throughout the 'lost decade' of the 1980s. Later, Ford did not really derive maximum benefits from the rise of Mercosur (1990–7), and ran loss-making operations from 1995 onwards. It reached a nadir of US$642 million in 1996, with the firm subsequently having to take the full brunt of the 1998–9 Mercosur crisis. In comparison, Asian subsidiaries turned out to be much more profitable and were hardly affected by the Asian crisis (1997 a loss of US$33 billion; return to profit in 1998). But Asian profits did not in general suffice to offset South American losses. From 1990 to 2000, the whole of South America and Asia/Pacific/Africa recorded three years in the black, totalling US$116 million, and eight years in the red, totalling US$1.6 billion. Instead of offsetting European losses, losses in the developing countries compounded them.

Above and beyond temporary vicissitudes, there is also a structural problem. It is surprising that the main and almost sole profit source of the world's second leading automaker, whose internationalization goes back a long way, is its domestic market.

GM has to a certain extent had the opposite experience. Its North American subsidiaries overcame the second global recession better than did its foreign subsidiaries. In 1981, GM's North American contribution to world profits was about 200%, more than offsetting the negative contribution of its loss-making overseas operations (around 100%). This allowed GM to record an overall profit. During the 1980s, earnings from foreign subsidiaries (which initially were mediocre) improved up to 1987, first reaching and then surpassing 50% of world profits. At the same time, profits from North American subsidiaries developed a downward trend. Profits from foreign subsidiaries helped GM partially to absorb the shock of the 1992 recession in North America, accounting for 100% of world profits in 1997 (before collapsing in 1998–9). As in the case of Ford, these changes were mainly a reflection of the European subsidiaries' behaviour. It is specifically because of European losses that overseas activities made an overall negative contribution to GM's world profits in 1979–82, and it is thanks to Europe's positive contribution that GM was able to limit the impact of American losses in the early 1990s. South America and Asia/Pacific/Africa made a marginal but almost always positive contribution during the 1970s and 1980s. South America's contribution rose after 1992, with a jump of more than 150% in 1997, a year when South America was the only region where GM recorded net profits. This shows that GM (unlike Ford) was able to take full advantage of South America's return to growth after the 'lost decade' of the 1980s. However, the 1997 Asian crisis, which led to this region making a negative contribution equivalent to 50% of world profits, soon had a knock-on effect in South America, whose contribution became negative in 1998. The speed with which this crisis spread, characteristic of financial globalization, demonstrates the fragility of the profit opportunities that emerging countries offer to multinational firms. Even more surprising is Europe's mediocre profit contribution. Throughout the 1990s this remained below 30%, and it continued to decline in 1998, despite Europe's return to growth. This is another sign of the structural difficulty of satisfying European demand.

In sum, the results have been more positive for GM than for Ford. Foreign subsidiaries played a positive role in term of profitability during the 1980s–1990s, a period of decline for GM in North America. Renewed growth in this region during the 1990s meant that US profits superseded foreign profits from 1998–9. In 1990–2000, GM accumulated around US$18 billion of profits in North America versus nearly US$13 billion of losses. Overseas it accumulated nearly US$14.4 billion of profits versus US$883 million of losses. Internationalization has indeed been very profitable.

Japanese firms' international profits[31]

In recent years, the Japanese economy has been characterized by the strong rise of the yen versus the dollar in 1986–7, and then, during the 1990s, by the country's entry into a period of slow growth triggered by the 1991 bursting of the financial bubble (followed by recessions in 1993 and above all in 1998). In 1998–9, new vehicle sales in Japan fell below the 4 million unit threshold for the first time since 1984, and production levels dropped back to their level of the early 1980s. Against this backdrop of Japanese economic crisis, foreign markets represented a crucial source of profit.

From this perspective, Japanese automakers can be divided into two categories. On the one hand there is a sub-set with Toyota (1982–99) and Honda (1972–99), who were profitable the whole time (whether profits came from Japan or from abroad), and who were not really affected by the recent macroeconomic shocks. Suzuki is also part of this sub-set, even though its profitability is less clear-cut. Inversely, there is a sub-set with Nissan, Mitsubishi and Mazda whose internationalization strategies ended in failure (inasmuch as overseas activities almost always recorded losses that were difficult to offset with domestic profits). Subaru is in an intermediate position, having recently succeeded in rebuilding an overseas activity that had long been a loss-maker.

Toyota is a paragon of regularity (see Figure 2.5), with profits from domestic activities varying between 70% and 90% of total profits, and leaving overseas profits to make a contribution of 10% to 30%. Toyota thus remains highly dependent on its country of origin in profit terms, but is one of the few firms to have a regular flow of profits from abroad. These foreign profits stem almost

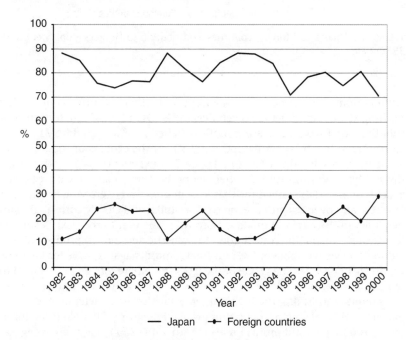

Figure 2.5 Japan's and foreign countries' contribution to Toyota's global net profit, 1982–2000

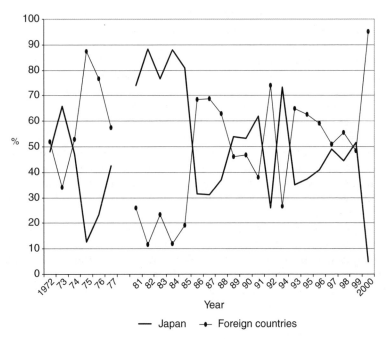

Figure 2.6 Japan's and foreign countries' contribution to Honda's global net profit, 1972–2000

entirely from North America, with Europe and 'other countries' contributing nothing at all, and sometimes even negatively. Over 1997–2000, foreign contributions to Toyota's operating profits reached 21.6%, including 21.5% for North America, −0.7% for Europe and 0.8% for the other countries.

On the other hand, Honda (see Figure 2.6) experienced a period of great instability. Apart from 1981–5, when net profits from Japan were increased by a factor of 2.4 (at the same time that foreign profits were growing slowly), net Japanese and overseas profits evolved in a similar and closely correlated manner, but with hierarchical modifications from one year to the next.[32] This led to a strongly oscillating contribution to domestic and foreign profits, rotating around an average value of 53% for foreign profits against 47% for Japanese profits in 1990–9. Honda is one of the few firms where foreign profits tend to represent more than 50% of world profits. This is the highest value found in our sample, confirming the highly internationalized character of this particular firm. With respect to operating profits, foreign profits accounted for as much as 60% of world profits on average in 1994–2000, and even as high as 63% in 1997–2000, because of substantial profits in North America (where Honda makes 50% of its total sales). North America made a contribution of

57.5% against 8% for 'other countries', and there was a loss of −2.3% in Europe, where the euro's weakness against the pound sterling, Japanese yen and US dollar weighed heavily on profitability. According to Honda's managers, the unfavourable impact of the euro's weakness should be offset in the future by internal productive flexibility (known as the 'takai' system) in factories in Great Britain, making it possible to manufacture different models using a single production line.[33] Instead of making a small passenger car aimed at the Continental European market where profit margins that were at best mediocre have been wiped out by the pound sterling's strength against the euro, the British subsidiary might choose to manufacture SUV's with their higher profit margins, and then to export them to the United States where there is strong demand (the dollar also being strong against the pound). Room to manoeuvre is limited, however, and Honda was unable to avoid losing money in Europe in 2000.

These European losses are going to weigh more and more heavily on profitability since the slowdown in North American growth means that profits in this latter region will no longer be enough to offset deficits elsewhere. Honda's extreme dependency on North America might in fact turn into a weakness.

Suzuki (see Figure 2.7) is characterized by a successful internationalization strategy, with the exception of two interludes: 1982, when heavy foreign losses were offset by higher profits in Japan; and then briefly in 1988–9, when overseas activities made a negative contribution to profits. All in all, foreign profits contributed positively and regularly to world profits, reaching 22% on average between 1983–9, and 60% over 1990–9 (this being the record among Japanese automakers). In terms of operating profits, the foreign contribution was more modest (16.7% over 1997–9) but more geographically diversified, with 9.7% emanating from Europe and 7% from North America and Asia.

The other Japanese automakers are characterized by the mediocre contributions of foreign profits, and even by the magnitude of overseas losses.

Subaru (see Figure 2.8) recorded negative contributions from net overseas profits up to 1995. This is mainly because of an inappropriate product offer in the United States combined with a rising yen.[34] Foreign losses were difficult to offset, with (lower) profits in Japan, especially during the domestic crisis of the early 1990s. As a result, Subaru recorded a net world loss over the period 1987–94. It was finally able to recover, with overseas profits making a contribution of 40% (and national profits a contribution of 60%) over the period 1995–9. Subaru was not affected by the Asian crisis of 1997–8, as Asia accounted for only a small percentage of its sales. More surprising is the fact that it was not harmed by the Japanese recession of 1998. A geographical breakdown of the firm's operating profits again highlights Japanese firms' significant dependency on the North American market for foreign profits: over 1997–9, North America's contribution was 29.5% versus a total foreign contribution to world profits of 30.5% (Europe and the rest of the world thus representing only 1%).

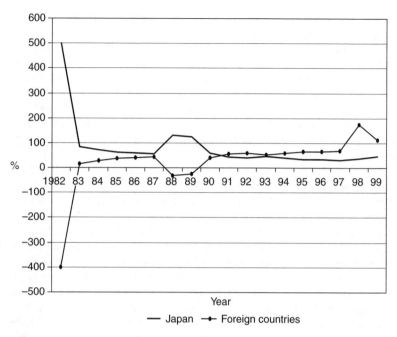

Figure 2.7 Japan's and foreign countries' contribution to Suzuki's global net profit, 1982–99

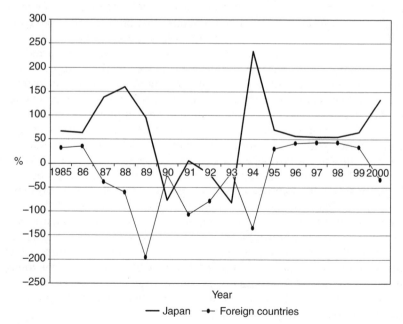

Figure 2.8 Japan's and foreign countries' contribution to Subaru's global net profit, 1985–2000

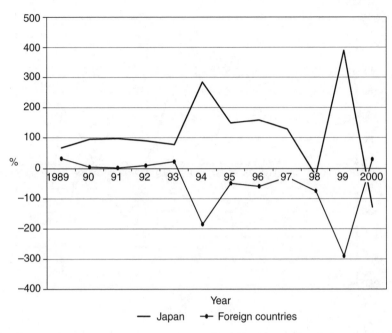

Figure 2.9 Japan's and foreign countries' contribution to Mitsubishi's global net profit, 1989–2000

The example of Mitsubishi (see Figure 2.9) is much less clear-cut. Overseas activities made only a modestly positive contribution (13%) to the firm's net world profits in 1989–93, and then made a negative contribution (−224.5%) in 1994–9. This could no longer be offset by the positive contribution (+124.5%) of the net profits realized in Japan, leading to a negative world income (−100%) over the recent period.[35] Mitsubishi was hit hard by the Asian crisis[36] and subsequently by the recession in Japan. Nevertheless, from 1998 onwards the firm's overseas activities were again in the black, thanks to strong growth in the North American market. The 1997–2000 geographical breakdown and operating profits shows a negative contribution from Japan (−1858.3%) that was offset by a foreign contribution of 1958.3%. However, this performance can only be explained by an excellent performance in North America (2988%) and to a lesser extent in other countries (30.1%), offsetting European losses (−1061.1%).

Nissan and Mazda are characterized by the almost systematically negative contribution of their foreign subsidiaries. For Nissan, the late 1970s and early 1980s were marked by foreign earnings' positive but modest contribution (12%) to world profits (see Figure 2.10), with domestic profits accounting for between 90% and 100% of this total. The situation took a turn for

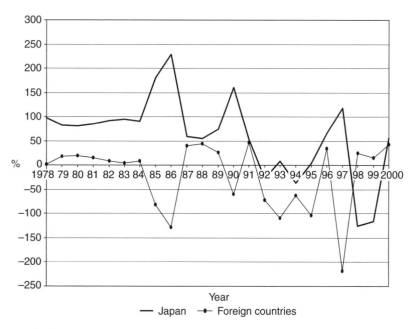

Figure 2.10   Japan's and foreign countries' contribution to Nissan's global net profit, 1978–2000

the worse in the 1980s, however, and deteriorated even further in 1992–5, when foreign losses could no longer offset domestic activities that had been hard hit by the Japanese economic crisis. The 1997 Asian crisis had an even greater impact on Nissan's foreign activities, although Japanese operations were profitable that year. From 1998 onwards, foreign profits (largely the result of good performances in the American market) were able to offset losses in the Japanese market, albeit only partially. This improvement continued through 2000, when Nissan's Japanese activities started to make money again. A geographical breakdown of operating profits again reveals a dependency on the North American market, which made a contribution of 36.9% to Nissan's global operating profits over 1997–2000, against a total foreign contribution of 37.7%. Europe was again a source of losses (−5.6%), and the rest of the world made a modest contribution (2%).

Mazda (see Figure 2.11) has a similar story. Overseas operations made a modest contribution to profits (12%) between 1983 and 1989, but almost none at all in 1990–2. From 1993 onwards, contributions became increasingly negative. The domestic profits that used to offset mediocre foreign earnings could no longer stave off the losses, given that Mazda was also a victim of the Japanese economic crisis. Despite a 1995–7 rationalization-driven recovery in Japanese profits, Mazda (like Mitsubishi) was particularly hard hit

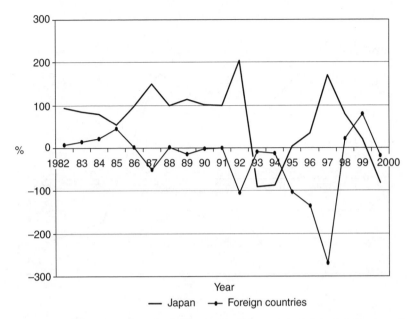

Figure 2.11 Japan's and foreign countries' contribution to Mazda's global net profit, 1982–2000

by the 1997–8 Asian crisis. In addition, Mazda is very sensitive to exchange rate fluctuations, as it depends on exports more than any other Japanese automaker (exporting more than 60% of its domestic Japanese production, compared to 50% for Toyota and 40% for Honda). It is expensive to manufacture in Japan; and the exports were being sent to countries with currencies that tend to be weak. As a result, net earnings in Japan plummeted from +30.5 billion yen in 1998 to −127.6 billion yen in 2000, whereas net foreign profits (which had recovered to reach 21 billion yen in 1999) fell back again to −27.6 billion yen in 2000 as a result of the rise in the yen.

The geographical breakdown of operating profits over this period (1997–2000) shows modest overseas contributions (3.1%) thanks to Europe (6.8%) and other countries (1.5%), and despite losses in North America (−5.2%). Mazda is the only Japanese firm that was unable to benefit from North America's long period of growth to offset the losses it was making in the Japanese and Asian markets.

Isuzu provides us with a final example of a relatively unsuccessful internationalization. A commercial vehicle and SUV maker, the firm suffered the full impact of the slowdown in Japanese growth, and above all of the 1998–9 recession (see Figure 2.12), during which time net losses reached 104 billion yen. Overseas subsidiaries made a negative contribution to net global profits

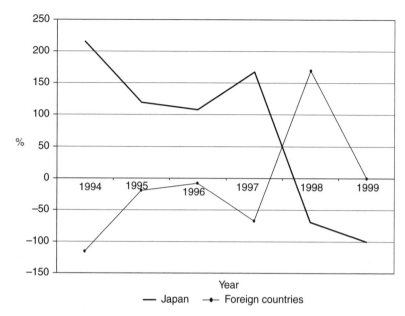

Figure 2.12 Japan's and foreign countries' contribution to Isuzu's global net profit, 1994–9

from 1994 to 1997; offset Japanese profits in 1998; and made a zero contribution in 1999. A geographical breakdown of operating profits shows that over a very short period of time (1998–9), North America and the rest of the world's contributions to foreign profits (5.1% and 2.7%, respectively) were small and in any event insufficient to balance out Japanese losses.

Changes in European firms' international profits[37]

European firms can be divided into two categories. On the one hand, French firms remained highly dependent upon Europe until the late 1990s, but on the other, Fiat, VW and Scania experienced an earlier and more successful internationalization outside Europe.

For Renault, foreign profit contribution over 1982–98 was almost always positive (see Figure 2.13). From 1982 to 1989 the average contribution of foreign profits was +59.6%, while domestic French contribution was negative (−159.6%). From 1990 to 1998, with foreign contributions remaining at 54.8%, a positive French contribution of 45.2% enhanced overall operating profits. Moreover, foreign profits played an important counter-cyclical role during periods of recession in France (1982–4 and 1992–5). However, this role was limited by the fact that Renault's foreign profits were primarily European in origin: 43.8% out of total foreign profits of 54.8% over the

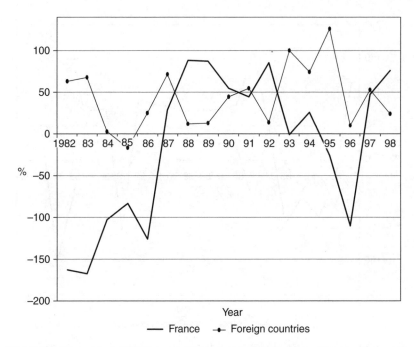

Figure 2.13 France's and foreign countries' contribution to Renault's operating profit, 1982–98

period 1990–8. As such, it was the gap (or uncoupling) between French and European growth that allowed European profits to offset French losses. Finally, the overseas subsidiaries' ability to absorb potential French losses was hampered by the fact that Renault's centre of gravity was still in France at that time. From 1987 to 1998, foreign profits remained surprisingly stable, revolving around an average value of 1.7 billion French francs, whereas French subsidiaries' profits fluctuated wildly around an average value of 2.5 billion French francs.

As was the case with Renault, after the 1979–85 crisis years, foreign profits almost always made a positive contribution to PSA's world profits. During the era of economic recovery (1985 to 1999), they accounted for 36.1% of PSA's overall earnings, against a contribution of 63.1% by French profits (much lower than for Renault). In addition, PSA's geographical diversification was limited almost entirely to Europe, meaning that foreign profits were basically tantamount to European profits (see Figure 2.14). This dependency on Europe, which became a handicap once European growth began to slow, turned out to be an advantage when European growth accelerated, thus allowing PSA to avoid the negative effects of the emerging country crisis. This explains why PSA's foreign profits rose continually after 1993, enabling it

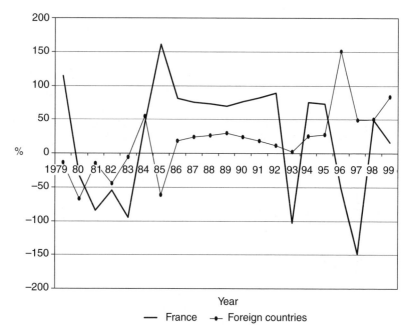

Figure 2.14 France's and foreign countries' contribution to PSA's operating profit, 1979–99

both to partially offset French losses in 1996–7 and to enjoy much higher world profits in 1998–9. However, such a favourable set of circumstances does not happen all that often, and the rest of the world's marginal but negative contribution to global profits (−2% in 1985–99) represents a structural weakness (one that could, however, be overcome if PSA reinforces its presence in South America and Asia).

The Fiat Group's operating profits are also highly dependent on Europe, despite the geographical diversification efforts Fiat has undertaken. Over the period 1995–2000, European operating profits represented 66.2% of world operating profits compared to 33.8% outside Europe (including 18% for Mercosur, 16.7% in North America and −1.1% in other countries). This limited diversification by the Fiat Group turned out to be very useful in overcoming the 1996 European recession (see Figure 2.15). A drop in operating profits from 2,500 billion lira in 1995 to around 1,000 billion in 1996 was offset by continued strong operating profits outside Europe (staying slightly above 1,000 billion lira; that is, around 500 million euros). However, the 1997 Asian crisis and its 1998 contagion to Mercosur highlighted the fragility of this result. In 1998–9, operating profits outside Europe were split in half and their contribution to world profits fell back to 30% (and then to

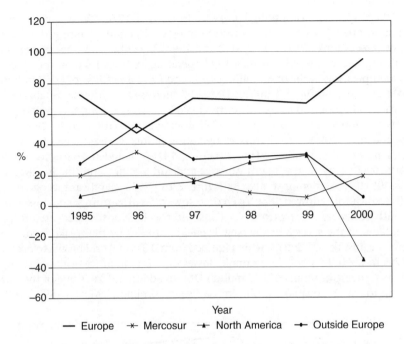

Figure 2.15 Europe's, Mercosur's and North America's contribution to the Fiat Group's operating profit, 1995–2000

5% in 2000). These developments are explained by the collapse in North American profits, which had risen between 1995 and 1999, ultimately accounting for 32.5% of the Fiat Group's world operating profits – previously, North American profits had been able to offset a drop in earnings in Mercosur and in the other countries. As for Fiat Auto, the foreign profits' fragility has been aggravated by the absence of any profits in North America and by the fact that activities are concentrated in Europe and South America. Note that Fiat Auto suffers from chronic mediocre profitability in Europe.[38] Although Fiat Auto's large profits during the Mercosur automobile market's growth phase (1994–7) made it possible to remedy this shortcoming, the 1998–9 Mercosur crisis exacerbated for Fiat Auto the effects of its shortfall in European profitability. As a result, Fiat Auto made an operating loss in 1998 and 1999, and only turned a small profit in 2000, a result of the cost savings generated by its new partnership with GM. Between 1998 and 2000, the only profit sources were the group's non-automobile business, under-lying the usefulness of the Fiat group's industrial and geographical diversifi-cation, as well as Fiat Auto's difficulty in sustaining a successful long-term emerging-country internationalization drive (even as European heartland profits were coming under attack).

VW is a special case among European firms. Since 1970, VW has only experienced operating or net losses for the briefest of periods – during the three global recessions of 1974–5, 1981–2 and 1993. Since then, VW has broken all earnings records, moving from a 1993 operating loss of −1.6 billion DM to a 2000 operating profit of 6.7 billion DM, and from a net loss of −1.9 billion DM to a net profit of 4 billion DM. VW increased its internationalization efforts in Europe and across all continents of the world during this period, yet was not too severely hurt by the 1997–9 emerging-country crisis. Over the period 1997–2000, VW's European operating profits represented 85.6% of its global operating profits.[39] The remaining 14.4% included 16.9% in North America, −2.4% in the 'South America and Africa zone', and finally 7.8% in Asia/Pacific. As demonstrated in Figure 2.16, VW's significant geographic diversification allowed it to overcome lower Asian earnings and losses in South America/Africa through a constant rise in North American profits (because of the success of the New Beetle, reinforced by the weakness of the euro against the US dollar), which jumped from 0.3% of world profits to nearly 17% in 2000. In 1999, for example, losses of 710 million DM were offset by North American profits of 727 million DM. In addition, VW is one of the few firms to have made major profits in Asia/Pacific (2 billion DM over 1997–2000)

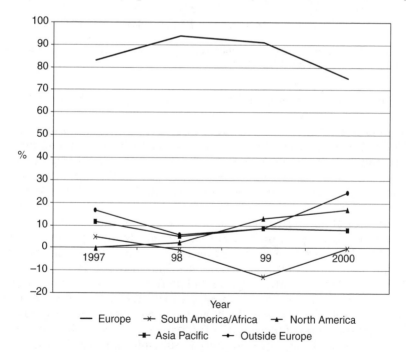

Figure 2.16   Europe's and other geographical areas' contribution to VW's operating profit, 1997–2000

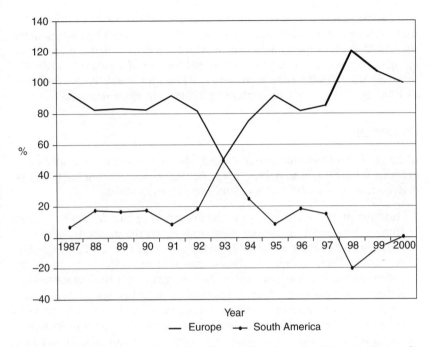

Figure 2.17 Europe's and South America's contribution to Scania's operating profit, 1987–2000

without having suffered any losses, even during the worst of the Asian crisis. Of course, the period under examination is very short, although it does cover a crucial time in the late 1990s crisis in the emerging countries (and in Japan). Still, our study does at least contain an example of successful internationalization, at least in profitability terms (as with Toyota and Honda).

Finally, Scania is another example of a successful internationalization (see Figure 2.17). A commercial vehicle specialist since 1991, Scania, like most capital goods producers is very sensitive to fluctuations in growth rates (since this sector tends to anticipate and accentuate recession and recovery phenomena).

Moreover, the only Scania facilities outside Europe, where the company realized around 16% of its production revenues in 1995–9, are found in Mercosur, a market characterized by great instability throughout the 1990s. In fact, Scania's global operating profits dropped from 3 billion to 1 billion kroners between 1989 and 1993; rose to 5 billion in 1994; suffered from the effects of the 1996 European recession; and finally recovered in 1997–9. In studying geographical contributions to Scania's global profits, note that, despite the highly unstable nature of the market, the firm did not experience any losses in 1987–97, either in Europe or in Mercosur. Europe accounted for around 82%

of its world profits and Mercosur the remaining 18%. In 1993, Mercosur profits, which because of the general recovery in South America had just doubled
their 1992 levels, helped Scania to cope with the recession that was just developing in Europe. Eventually, they accounted for 50% of Scania's world profits.
Inversely, the 1998–9 Mercosur crisis created losses for Scania that reached 20%
in 1998, but these were largely offset by higher earnings in Europe.

Conclusion

Although the information at our disposal was neither exhaustive nor homo-
geneous for all the automakers, the following lessons can nevertheless be
derived from our analysis of levels of internationalization:

1. Automobile firms, perhaps with the exception of Honda, are not global
   firms. Commercial internationalization is by far the most advanced with
   Japanese (57%) and European (73%) firms, but for the Americans (24.5%)
   the focus of activity remains their domestic market. The large size of the
   American market does not explain all this, given that the European market now accounts for equivalent volumes (around 20 million units per year).
   Productive internationalization outside a firm's country of origin remains
   below 45% on average according to our production revenue criterion.
   Moreover, according to our overseas production criterion, it only surpasses
   50% in Europe.[40] Capital internationalization is even less developed –
   foreign assets only represent 30% or less of American or Japanese
   firms' total assets (although this number does rise to 54% for European
   firms). Table 2.7 provides a synthesized vision of the various forms of
   internationalization by means of a synthetical global index, which adds
   the proportion of overseas production to the synthesized UNCTAD index
   we have shown for comparative purposes.[41] Globally, we find that the
   average level of internationalization is 43.2%; 50% of all firms feature a
   level of internationalization of more than 41.5%, and only five out of sixteen firms feature an internationalization of more than 50%, regardless of
   the index being used. This includes three European and two Japanese
   firms that are not necessary the largest ones in terms of their overall production volumes. These firms also have in common the fact that they
   market least a quarter of their revenues and manufacture at least a quarter of their output outside their region of origin.[42] Toyota and the Fiat
   Group, with a global index of around 47% and UNCTAD index values
   of 52% and 49%, respectively, are very close to this leading group, and
   present similar characteristics. But we cannot call the seven most
   internationalized firms 'global firms'; instead, they should be called multi-
   regional firms, given that they run at least one major facility on another
   continent (Honda, Toyota, Nissan and DaimlerChrysler) or else several
   significant but smaller facilities on different continents (VW). The new

Table 2.7 Ranking of firms according to the synthetical indexes

Firms	Global	UNCTAD
DaimlerChrysler (97–99)	69.8	67.4
Honda (95–99)	60.7	65.3
BMW (95–99)	56.0	58.3
VW (95–99)	55.8	56.6
Nissan (95–99)	51.1	54.9
Fiat Group (95–99)	47.2	49.2
Toyota (95–99)	46.8	52.1
Isuzu (96–99)	41.9	41.9
Renault (95–99)	41.2	45.8
Ford (95–97)	38.6	36.1
PSA (95–99)	36.8	41.4
Mitsubishi (95–99)	35.6	37.5
GM (95–96)	33.8	30.0
Subaru (95–99)	32.3	37.6
Mazda (95–99)	29.9	33.8
Navistar (96–98)	13.7	9.5
Average	**43.2**	**44.8**
Median	**41.5**	**43.9**

Source: Our own calculations from the firms' financial reports. For methodology see Table 2.2.

merger/acquisition or partnership projects, which can be based on capital stakes being taken with or without a controlling participation, presuppose that the internationalization trend will continue, but that it will sometimes take the shape of original forms that will make it more difficult to identify the exact dimensions of the new entities being created.[43] The profitability of this new stage of internationalization also raises a number of issues, especially since it has been shown that those firms that are the most internationalized are not necessary the most profitable.

2. We note that few firms have succeeded in transforming foreign operations, all regions combined, into a durable source of profit. Among the American firms, and unlike Ford, GM (despite the fact that it has long been described as a leader in decline) was able to achieve this not only during long post-war period of high growth but also over the course of two decades (1980–2000) of slow and unstable growth. In Japan since the 1980s only Toyota, Honda and Suzuki were able to achieve this. All the other Japanese firms' performances were either mediocre (Subaru, Isuzu) or even negative (Mazda, Mitsubishi, Nissan). In Europe, French firms have only been making a profit on their foreign operations since 1986. Scania (and probably VW) had similar results. Table 2.8 provides a synthetical view of this result

Table 2.8   Number of loss-making years, 1990–9, by geographical zone

Firms	Overseas	Country of origin	World
Toyota	0	0	0
Honda	0	0	0
Suzuki	0	0	0
VW	probably 0	1	1
Renault (1990–8)	0	3	1
PSA	0	3	2
GM	0	4	3
Scania	2	0	0
Isuzu (1994–9)	5	2	1
Ford	5	3	2
Subaru	5	3	4
Mitsubishi	6	1	1
Nissan	6	4	7
Mazda	7	2	5

Source: Our own calculations from the firms' financial reports.

for 1990–9, a period covering an entire cycle of growth in North America; a period of slow growth and then recovery in Europe;[44] and the beginning of an extended period of stagnation in Japan. Seven out of thirteen firms did not make any foreign losses at all over this decade, including three Japanese, three Europeans and one American. These are firms for which internationalization has generally developed into an additional competitive advantage. The three Japanese firms present the particularity of not having suffered any losses in their market of origin, in spite of the Japanese economic crisis and the country's weaker automobile market. In Europe, only VW has achieved a similar performance. French firms and GM only lost money in their domestic markets, and this was offset occasionally by foreign profits. Scania is close to this first group – the Mercosur crisis caused it to lose money for two years in its number two market, yet it did not record any overall losses, coming out ahead both in its market of origin and globally.

This initial category is followed by a group of firms (almost all of whom are Japanese) that lost money during at least half of the 1990s, something that cannot be explained solely by short-term fluctuations. For these firms, internationalization has represented a handicap that has often compounded a precarious national situation.

Ultimately, we know that there is no clear and linear relationship between levels of internationalization and profitability. Honda, VW, and to a lesser extent Toyota, are members of a category comprised of the world's most internationalized firms (using a classification derived from synthetical indexes) but Renault and PSA are not really members of this group (given their average level of internationalization), and GM even less so.[45] Similarly, within the group of those firms for which internationalization has been the least successful, we find relatively less-internationalized firms such as Mazda, Mitsubishi and Subaru as well as a firm that is highly internationalized (Nissan). A firm can fail as a result of insufficient internationalization (that is, Mazda) or else because of its high but inappropriate degree of internationalization (that is, Nissan). In the same vein, a firm can obtain profits from abroad because it has a low level of internationalization (PSA) – or else its higher level of interna-tionalization can expose it to greater possibilities of losses (Fiat Auto). Internationalization is truly a risky business, and not always a source of advantage. More than the actual level of internationalization, it is the quality of this status, its appropriateness to the firm's specific resources, to the competitive environment and to the characteristics of market demand that leads to success or to failure – an observation that raises questions about the organizational characteristics of those firms that have been the most successful.

3. The three firms (Toyota, Honda and VW) whose productive models have turned out to be the most relevant and coherent (Boyer and Freyssenet, 2002) are among the most internationalized firms of all (Honda and VW) or at least belong to the upper tier in this category (Toyota). These are firms where internationalization has become a durable source of profit. Should we consider this to be a confirmation that their respective productive models, built within a national framework, have been reinforced by the international situation post-1974? The figures sustain this thesis but do not suffice to prove it. Indeed, when these firms internationalize, their national productive model undergoes an inevitable hybridization that can vary depending on the region in which they have set up facilities. This hybridization affects their initial 'profit strategy' and 'company government compromise' – these being the two preconditions for a firm's profitability. Will Honda be able to pursue its 'innovation – flexibility' strategy in those regions where it has set up operations, or else is it going to change strategy? If so, how can we be certain that the successes these firms have achieved abroad are the consequence of an original productive model? Might they not be a hybrid variant that is quite distinct from the original model? To answer these questions, we need a specific in-depth analysis of firms' internationalization trajectories – something that can be found in the later chapters of this book.

Translated by Alan Sitkin

Methodological appendix

Sources

National and world production data of automobile firms are taken from: '*L'industrie automobile française*', several years completed by *le Répertoire Mondial des activités de production et d'assemblage des véhicules automobiles*, CCFA, 2 rue de Presbourg, 75008, Paris, France (www.ccfa.fr). All other data are taken from the financial reports published by firms every year.

Contribution index to world profit

We have tried to determine whether national or foreign profit contributed to increasing or decreasing world profit, or to reducing/worsening world loss. To do so, we have divided the foreign profit or loss by the absolute value of the world profit or loss. We have done the same with the national profit or loss. We can therefore take into account all possible cases.

Two examples are given here:

1. If the national and foreign profits are worth 50 each, world profit is worth 100, and the contribution of national and foreign profit is 50%.
2. If national profit is worth 50, and a foreign loss worth -70 is registered, there is a world loss of -20. The contribution of national profit is 50 divided by the absolute value of -20, (equal to 20), which gives a positive contribution of 250%. The negative contribution of the foreign loss is -70 divided by 20, which gives -350%. Finally, the sum of the contribution of the national profit (250%) and that of the foreign loss (-350%) gives a negative balance of -100%, pointing to the fact that the firm has suffered a world loss. The national profit has contributed to reducing this world loss; but the foreign loss has contributed to worsening it.

We can also imagine the case of a world profit resulting from a foreign profit despite a national loss, and so on.

Notes

1 Unfortunately, we have not got at our disposal sufficient information on Fiat or the German firms.
2 The transnationality index is calculated as an average of three relationships: foreign assets versus total assets; foreign sales versus total sales; and foreign staff versus total staff (cf. UNCTAD, 1999).
3 GM, Ford, Toyota/Daihatsu/Hino.
4 GM (Isuzu included), Ford (Mazda included), Toyota/Daihatsu/Hino, DaimlerChrysler, Renault/Nissan, VW.
5 Nissan and VW.
6 Fiat, PSA, Honda, Mitsubishi.
7 Chrysler, Renault, PSA, UAZ, Fiat, Honda, Mazda, Mitsubishi.
8 Suzuki-Maruti, Hyundai-Kia-Asia, Daewoo-Ssangyong, Avtovaz.
9 Suzuki, Daimler-Benz, Isuzu, Subaru, British Leyland, Volvo, BMW.
10 Avtovaz, Subaru, Volvo, Proton, Gaz, ChinaFirst.
11 The 'commercial revenues' indicator allows us to break world sales down into their component parts (all products combined) by place of sale, regardless of

where the product was manufactured. A product can be sold in a given foreign country after being made in the firm's country of origin or in third country.

12   The 'production revenues' indicator allows us to break global sales down into their component parts (all products combined) by the location in which the firm's subsidiaries have set up operations. One product can be manufactured by an overseas subsidiary of the firm, and sold in the same country, or in another country.

13   These are personal calculations based on the fifteen automobile firms that appear among the 100 leading multinationals comprising the UNCTAD sample.

14   Korean firms were not included because of the insufficiency and unreliability of relevant statistical information. The same applies to Russian, Chinese and Indian firms. Often smaller than average, these firms are barely internationalized and their future as independent concerns remains in question, particularly in South Korea.

15   This number can be obtained from the average of Averages (1), (3) and (5). (See Table 2.2.)

16   During the 1970s, North America was limited to the United States and Canada. Since the creation of NAFTA, however, Ford includes Mexico as part of North America.

17   In 1990–9, 69.8% for NAFTA, 23.7% for Europe and 6.5% for the rest of the world, including around 3% in South America and 3.5% in Asia/Africa/Pacific. Sources: personal calculations based on financial statements.

18   Like Paccar and Navistar (see Table 2.2) and in particular the Japanese commercial vehicle makers. Hino, Japan's top automaker, made only 12% of its total sales overseas in 1998–9.

19   Fiat's example shows the usefulness of industrial diversification, as 6.8% of the group's revenues in North America are not made by Fiat Auto, the group's passenger car subsidiary, but by other units within the group.

20   French firms, for example, make 25% of their total sales outside Europe.

21   By the year 2010, GM plans to realize 10% of its total sales in Japan.

22   If we include the Korean firms, overseas production reached an average of 24% in 1990–4 and 36.3% in 1995–9.

23   As a result, BMW's percentage of overseas production dropped sharply below 50% in 2000.

24   Here we are defining the term 'region' in the broadest sense of the term. For American firms, this means NAFTA plus South America. For European firms, it is the European Union (EU) plus other countries in Europe (including Turkey). For Japanese firms, it means the other countries in Asia, plus Oceania and Africa.

25   That is, outside NAFTA and South America.

26   Here we could mention the Renault/Nissan grouping, linked to the Volvo/RVI/Mack/Nissan Diesel grouping; DaimlerChrysler/Mitsubishi; and other groupings such as VW/Scania and GM/Fiat (or even the take-over of Navistar by Hino).

27   Sales by zone of production is a measurement that includes all the products (complete passenger cars, commercial vehicles where applicable, motorcycles, motors and spare parts) that are used in all the business lines (automobiles, other manufacturing activities and services).

28   The periods that Tables 2.2 and 2.6 cover in terms of commercial revenues and production revenues are different from the ones referred to here, since information on breakdown by geographic zone has only been available since 1997 for Japanese firms (with VW and Renault no longer providing this information from 1997 and 1998 onwards, respectively). Generally speaking, this has had a minimal impact on the exportable surpluses (commercial revenues – production revenues) that we have calculated.

29 The revenues 'produced' by foreign subsidiaries (see revenues by production facility, Tables 2.2 and 2.6) modify the hierarchy of productive internationalization (when measured by overseas production and calculated in physical terms). This applies mainly to European firms. Several reasons explain this phenomenon: the nature of the product range that is being manufactured; average purchasing power in each operational zone; the foreign production's rate of integration; variations in exchange rates and so on. There is not enough space in this chapter to do justice to all these considerations.

30 For the American and Japanese firms, we can make use of long series of net profit statistics. For European firms, we have series of varying lengths covering operating profits. These two measurements of profit are clearly not the same. The point, however, is not to compare them, but instead to study, with the help of our indicator, overseas contributions to profits.

31 To analyse Japanese firms' world profits, we dispose of two sources of information. On the one hand, we have net consolidated world-wide earnings, and net unconsolidated earnings (reflecting changes in Japan itself). To calculate net foreign earnings we subtract net unconsolidated earnings from net consolidated earnings. Using these two time series we calculate an indicator of contributions by net national and foreign profits to net world profits. This is, of course, a rough assessment, but it is an accurate one that is particularly useful in analysing long term trends. In addition, we can break operating profits down by geographic zone from around 1995–6 onwards. By definition, operating profits are a truer reflection of a firm's productive activities – but our information is more recent. Net profits, which include financial income and charges, tax, and extraordinary income and costs, reflect a firm's final earnings. We have tried to combine the two sets of information. The only numbers represented in graphic form are changes in net profits.

32 The sharp drop in Honda's net earnings in Japan are explained by an exceptional domestic loss of 109.4 million yen.

33 Reuters interview with M. Davies, General Manager Honda UK, 21 December 2000, http://just-auto.com/features.

34 US sales reached a peak of 183,000 units in 1986 and fell to a low of 100,000 in 1995 before going back up to 172,000 in 2000 thanks to a rejuvenated product range.

35 In 2000, Mitsubishi's sales in Japan suffered as a result of a scandal involving the recall of faulty vehicles. Passenger car and truck sales fell by 8.6%, and mini-car sales by 7%.

36 Its subsidiary in Thailand suffered a loss of 43.7 billion yen (around US$350 million) caused by the impact of the baht devaluation on dollar-linked debt (and because of the collapse of the local market).

37 Operating profit is the only geographical zone information available on European firms. Renault and PSA stopped publishing this data in 1998. Fiat and VW started to publish it in 1995 and 1997. Volvo does not publish it at all.

38 Despite major productive modernization initiatives during the 1990s, Fiat Auto is still handicapped by its specialization (70% of the firm's sales) in a small-car sector that is marked by weak profit margins. The firm does not achieve sufficient economies of scale compared to its European rivals. Turnover was increased by a factor of 1.8 between 1990 and 2000 but operating profits never returned to the level they had reached in the late 1980s.

39 To break the VW Group's pre-tax operating profits down on a geographical basis, we have used the following method (based on the segment analysis contained within the company's annual report): (i) we use only gross profits for manufacturing activities, thus excluding financial activities; and (ii) we consider that each

marque (VW, Audi, Skoda, Seat, Rolls-Royce/Bentley) made its profits in Europe, with the world's 'other regions' being presented as such in the report.

40 If we exclude firms specializing in commercial vehicle production, overseas manufacturing represents around 45% of world output for European and American firms, but only 31% for Japanese firms (see Averages (2), (4) and (5) in Table 2.2).

41 We have sometimes supplemented the UNCTAD calculations, for example, by incorporating Honda Motor's number of overseas staff members. Where information is lacking on assets or staffing, we did not calculate the UNCTAD index, in contrast to the UNCTAD itself, which calculates this index even when it only has available two out of the three necessary pieces of information.

42 Apart from BMW, which has an extra-European production of only 6.3%, BMW's 2000 divorce from Rover does not seem to have undermined the group's level of internationalization. Quite the contrary, in fact: it diminishes Europe's role. BMW has continued to stress its internationalization drive in North America, with the proportion of total assets located in this region rising from 23.7% in 1999 to 30.3% in 2000.

43 For example, there was no ambiguity during the DaimlerChrysler merger, given the length of time that the illusion of a 'merger among equals' lasted. Less straightforward was the take-over of Mitsubishi by DaimlerChrysler, and of Nissan by Renault. Although there is no ambiguity with respect to the leading role played by DaimlerChrysler and by Renault in these operations, the new groupings do not (yet?) constitute jointly operating firms, and may never reach that stage. The Fiat/GM agreement (not to mention the increased number of *ad hoc* partnership arrangements) raises the same types of issue.

44 This is the only period where available information allows the comparison of the greatest number of firms.

45 We have not been able to calculate the synthetical index for Scania and Suzuki, since one of the necessary pieces of information is not available. Based on three elements out of four, Scania's overall synthetical index value is 71.5%, and Suzuki's 35.2%.

References

Boyer, R. and Freyssenet, M. (2002) *The Productive Models: The Conditions of Profitability*, London/New York: Palgrave.

Chesnais, F. (1994) *La mondialisation du capital*, Paris: Syros.

Economist Intelligence Unit (2000) *The Automotive Industries of Asia-Pacific: Prospects for ASEAN and the emerging markets to 2005*.

Economist, The (1999) 'How to Make Mergers Work?', *The Economist*, 9 January.

Financial Times Auto Survey (2000) 'Brazil: Sights Set to Give Exports Needed Boost'. Website: www.ftsurveys/industry/sccc0a.htm.

Friedman, J. (1983) *Oligopoly Theory*, Cambridge University Press.

Lung, Y. (2000) 'Towards a Worldwide Oligoply in the Automobile Industry?', *La Lettre du GERPISA*, no. 143, June. Website: www.gerpisa.univ-evry.fr

Ohmae, K. (1985) *Triad Power*, New York: The Free Press.

Porter, M. (1986) *Competition in Global Industries*, Boston, Mass.: Harvard Business School Press.

PricewaterhouseCoopers (1999) *Global Automotive Industry Review 1998*.

UNCTAD (1998) *World Investment Report: Trends and Determinants*, New York/Geneva: United Nations.

UNCTAD (1999) *World Investment Report: Foreign Direct Investment and the Challenge of Development*, New York/Geneva: United Nations.
UNCTAD (2000) *World Investment Report: Cross-Border Mergers and Acquisitions and Development*, New York/Geneva: United Nations.
Ward's Automotive Yearbook (2000).

Part I

Towards the Regionalization of the Global Strategies of US Automakers, Suppliers and Dealers

3
The Twin Internationalization Strategies of US Automakers: GM and Ford

Gérard Bordenave and Yannick Lung

Introduction

By the latter half of the 1990s, when, against a background of increasingly deregulated markets, people were beginning to talk more and more about the phenomenon of globalization, General Motors (GM) and Ford had already accumulated long experience in international markets. The two groups, respectively the largest and second-largest vehicle manufacturer in the world, are arguably the most internationalized as well (given the geographic dispersion of their sales, productive capacities and resources).[1] Their adventures overseas date from early in the twentieth century, shortly after these two pioneers of the automobile industry had first started in business (Bardou *et al.*, 1977; Hounshell, 1984). Before GM was reorganized by Alfred P. Sloan, Henry Ford had already opened the sector up to the British market, later moving into other European countries and indeed into other continents (Wilkins and Hill, 1964; Laux, 1992; Tolliday, 1998). He soon launched a number of overseas assembly operations, and subsequently began to manufacture locally, exporting to the best of his ability the rigid methods of mass production. GM, on the other hand, was born out of a conglomerate of firms. Because of the conditions of its birth, it has always diverged from Ford's monolithic structure, and under the organizational leadership of Sloan, it was soon able to achieve a measure of corporate stability (Chandler, 1962). In the early 1920s, GM was already in a position to be able to dispute Ford's hegemony, both domestically and internationally. Where Ford used to advance through internal growth, GM opted intentionally for external growth (Dassbach, 1989). It acquired Opel in Germany, Vauxhall in Britain and Holden in Australia, catching up with Ford within a very short period of time. In the 1930s, despite all the economic difficulties of the time, GM and Ford were already able to rely on the diversified and irreversible presence they had established overseas. The ubiquitous protectionist policies of the time had an impact on the two firms – and on Ford more than on GM, which was more willing to allow its subsidiaries to operate more autonomously (Bordenave, 1998).

The two firms' international presence also means that their industrial resources were used by both sides during the Second World War. Reunified once peace had returned, these overseas entities nevertheless continued, during the post-war years of reconstruction and until the late 1960s, to operate relatively independently from one another. GM's and Ford's subsidiaries had to report to their US parent company – otherwise their industrial behaviour was hardly distinguishable from that of local automakers. The organization of the two multinationals during this period can be deemed to be a multi-domestic one (Bélis-Bergouignan *et al.*, 2000).

Starting in the late 1960s and lasting until the late 1980s, the two firms' internationalization processes embarked on a new phase. The background for this was a context of renewed free trade, primarily as a result of the regional common markets that were starting to be developed. For GM and Ford, this was a time of regional integration. Each began to unify its product range, optimize its design and manufacturing resources, centralize its purchasing function and co-ordinate its distribution network on a continental scale. This trend was particularly strong in Europe. In 1967, Ford created Ford Europe. The aim of this managerial entity was to achieve the progressive integration of Ford's British and German subsidiaries, which had tended to see themselves more as competitors than as partners. The GM group, on the other hand, had to contend with the fact that Opel was larger than Vauxhall. Little by little, Vauxhall's vehicles were turned into re-baptized Opels (apart from being right-hand drive). When GM Europe was finally founded in 1987, it was more a question of consolidating an existing position than of creating a new one. In North America, integration was handled differently because of the United States' domination of the entire region. Once Canada was integrated into the North American market following the 1966 Auto Pact, the new aim was to develop a southern productive base, and this led to Mexico's inclusion in the regional system during the 1980s. Note that Europe had gone through a similar process with the industrialization of the Iberian peninsula (Layan, 2000). South America and Asia also furthered their regional integration, albeit to a lesser degree, as institutional ties between the various countries in these regions were less developed: some national markets (notably Japan's) maintained strong barriers; and GM and Ford had less-developed productive bases here. The transition from a multi-domestic to a multi-regional organization was the key trend of this era.

Yet the period running from the late 1960s to the late 1980s was also marked by other events that could not avoid having an impact on the automakers' internationalization processes. The first was the rise of Japanese automakers – and the second, compounding the effects of the first, was the succession of oil crises that occurred. Ford experienced a violent shock in the late 1970s but recovered relatively quickly. GM at first seemed to be spared such problems, but its situation deteriorated subsequently and continued to do so until the 1990s. The two automakers, like many of their Western competitors, were forced to rethink completely their models of industrial organization (Freyssenet *et al.*, 1998). In this sort of challenging environment, internationalization is an advantage, if only because it allows firms to benefit from variations in regional economic cycles, or else to try to redeploy their resources advantageously. In fact, firms' reaction to the crisis, which was to search for new alliances and co-operative arrangements (later followed by an industry-wide trend towards concentration), had the effect of perpetuating the crisis. Ford took a 25% stake in Mazda in 1979, thus paving the way for a whole range of current and future co-operative agreements with this Japanese automaker. GM moved closer to Isuzu and Suzuki, and even created a joint venture with Toyota. The US firms wooed the Japanese in an effort to appropriate their know-how – but they also approached other firms. In 1987, Ford merged its Brazilian and Argentine entities with Volkswagen's in a joint venture called AutoLatina. A more specific agreement covering a European niche vehicle (minivan) united the same two partners in an enterprise called AutoEuropa. These moves were then followed by a period of external growth. After failing in its negotiations to acquire Fiat, Ford bought two upmarket European specialists – Aston Martin and (even more importantly) Jaguar – in 1987. GM followed its example three years later by taking a 49% stake in the Swedish automaker, Saab. All in all, at the dawn of the 1990s, GM and Ford had already gone through a considerable amount of reconfiguration (Bordenave, 1998; Flynn, 1998). They had not only rebuilt internal coherency widely at a regional level, but had also strengthened their international networks through co-operative agreements and mergers.

This chapter will focus primarily on GM's and Ford's third phase of internationalization. This phase began during the latter half of the 1980s, and continues at the time of writing. It is commonly known as 'globalization' (Porter, 1986). One of the aims of this study will be to offer an extensive approach, based on GM's and Ford's most recent experiences, to a term that has become a relatively hackneyed expression. If we focus on the dynamics underlying the globalization process, it would appear that its aim has been a global integration of corporate management. For GM and Ford, who have completed their regional integration more or less successfully, the issue is one of benefiting from integration at a higher level. The strategies these two firms have been pursuing towards this end would seem to run along two main lines. On the one hand, there is a first line of action that revolves around what we can call the firms' operational core – that is, their central automaking activities in North America and in Europe (these being the zones in which most of their products, markets and resources are concentrated). On the other hand, there is a second line of action that revolves around what we can call the firms' borders – that is, everything that is peripheral to their main activity, in a geographical and economic sense. The words 'border' or 'periphery' should not be given a connotation of 'marginal' or 'negligible', since it is largely at this level that automakers' futures will be enacted. By advancing in both of these directions, automakers in general, and GM and Ford in particular, have been the main drivers behind the globalization process.

The two main points discussed above will constitute the heart of our study, a comparison of Ford's and GM's internationalization strategies. This comparison will highlight the high degree of imitativeness (Pointet, 1997) that both have displayed in their behaviour and their decision-making. This imitation is, first and foremost, predicated on the fact that both firms have been pursuing similar types of profit strategies, involving a combination of product variety and economies of scale (scope–volume). Both rely on a Sloanian productive model (Boyer and Freyssenet, 2000). Once the whiz kids and Henry Ford II had re-established Ford Motor Company in the aftermath of the Second World War, the firm as a whole adopted its main rival's Sloanian methods. Mimetic behaviour thus seems to be a logical outcome for firms that share the same economic environment; offer similar product ranges (products that are highly substitutable, hence they are in competition with one another); pursue the same types of profit strategies; and basically benchmark their activities according to similar methods and modes of organization. Clearly, a few elements of differentiation do exist, reflecting each firm's history and modus operandi. GM is more managerial than Ford, which basically remains a family-run company. The former is more apt to decentralize, while the latter more hierarchical and apt to homogenize. However, both have been developing since the early twentieth century in an identical institutional environment. They have been subjected to the similar constraints (the latest having been the increase in shareholder power). Shareholders basically forced G. Stempel's departure from GM in 1992. Moreover, given Ford's recent poor financial performances, the late 2001 return to power of a member of the founding family (W. C. Ford) probably met with approval from the company's institutional investors. The long and parallel internationalization paths that GM and Ford have been following are therefore extremely analogous. As globalization spreads its wings, it seems natural that both firms have come out in favour of a transregional type of configuration that offers, for each market segment, a real link between the different forms of globalization and regionalization. It remains that there has been a reversal in what had ostensibly been a clear trend.

The globalization of General Motors and Ford in their North American and European operational cores

In the late 1980s a new point of focus began to emerge at Ford and GM, one that would begin to grow and finally find its concrete expression during the 1990s. The project was based on an integration of those activities that were located on both sides of the Atlantic. Up to this point, the reciprocal relationship between these two geographic zones (which combined represented more than 90% of Ford and GM's global production and sales – that is, the vast majority of their activities) consisted of little more than a small and occasional trading in products. The desire to develop systematically a number of shared products (commonalized components and shared platforms) between the two continents constituted a quantum leap with respect to then current practices, even though the idea was not particularly new and had already, on several occasions, been taken into consideration, notably with the 'world car' concept. As such, this latest scheme should be analysed as something more than a simple initiative aimed at increasing the scale of a particular product's sales, thereby achieving economies of scale. It implies that there was a desire to exploit capabilities that were specifically regional – that is, that were continentally differentiated – and could be applied towards global optimization. This search for integration constitutes a globalization approach (locally adapted products on shared platforms) as opposed to a straightforward world-wide approach (identical products produced and/or marketed all over the world) (see Bélis-Bergouignan *et al.*, 2000). The present study will focus on the automakers' efforts to globalize by means of platform-sharing strategies (Bordenave, 2000). We start with Ford's approach, this firm having been a trailblazer with the way it globalized its North American and European activities. We then examine GM's approach, and end with a comparative conclusion.

Ford's approach to globalization

Ford is the first automaker to have developed a programme of shared global platforms for its two main North American and European zones of activity. As is often the case with Ford, this strategic development was rooted in an earlier, two-phase organizational evolution. The first phase was in 1987, with the appearance of the concept of responsibility centres. This was furthered in 1994 with the launch of the 'Ford 2000' reorganization plan. However, from 1998 onwards, the firm retreated from a plan that had come to be seen as something that was overly radical. Ford's organization then became a little unsettled, especially since, at the same time, it was having to deal with the consequences of the take-over of Volvo Cars and other luxury automakers. This led Ford to create a dedicated upmarket structure whose purpose was to develop synergies between all the brands it owned in this segment.

From responsibility centres to the first global platform

Back in 1987, the responsibility centres' early strategies revolved more around the way in which competencies were to be attributed to them than around any structural reorganization. Three poles of competency were named at this time: the Japanese partner Mazda (for smaller cars), Ford Europe (for medium-sized vehicles, four-cylinder engines and manual transmissions) and the American parent company (for larger cars, V6 and V8 engines, automatic transmissions, and electronic control and air conditioning systems). This vision expressed both the desire to develop jointly a number of high-volume vehicles and intermediary products, and a policy of allocating specialized tasks among the various centres according to the different types of capability that each possessed. As such, the basic elements of a globalization approach were already present in an outlook that essentially turned on the notion of a 'world car' (featuring locally adapted model variants). The actual materialization of this approach was, however, not without problems. The Ford Escort's replacement in 1990 was not done in the same way on both sides of the Atlantic. In North America and in Asia-Pacific, Mazda was in charge of a process that will remain for Ford's design teams the apex in their learning of Japanese product development practices. In Europe, the replacement of the small vehicle bearing the same name (a lower-mid-market vehicle in the European classification) was based on local developmental resources – thus revisiting a paradox that had first been witnessed ten years previously, when cars sold by one manufacturer under the same name did not in fact have anything in common.

The European programme was in the process of being strengthened when Ford's responsibility centres were first announced, and this factor, when added to Europe's distance from Mazda's sphere of influence (and probably also people's sensitivities and unwillingness to change their habits) would appear to have constituted an insurmountable obstacle. Ford did not bring out its first global vehicle until 1993 (the 1994 model year), when it launched the (CDW27 platform, upper mid-market) Mondeo in Europe. This car was introduced in North America the following year, having been slightly adapted to the local market, under the name of the Ford Contour and/or the Mercury Mystique. Small volumes were also exported to other markets, particularly to Asia. The car's transfer from Europe to the United States was achieved when the firm sent a European development centre team on a mission to its Kansas City (USA) plant. This team had previously been involved in launching manufacturing operations at Ford's Belgian plant in Genk. The programme amounted to a total cost of US$6 billion, but even though new transmissions and engines were included in this number, it was considered to be very high. The commercial performances of these American sister-cars were very disappointing, as it was difficult to find room for them in the product range between the small models (like the Escort) and the American market's main 4-door sedan segment (which Ford was already occupying with its successful Ford Taurus and Mercury Sable models). Global sales were far below 600,000 units per year, yet the target had been 800,000. In 1999, the Mercury Cougar was added to the CDW platform, leading to some improvement in the amortization of costs – but on balance, Ford's first global platform was at best a partial success. Eventually, Ford decided not to renew its experience with global platforms on this market segment. The replacement of the Mondeo in 2000 has been presented as a European operation – the car's platform is not meant to be used on the North American market.

The 'Ford 2000' reorganization plan

The 'Ford 2000' reorganization plan represented a significant and deliberate step towards globalization. Announced in 1994 and launched in January 1995, this plan effectively led to the merger of the North American and European regional organizations by placing all the major functional divisions (design, manufacturing, purchasing, marketing and so on) under the umbrella of a single entity named Ford Automotive Operations located in the United States. Ford Europe became a minor functional unit whose main responsibilities were sales-orientated. The reorganization created five vehicle centres characterized by the type of mutually dependent functions usually found in a matrix structure. At first, North America inherited four of these centres (large-sized automobiles with a front-wheel drive; large-sized cars with rear propulsion systems; light utility vehicles; and trucks) and the other centre (small and medium-sized cars) was located in Europe. This breakdown was soon to be reorganized, the vehicle-centres rapidly being restructured so that only three remained, two in North America (large-sized cars and utility vehicles) and one in Europe (unchanged). Note that the Asia-Pacific and South America zones were not affected by this restructuring, although it had been foreseen that they would be involved at some unspecified date in the future. In much the same way, Mazda, which had been designated a responsibility centre in 1987, no longer had a specified role, and had to wait for a new definition. Despite these limits, 'Ford 2000' was a significant reorganization action that was supposed to provide the firm with a straightforward transregional organizational structure, as opposed to its previous multi-regional structure.

This plan committed the firm to a centralized type of general management – a move that was reminiscent of its actions at the time when its founder Henry Ford had first started operating in Europe. There was one main difference, however. Europe had in the meantime developed an exhaustive productive apparatus and was now capable of total autonomy. As such, this latest departure from Ford's established operational modes was probably a step too far, and the firm retreated somewhat in 1999, reallocating to Ford Europe its traditional role. However, the inter-continental sharing of platforms was not abandoned. The replacement of the Escort by the Focus (on the platform CW170), launched in Europe in time for the 1999 models, and in North America the following year, was encouraging. Designed under the aegis of 'Ford 2000' by Europe's small world car centre, this automobile (marginally differentiated for the various continents) was first greeted favourably by the markets, particularly by the American one. With more than 900,000 units sold worldwide in 2000, this second global platform to have been developed by Ford may well reach the output levels that had been anticipated for the first, especially since a number of new models and cars are to be developed on it (primarily convertibles and coupés, with substantially differentiated product lines). Still, these future developments remain uncertain, since they depend on the capacities of a reconstituted regional entity, Ford Europe, that is being pressurized both into regaining a market share that began slipping away in the late 1980s, and into increasing its structurally low profit rate. In addition, Ford Europe's priority is to sort out the renewal of its small regional model, the Fiesta, in 2002. It has already announced that its long-established Dagenham plant in England would no longer be manufacturing this car, and that it would as a result lose its status as an assembly site. In any event, Ford's first two global platforms have two interesting elements in common. The first is that they were both inspired by the vision of a world car, inasmuch as the vehicles built thereon were barely differentiated by continent. The second is that both were first designed in Europe and subsequently sent to the North American market, exemplifying a situation in which a parent company is seeking to exploit the resources located at a group's periphery, rather than the reverse. Even as it was dreaming of becoming global, the firm did not lose all its ethnocentricity, at least not during its initial experiments in globalization.

Strategic and organizational reorientations in the aftermath of the Volvo acquisition

The third sequence in Ford's globalization process was based on a conjunction of factors: people's increasing scepticism as to the viability of the 'Ford 2000' plan; and Ford's participation in the mergermania that was so characteristic of the late 1990s. To be more specific, this latter trend altered the portfolio of marques that automakers were building up and created new strategic challenges for them. Arguably, it was launched in 1996 when Ford raised its stake in Mazda from 25% to 33.4%, thus effectively taking control of the Japanese automaker. One of Ford's American executives came in to run the Japanese firm, and after that time Ford officially included Mazda in its portfolio of marques. However, the ultimate denouement of what had been a long and fruitful co-operation between Ford and Mazda did not lead to any particularly spectacular results, at least not in the short run, as regards any integration between these two firms. It is true that Ford's prime objective was to help Mazda, which had been experiencing serious difficulties, to recover – and in this respect the operation has been moderately successful, with Mazda, having suffered losses for five years in a row, becoming profitable again in 1999. As regards co-operation in vehicle design or sharing, note Ford's involvement in developing the sports utility vehicle that Mazda launched in 2000 on the North America market. Moreover, Ford has been building a small-sized car in small volumes for Mazda in Europe. In 1999, Ford Europe's general management let it be known that it was working closely with its Japanese partner in Ford's European development centre on a project involving a mini car that the two marques are going to share. Ford and Mazda's collaboration in vehicle sharing would therefore appear to be relatively niche-orientated. Mazda's identity and the specificity of its distribution network are supposed to remain untouched. Be this as it may, it seems that Ford, a company that is not known for the longevity of its alliances, is eager to keep Mazda as a means of entering the Japanese market. Note that AutoLatina and AutoEuropa, the two joint ventures that Ford organized with Volkswagen in the late 1980s, were both dissolved by the late 1990s.

The second major event of this recent mergermania took place in February 1999, when Ford took over Volvo Cars for US$6.45 billion. It should be noted that this operation excluded Volvo's truck division, which was to merge the following year with Renault Véhicules Industriels, thereby creating a unique situation wherein cars and trucks carrying the same brand name would from then onwards be leading entirely autonomous lives. At the time of the acquisition, Volvo Cars was a specialist top-of-the-range automaker with a strong brand image. Its production, based on two platforms, was close to 400,000 units per year. Volvo exported more than 40% of its output outside the continent of Europe, mainly to North America. This considerable reinforcement of Ford's upmarket presence coincided with its decision to stop producing the European model (the Ford Scorpio) that it had been using to attack this segment – a model that Ford had no intention of replacing. The firm's immediate reaction was to create, less than three months after the take-over, a new entity called the 'Premier Automotive Group'. This was an autonomous entity responsible for the direct management of Lincoln (a prestige American brand) and the entire top-of-the-range European portfolio (Jaguar, Austin Martin and Volvo). In 2000, this entity was again reinforced through the purchase of Land Rover from BMW, after the latter firm had decided to separate from the Rover Group – only six years after having acquired it. The reason for combining the whole of the Ford Group's top-of-the-range business line was to create a situation in which the many marques it owned on this very specific market segment would be able to expand coherently. The main goal was to avoid any possible cannibalism while preserving as far as possible each entity's identity. In the market's upper segments, commercial performances are particularly dependent on ongoing differentiation and on the longevity of brand images, and this does not mesh well with a search for synergies, or with a policy of developing shared platforms.

It would appear that the first synergies to be discovered involved shared systems, reflecting a long-term trend in which automobile manufacturing has increasingly become a question of system integration. It is also possible to share certain specific types of capabilities. Ford emphasized this during its acquisition of Volvo, when it highlighted its interest in the Swedish automaker's experience in vehicle safety. Given the reputation that the Swedes have acquired in this area, we can almost consider that this take-over was tantamount to a technological investment, similar to Ford's purchase of the Norwegian company Pivco AS, when it tried to develop the Think, a small electric car. Volvo's commercial size clearly precludes this sort of assimilation, but the underlying logic is not dissimilar. Other possible areas of co-operation between Ford and Volvo are logistics management, or certain manufacturing activities (given the proximity between the two automakers' German, Belgian and Dutch plants). With regard to platform sharing, finally, there is less room to manoeuvre, but one of the experiments that has been initiated by the American large-sized car centre under the aegis of the 'Ford 2000' plan offers some interesting possibilities. The Lincoln LS (DEW) platform, launched in 1999 (in time for the 2000 new car sales), handled a number of differentiated models: the Jaguar S-type (in 1999) and the Ford Thunderbird (in 2000). The presence of a Jaguar provides the platform with a global character, especially since it is planned that within a few years the Lincoln LS is to be exported to Europe.

The example of Jaguar is interesting as it may be the forerunner of one of the configurations that Volvo could be assuming in the future as a member of the Ford group. First, it is noteworthy that ten years have elapsed since Ford acquired this specialized English automaker. This was before platform sharing became an explicit goal. At the time of writing, Ford is clearly committed to an extension of the Jaguar range, to which it added another, smaller model in 2001 (the X-Type), one assembled on Ford's old Halewood site. Jaguar will then possess four basic models instead of the two it had initially – and its output could exceed 150,000 units per annum instead of the 40,000 that had originally been foreseen. Note that the relationship between this small Jaguar model and the new Mondeo platform has not been clearly specified but the two vehicles have a number of components in common. Ford may ultimately seek to extend Volvo's range, just as it has done with Jaguar. There is a great deal of conjecture on this point, including the diametrically opposed possibility that Ford will again use the flexible new (1999) Volvo S80 platform for its own purposes, conceivably to replace its signature car product in the United States, the Taurus. The choices that are being made here have not been finalized or communicated and it would probably take quite a long time before such sharing policies could be implemented. What has happened with the Lincoln LS shows in any event that global platform sharing is feasible for top-of-the-range cars, as long as this is achieved through the use of highly differentiated models; that is, as long as there is no real attempt to repeat a 'world car' approach. Another possibility could involve the sharing of technologies and modules instead of platforms. This is something that Ford announced on April 2001 with its 'C1 Technologies programme' relating to the replacement of the middle-range passenger cars for three brands, Volvo (S40 and V40), Mazda (323) and Ford (Focus).

Ford's October 1999 reorganization was basically a materialization of its decisions in this domain. Brand management, a concept that GM also likes to stress, has been delegated to Ford's six business units: the four geographic zones where the brand appears in its own name (North America, Europe, South America and Asia-Pacific); the Premier Automotive Group; and Mazda. This structure should probably not be viewed as anything more than a straightforward reversion to a regional approach, even though it clearly strengthens the Ford brand's regional organizations – entities that continue to reaffirm the principle of a global platform (in that each possesses its own strategic thinking unit). However, a case could also be made that one objective of this approach is to make it possible to reconcile global and regional considerations even as business units are being allowed to oversee products that are intended for their local markets. The Ford example shows in any event that the globalization of the automobile industry is not a foregone conclusion. Globalization creates serious problems for management, subjecting firms to intense pressures because they must constantly assess and reassess whether their strategies and structures continue to be relevant.

General Motors and its global platforms

On the one hand, GM has been slower than Ford to adopt explicitly a platform sharing approach in the main continental markets. But on the other, it is true that GM's policy in this area was formulated as a master plan that was first announced in 1996. Moreover, compared to Ford, it would also appear that GM has acted in a more systematic and ambitious manner, at least in terms of the number of platforms and models concerned. It has also been more aggressive, in that its platform-sharing plan is supposed to be operational for a relatively longer period of time (until well beyond the first decade of the twenty-first century). Unlike Ford, the GM plan does not coincide with any international reorganization, but relies on a pre-existing internal division of labour that has allocated to GM Europe (and in reality to its Opel subsidiary) the responsibility for international affairs – for the whole world outside North America. This arrangement caused an organizational crisis, leading GM in 1998 to adopt a structure that was better adapted to its globalization drive. Finally, GM's acquisition in 2000 of a 20% stake in Fiat Auto has paved the way for a whole range of new possibilities involving the sharing of platforms with this other large European generalist automaker.

The 1996 master plan and its various incarnations

Except for its well-established practice of exporting small residual volumes of different American models to Europe, GM had already accumulated a modicum of relevant experience before announcing in 1996 that it was coming up with a master plan for global platforms. The volumes involved meant, however, that the previous impact had been minimal. In 1996, GM began exporting to the United States a top-of-the-range European car called the Opel Omega. This car had already been launched in Europe in 1994, but in America it was sold through the Cadillac network and called the Catera. In terms of the direction of the flows involved, this was a relatively novel approach – but in fact it was more of an example of residual exports rather than global platforms. The 1996 plan was primarily noteworthy because of its magnitude. After all, it had a simultaneous effect on the three global platforms that were supposed to cover all the manufacturer's future small and medium-sized cars. It should also be analysed in the light of GM's overall goal of reducing the number of platforms it operated (from fourteen to seven). These global platforms were each named after a Greek letter. Starting with the smallest, they were called the Gamma, Delta and Epsilon platforms, and each was sub-divided by type of market (this being yet another original point): A for emerging markets, B for North America and C for Europe. In GM's existing structure, responsibility for international affairs had been given to Europe. In addition, the platforms mentioned above corresponded to the types of capabilities that could be found in Europe. The combination of these two factors meant that the responsibility for the platforms' development was allocated to Opel (and to the resources it was able to mobilize). Inversely, the North American developmental resources inherited the other platforms (large-sized cars, utility vehicles) even though this had not been specified in the plan. It remains that with each platform being sub-divided into the three described market categories, people were being lead to believe that above and beyond their main responsibilities, centres located on different continents would engage in a joint product-development processes.

In the years that followed, GM would become convinced, even as it was maintaining its overall strategic line, that it should flesh out the contents of its 1996 plan – as well as partially amending it to reflect the operational adjustments that its development programme was having to make. This was particularly true for the Delta and Epsilon platforms. For the smallest platform (the Gamma), things were in a far greater state of flux. As for the Delta platform, its launch was disturbed by the extremely short delay between the master plan announced in 1996 and the 1998 launch (six months later than originally foreseen) of the Opel/Vauxhall Astra – a vehicle that belonged to the medium/low European range, and which was destined because of its size and production volumes to be the Delta platform's signature model. The Astra is not sold in North America, but it is marketed in South America and Asia under a variety of different brands (Opel, Chevrolet or Holden), depending on the market.[2] Following the Astra (which was launched in 1998), the next models to be designed on the Delta platform were intended as a replacement in 2001–2 for American models such as the Chevrolet Prizm and Cavalier or Pontiac Sunfire that have all been commercial disappointments. In 1999, GM informed its suppliers that it would be postponing production of these replacement models by at least two years. As a result, the European Astra is apparently no longer going to be used as a vehicle for satisfying the American marketplace. Other reasons, more transitory in nature, have also had an impact, including the desire to concentrate those resources that can be used to develop light utility vehicles (which have experienced a commercial boom in the United States). In addition, GM wants to bide its time, to be able to assess whatever innovative models its competitors might be launching in this segment (for example, the Ford Focus and

Chrysler PT Cruiser). In 2000, a GM communiqué officially relaunched and repositioned the timing of the Delta platform. GM Europe was reaffirmed as being in charge of this platform and its two key models, the Astra and the Zafira minivan. However, the first car to be launched on the Delta platform was a Saturn product. We should also mention the forthcoming European and American replacement models, although things may still change for the latter. The Chevrolet Cavalier and Pontiac Sunfire are both to be made on the Delta, while the Prizm could disappear and be replaced by a hybrid vehicle that may be manufactured and even designed in co-operation with Toyota (as part of the NUMMI joint venture). Nevertheless, as a result of the GM–Fiat deal concluded in 2000, the Delta plans will have to be revised. The stake taken by GM in Fiat during that same year creates new co-operation possibilities, which will inevitably interfere with this platform.

As regards the largest of the three platforms mentioned in the 1996 plan (Epsilon) GM did not specify its contents and scheduling until the year 2000. It was decided that the leading European car, the Opel/Vauxhall Vectra, should not be allocated to the platform this time, as the model had already been renewed one year before the 1996 plan was announced. The Epsilon platform's launch would therefore have been postponed until the new decade (when the Vectra is up for another renewal) had it not been for Saturn's decision to launch a new range in 1999 (2000 model). Because of the slightly larger size of the new Saturn L-Series, the Epsilon platform was intended to be used. In fact, however, it was developed along the lines of the current Vectra series, even though, during its development phase, Saturn had tried to emphasize its differences from the European model. The L-Series is basically a larger car: various structural modifications have been made, the body has been completely changed, one of the driving systems has been specifically Americanized and only a very small percentage of the Vectra's components have been used (80 out of a total of 1,900). It is true, however, that some real co-development has taken place. Saturn's engineers, working together with their European colleagues in a 50-strong team, were sent to England, to the premises of Lotus, a British design and engineering company. This work organization can be seen as a precursor of the way, or of one of the ways, in which GM intends to shape the co-development of its global platforms. Whatever the status of the 1999 Saturn L model as regards the Epsilon platforms, GM's year 2002 forecasts confirm that its future replacement will indeed be made on this platform. Several models will supposedly be tied into the Epsilon: in Europe, the new Opel/Vauxhall Vectra and the Saab 9-3 (2002); in North America, the Chevrolet Malibu, the Pontiac Grand Am and the Saturn L (to be launched around 2004–5). Finally, for the upscale segment of the European car market, GM could use a North American platform, replacing the Opel/Vauxhall Omega using the Sigma platform (which initially was not intended to be shared on both sides of the Atlantic).

The contours of the Delta and Epsilon platforms may have become more specific, but Gamma, the smallest of the three global platforms, has not yet benefited from this level of definition – despite the fact that the Opel/Vauxhall Corsa, which is to be made on this latter platform, was renewed in 2001. This launch might be an opportunity for GM to respond to a certain number of ongoing questions relating to this platform. First, there is the issue of whether the platform's A, B, and C organization, discussed above, truly lends itself, given its small size, to this type of sub-division. Are we talking about a world car or about models that are becoming more and more differentiated? Given the potential volumes and markets, differentiation would seem to be the answer. Europe is in great need of equipment (the C models); North America, where these vehicles are less crucial, has a somewhat lesser need for them (the B models); and the emerging markets, where purchasers' budgetary constraints are more stringent, has little need for them (the A models). If GM develops adapted variants (hatchbacks, pick-ups) from the European Corsa, and produces and sells them in the emerging markets, North America will probably remain outside this project. Second, what treatment is going to be reserved for those vehicles that are even smaller than the Corsa? After all, this is a segment that GM would be ill advised to ignore. Will these be Gamma vehicles, or will a more specific approach be followed? Third, what about the future of GM's collaboration with the Japanese firms Isuzu and Suzuki, or even with Toyota (NUMMI), on this automobile segment? Will these be integrated into Gamma or will they run alongside it? GM has introduced in Europe a smaller vehicle that Suzuki helped to develop – in addition to the replacement of the Corsa. Last, but not least, what contributions will Fiat Auto's competencies make to GM's products in this segment (see below). All in all, many questions remain unanswered, and some difficult decisions are going to have to be made. Note that the insufficient transparency of GM's global strategy for this segment is similar to the situation at Ford, which has also been getting ready to renew its European Fiesta for an introduction that will be more or less concomitant.

A global reorganization that has become a necessity

In terms of the organizational aspects of its global strategy, GM, like its rival, Ford, has experienced a number of problems, albeit of a different nature. Whereas Ford's decision to adopt a trans-regional structure would appear to be a case of 'too much, too soon', GM can be criticized for not having done enough. In its 1996 global platform plan, GM announced its intention to organize its activities around the international structure it first set up in the early 1990s – an organization that, with hindsight, would seem to have been overly simplified. In 1992, probably influenced by the contrast between its highly profitable European subsidiary and poorly performing American parent company, GM decided to set up GM International Operations in Zurich, Switzerland, in juxtaposition with (and basically overlapping) the attributions of GM Europe's headquarters. GM International was intended to manage all of GM's activities outside North America, and serve as a catalyst for the rest of the group. In addition, the approach probably stemmed in part from the assumption that European products could easily be adapted to the demands of the emerging markets. This put a lot of pressure on Opel's development centre in Dudenhofen (near Frankfurt, Germany), compounded by the 1996 plan to sub-divide platforms by market types. A serious internal crisis erupted in 1997, with Opel's senior management starting to fight openly with Zurich, arguing that its development centre's resources were being consumed by GM International to the detriment of Opel's own requirements. This crisis coincided with the sudden losses that the group made in Europe that year.

GM's spontaneous reaction was to try to allocate the Dudenhofen centre's resources better between Opel's needs and the group's international needs. In addition, GM International was repatriated to the group headquarters in Detroit. Subsequently, in October 1998, the group's global structures were reorganized, with GM International totally disappearing. The four regional presidents (North America, Europe, South America and Asia) were made directly accountable for operations in their respective zones, but on a parallel rather than on an integrated basis. Thirteen 'global process leaders' were named, each in charge of the global co-ordination of a particular function (that is, product development, manufacturing, sales, purchasing, quality and so on). The thirteen global process leaders and four regional presidents together formed an 'automotive strategy board' placed under the direct authority of GM's president and head of operations. As regards GM Europe's role in the new structure, the subsidiary no longer influenced the world outside America to the extent it had previously. The new structure is much more multi-regional than the old one, which tended to be bi-regional. Ford probably had an eye on GM's new organizational structure when it undertook a similar operation a year later. With these new organizations, what the two firms have in fact been striving to do is to balance global and regional considerations.

GM's stake in Fiat Auto

The final chapter of our study of GM's globalization of its main markets looks at the impact of globalization-related mergers or strategies. As Ford had done with Mazda, in 1998 GM reinforced its stakes in its Japanese partners, Isuzu and Suzuki, increasing them to 49% and to 10%, respectively (and the latter to 20% two years later). This made it seem as if there was going to be greater co-operation between GM and the two Japanese firms, a collaboration that had already borne fruit in the small vehicle niches, notably with the light utility vehicles that had been co-developed with Isuzu. In 1999, GM also acquired a 20% stake in Fuji Heavy Industries, which controlled Subaru. As mentioned above, however, GM's ultimate intentions for these Japanese automakers have yet to be specified. Elsewhere, GM took total control of Saab in 1998. Aside from this one move, however, it did at first seem that GM would not be participating in the mergermania of the 1990s, which had been exemplified by the spectacular deals between Daimler and Chrysler in 1998, and between Renault and Nissan, and Ford and Volvo, in 1999. Then, in March 2000, GM took a 20% stake in Fiat Auto with an option to purchase the remaining 80% (Volpato, 2003). Above and beyond the fact that the American company did not, because of its mediocre profitability for the previous fifteen years, have enough cash to purchase the Italian firm outright, the deal confirmed GM's willingness to exchange capital stakes (unlike Ford, which has always preferred outright take-overs). By taking a significant stake in the capital of a generalist European automaker which produces more than 2.5 million vehicles per annum (of which 40% are sold in emerging countries), GM has made it difficult to ascertain who is the world's largest automaker. After purchasing Volvo and including Mazda, Ford was able to fight back to GM's level – and as the 1990s drew to a close, each firm was producing more than 8 million vehicles per annum.

In addition to this symbolic battle for supremacy, we can anticipate that this alliance will over time have an effect on GM's globalization strategy. After reaching an agreement, the new partners announced the creation of a joint venture that should enable them to share engines and transmissions (Fiat-GM Powertrain) as well as another joint venture specializing in purchasing activities. Fiat may even receive some support from GM's distribution network and thus re-establish itself in North America. With respect to platform sharing, certain observers have underlined the fact that GM might be interested in the flexible platforms that Fiat has developed using its own technology. In fact, in 2000, GM Europe and Fiat created a common vehicle architecture team based at the Saab works in Sweden, with a mandate to develop a common platform for premium vehicles (replacement of Saab 9-5, Lancia Lybra and so on). However, co-operation between the two automakers seems to have increased more strongly than expected initially, following the announcement made in early 2002. A small-car team based in Turin has begun to work on a common platform to replace the Fiat Punto and 178 and the GM Corsa, which are being planned for 2005–7. At the same time it has been announced that Fiat's new large car (due in 2003–4) will be based on GM's Epsilon platform which was launched in 2002 with a view towards replacing the Vectra. Finally, as yet unconfirmed information indicates that the next Astra to be launched, in 2004–5, will be based on the Fiat Stilo platform. In such a case, the failure of GM's strategy of global platforms would be evident, with only one common transatlantic platform (Epsilon) rather than the three global platforms planned initially: Gamma (Corsa) and Delta (Astra) platforms are becoming more and more regional and less global (in terms of reinforcing the integration of Europe and North America).

In any event, it was no surprise that the integration team, comprising people from both firms' upper echelons and intended to guide discussions on possible synergies, included, above and beyond representatives from the various parent companies, senior managers who have been working for the two firms in Europe and South America. These two zones (including Eastern Europe) are the areas where Fiat has concentrated most of its resources, and where the two firms have the greatest opportunities for co-operation. Supposing that Fiat and GM wished, and were able to, increase the co-operation that exists between Europe and South America, it would be interesting to see whether this could be achieved without damaging GM's Europe–North America axis. It is possible that major strategic changes of this nature may occur over time.

Imitative behaviour converging in intent, yet with each party maintaining its own trajectory and modalities

Comparing the chronological sequence of events with regard to the globalization and organization of GM and Ford (see Table 3.1), we see an overall congruence between the trajectories of the two automakers. It is clear that GM's 1996 plan was a response to Ford's first global platform and to its 'Ford 2000' reorganization. Similarly, there is a clear tie between Ford's reinforcement of its links to Mazda and GM's reinforcement of its links to Isuzu or Suzuki; like Ford's purchase of Volvo and the stake that GM took in Fiat a year later. In the first chronology, note that Ford was the forerunner and GM the follower, which would tend to suggest that Ford achieved strategic superiority over its rival during this period, at least in the competitive fields that this chapter covers. The other major argument substantiating this contention is that, even though Ford did indeed exploit all the market potentialities of its three North American/European global platforms, GM has always basically lagged behind in this respect. Nevertheless, it is evident that the two firms' respective positions are very unstable. Even after 'Ford 2000' started to come under criticism, it took Ford until 1999 to decide to undertake a reorganization that could reconcile its diverging global and regional considerations – in other words, it acted a year later than GM, which had been trying to respond to its own internal crisis. The two automakers also began to converge in terms of the areas they were trying to change, and in terms of the types of problems that they were facing while trying to carry out these strategies. Both had problems in deciding how to attack the American downmarket range and, to lesser extent, the European upmarket range. It was also difficult to define the role to be assumed during this globalization drive by the two firms' Japanese partners, who are, it must not be forgotten, their direct rivals in terms of European-located competencies. It also seems paradoxical that GM's and Ford's globalization drive did not affect their utility vehicles (especially their various types of sports utility vehicles) or their minivans, given that both firms had strong positions in North America for this type of product. GM's and Ford's highest volume platforms (with an annual output of around a million units) have, in fact, been the regional ones where light utility vehicles are being produced with no regard being paid to a European-centred globalization drive (aside from a few small residual exports). It is true that utility vehicles account for

Table 3.1   Globalization and organization timeline, 1990s–2001

Ford		GM	
1993	Senior management changes (A. Trotman)	1992	Senior management changes (J. Smith)
1993	Mondeo launched in Europe	1992	Founding of 'GM International Operations' in Europe
1994	'Ford 2000' announced: global operations integrated; three responsibility centres organized by vehicle type and by main functions to be globalized	1996	Announcement of global platform policy for small and medium-sized cars, with three market variants (North America, Europe, emerging markets)
1996	Stake in Mazda rises to 33.4%	1997	Cohabitation crisis in Europe; repatriation of GM International to Detroit
1997	End of AutoLatina JV with VW (followed by 1999 closure of AutoEuropa)	1998	Increased stakes in Isuzu (49%), Suzuki (10%) and Saab (100%)
1998	Senior management changes (J. Nasser); Kia withdrawal	1998	Reunification of global operations; integration of four regional entities including main functions to be globalized
1999	Purchase of Volvo Cars and creation of 'Premier Automotive Group' (PAG)		
1999	Reorganization: creation of six Business Units' (four geographical regions, Mazda and PAG) focusing on brand management and integrating globalized functions	1999	20% stake taken in Fuji Heavy Industries (Subaru)
2000	Purchase of Land Rover from BMW; negotiations on take-over of Daewoo (abandoned September)	2000	Participation in capital of Fiat Auto via exchange of shares
2001	Senior management change (William Clay Ford, Jr)	2000	Increased stake in Suzuki (20%); expresses interest in taking over Daewoo

50% of total unit sales in America, against barely 10% in Europe. A disparity of this order is unlikely to lead people to conceive of the two zones in an integrated manner.

GM's and Ford's imitativeness did not prevent each from maintaining its own specificities. With respect, for example, to the aforementioned lag between the two firms as regards the execution of their globalization projects, Ford and GM can be differentiated by the way in which each has broached the issue of platform sharing (see Table 3.2). Ford basically started out with a programme for sharing competencies, allocating to each specific centre the responsibility for a given platform – whereas GM defined a platform globalization plan without devising any definitive solutions for the problem of responsibility sharing (particularly as its main concern was the need to

Table 3.2 Sharing platforms between Europe and North America

Ford	GM
1 Eur 1994: CDW27 (upper mid-scale) Eur 1994: Ford Mondeo NA 1995: Ford Contour, Mercury Mystique NA 1999: Mercury Cougar Eur 2000: CD132 (replacement) Eur 2000: Ford Mondeo II	1 Eur 1994: Opel OMEGA (upper scale) Eur 1994: Opel/Vauxhall Omega Eur/NA 1997: Cadillac Catera
2 Eur 1999: CW170 (lower mid-scale) Eur 1999: Ford Focus NA 2000: Ford Focus	2 Euro 1994: Opel VECTRA (upper mid-scale/upper scale) Euro 1994: Opel/Vauxhall Vectra Euro/NA 1999: Saturn L
3 NA 2000: Lincoln-LS (upscale) NA 2000: Lincoln-LS Eur 2000: Jaguar S-type NA 2001: Ford Thunderbird	3 Planned for 2001 and beyond: (a) GAMMA (downscale) Eur-2001: Opel/Vauxhall Corsa NA ?: Chevrolet Metro ? Eur 2005–7: common platform with Fiat, Fiat Punto & 178, new Corsa
4 Eur 2003 C1 programme: Ford Focus Volvo S40 and V40 replacement Mazda 323 replacement	(b) DELTA (lower mid-scale) NA 2003: Saturn S-series Eur 2004–5: Opel/Vauxhall Astra and Zafira or Fiat Stilo platform? NA 2004: Chevrolet Cavalier, Pontiac Sunfire ? (c) EPSILON (upper mid-scale/upper scale) Eur 2002: Opel Vectra, Saab 9–3 NA 2004–5+: Chevrolet Malibu, Pontiac Grand Am, Saturn L-series (d) SIGMA platform (rear-wheel-drive) NA 2003: Cadillac CTS, Seville, XLR roadster Eur 2005: Opel Omega

Note: Eur = Europe; NA = North America.

break each platform down by type of market). We can say that Ford's approach to platform sharing has, up to the time of writing, been heavily impregnated with the global car theme. This is true in particular for its first two platforms (the Mondeo and the Focus), but less so with its third (the Lincoln LS). GM appears, however to, have favoured a more differentiated approach to the various markets. This is reminiscent of Ford's more centralizing culture, although it remains possible that the firm will in turn evolve over time towards a more decentralized approach. GM and Ford are beginning to converge, now that Ford has started to withdraw from its focus on a 'world car' in favour of traditional high-volume saloon cars. Along these lines, we also note that are two firms are distinct in terms of their modalities of external growth. Ford prefers to gain control and where possible full ownership, whereas GM is more than ready to accept partial and even minority participation. The difference between the structure of the two automakers' shareholders (relatively dispersed for GM, but more concentrated for Ford, where the founding family continues to play an important role) may be an explanation for these specificities – but they have also been shaped by each firm's own historical trajectory. Despite its standardizing effect, globalization does not erase those behaviours that historical forces have allowed to ferment slowly.

General Motors and Ford's new corporate borders

For the last few decades of the twentieth century, the internationalization process that the Big Two American automakers, Ford and GM, have followed has also led to a redefinition of their corporate borders, in both senses of the word 'border':

- At a geographical level: the two groups' industrial presence has been extended and restructured, as each has moved into new countries and regions in line with what can be termed its 'world economy', the concept that was initially developed by Fernand Braudel and Emmanual Wallerstein (Lung, 1991); and
- At an economic level: since the activities involved in the firms' basic competencies (Dosi and Teece, 1998) have been redefined, there has also been a reshaping of the core businesses themselves. This movement has found its expression in the divestments and investments that the firms have made in new productive activities – as if the rampant 'financialization' that has been associated with the overall drive towards globalization has caused companies to reformulate the way in which they design their productive coherency.

The reconfiguration of the two firms' 'world economy'

Ford and GM clearly both have a long tradition of nurturing the international presence they have established. Since the 1920s, they have had a significant presence in South America, where they first built a number of assembly sites, and subsequently adapted themselves to local developments – each time taking stock of whatever national import substitution policies were being followed, particularly in Brazil and Mexico. In Asia, they have been able to achieve a dominant position, despite the presence of the

Japanese automobile industry. In fact, their entities in Australia, which has always been an important market in this part of the world, have long been market leaders (with Ford trading here under its own name, and GM in the name of Holden, thus following a strategy similar to its European one). Since the beginning, each firm has imitated the other's productive internationalization. This is characteristic of oligopolistic competition, where neither party wants to allow its rival to benefit exclusively from any source of profit. If one of the firms sets up operations in a given country, its competitor will have done the same within a short period of time, each acting alternately as first mover and as follower. The history of the rivalry between Ford and GM has been akin to a two-agent race, although there have been differences in the way that each has conducted itself during this confrontation: GM has often adapted more to the local environment (its own creation by W. C. Durant was based on a principle of diversity; cf. Madsen, 1999) whereas the Ford Motor Company has usually pursued approaches that have been more uniform, and even universal (reflecting the principle of homogeneity preached by Henry Ford I).

This rivalry continued throughout the post-war years, notably in Europe (Dassbach, 1989), and has persisted in recent times. It nevertheless remains true that a comparison of the two firms' geographic border redefinition strategies reveals an increasing convergence – each firm has committed itself to pursuing new areas, and to reorganizing its older units (in regions such as South America and Asia-Pacific).

Opening up towards new areas

The 1980s and 1990s were marked by the redefinition of central regional spaces. Firms tried to integrate peripheral regions – and they made of number of (up to now unsuccessful) attempts to gain a foothold in those emerging markets that offer the greatest potential for growth: namely, continent-sized countries.

In regional integration matters, Ford Motor Company has played a leading role, having opted for the construction of a vertical regional division of labour between the various sites it runs in its central industrialized regions of Europe and North America. Having anticipated the enlargement of the original six-member Europe Union (EU) towards the Iberian peninsula, Ford was responsible for triggering the loosening of Spain's foreign investment control laws in the early 1970s. Its decision to build a manufacturing unit in Valencia to make a small-sized, bottom-of-the-range Fiesta model was mirrored by Opel's decision to set up its own operations in Zaragossa, in the hope of assembling the same type of product (the Corsa model) at this location. Towards the mid-1980s, when Mexico's integration into the North American (NAFTA) system was just becoming an issue, Ford was once again the firm that was most willing to make a direct commitment to the constitution of a regional productive system, first building a plant in Hermosillo, Mexico

(Carrillo and Montiel, 1998) and then (in the 1990s) shifting its production around between the various sites it runs in the three NAFTA countries. General Motors, also committed to a southerly relocation (starting with the American states that lie to the south of the state of Michigan), was more prudent in its approach because of the sensitive nature of the relationship it entertains with the American labour union, the UAW. It was primarily through its component-making activities (that is, through its GMAC/Delphi subsidiary before this was spun off) that GM was able to consolidate its presence in northern Mexico. At the time of writing, 80% of all vehicles coming off GM's North American lines are equipped with multiplex systems assembled in *maquiladoras*, and Delphi's multiplex R&D centre is also located south of the Rio Grande (Carrillo and Hualde, 1997).

It is also through their building of component-making plants in Central and Eastern Europe that the two American firms were able, during the early 1990s, to gain a presence in countries that have committed themselves to making the transition to a market economy (see Table 3.3). With respect to the automobile production activities themselves, Ford has been extremely cautious, displaying a great deal of risk aversion in an environment marked by its centralized management of localization choices (that is, following the implementation of its 'Ford 2000' plan). The firm has opted for an incremental development strategy, with commercial activities coming first, and productive ones later (if ever). Ford's commercial presence is on the whole very satisfactory in this part of the world (having been evaluated at 5% of the Central European market) but even now – more than a decade after the fall of the Berlin Wall – the second (productive development) phase has not really started, with regard to assembly operations at least. In fact, the assembly plants that Ford opened in Poland in 1995 and in Byelorussia in 1997 (CKD) were closed five years later as part of a 1999–2000 plan aimed at restructuring the firm's European activities.

Conversely, through its German Opel subsidiary (which has been very active in Central and Eastern Europe), General Motors has made a heavy commitment to modernizing and consolidating the automobile industry in countries that have committed themselves to making the transition to capitalism. One example is the pilot site it opened at Eisenach, in (the former) East Germany, where organizational innovations have created one of Europe's top-performing assembly plants, a model for the rest of the group (Jürgens, 1998). GM has also developed its productive activities in the region's other countries: an assembly unit in Poland; an engine plant in Hungary, now managed by the Fiat–GM Powertrain joint venture (its low volume activities of CKD assembly having been stopped in this country); not to mention its numerous Delphi sites or the units that are run by its strategic partners (Suzuki, Fiat). In 2000, aggregate sales of Opel, Fiat and Suzuki brands represented 14.3% of the Central and Eastern European passenger car markets (including Russia), whereas total market share was about 2.5% for the Ford, Mazda and Volvo

Table 3.3 Ford and GM's new productive areas: current and future projects as at September 2000, in units/year (u/yr)

Country	Ford	General Motors (GM)
East Germany		Opel, Eisenach, since 1993. Theoretical capacity 177,000 u/yr
Byelorussia	Ford Union (J.V., Ford 51%), 1997. CKD 6,800 u/yr. Closed in 2000	
Hungary		GM, Szengotthard, 1991. Assembly 15,000 u/yr (Opel Astra). Closed 1998–9 Fiat–GM Powertrain: production of engines (530,000/yr) and transmissions (250,000/yr starting in 2001)
Poland	Ford. Assembly unit at Plonsk opened 1995. Theoretical capacity: 30,000 u/yr. Maximum: 14,000 in 1997. Closed down in 2000	New plant opened at Gliwice in 1998. Theoretical capacity 72,000 u/yr (150,000 in time). Astra hatchback and Agila derived from the Suzuki Wagon R+ being produced in Hungary Assembly of Opel Vectra by DFM
China	Jiangling Motors Group Corp. (30% held by Ford since 1997. Assembly of Transit vans (target 60,000 u/yr). In the future: an additional jointly designed vehicle and capacity adding up to 110,000 u/yr Changan Ford Automobile: 50–50 J.V. with Changan Automobile to produce a small car: Ikon (hatchback derived from the Fiesta). Production to start by the end of 2002. Capacity: 100,000 u/yr	Shangai General Motors (50% with SAIC) founded in 1997. Production of Buick Century and Regal, Sail (Corsa hatchback) and minivan GL8 (capacity: 100,000 u/yr). V6 engine and automatic transmission plant Technical centre Jinbei GM Automotive Co. founded in 1992. Relaunched in 1998 (50–50): production of Chevrolet Blazer and S10 pick-up starting in 2001 (capacity: 50,000 u/yr) Negotiating a J.V. with Liuzhou Wuling Motors for production of low-price vehicles
India	Mahindra and Mahindra (7% stake), Escort assembly unit. New plant in Madras (Ford India). Assembly capacity of 50,000 u/yr (Ikon, derived from Fiesta)	General Motors India (50% in 1994 with Birla; 100% GM since 1999) Since 1996, assembly of Opel Astra hatchback. Capacity: 25,000 u/yr, rising to 100,000

Table 3.3   continued

Country	Ford	General Motors (GM)
Community of Independent States (CIS)	St. Petersburg. Joint venture with Bankers House SP. Starting in 2001, 25,000 Focus to be assembled per annum (ultimately rising to 100,000 u/yr)	Yelabuga (Tatar). Construction of the Yelaz complex (J.V., holds 25% of capital). Chevrolet Blazer assembly unit since December 1996 (Objective: 300,000 u/yr). Production stopped (to be abandoned) ZAO General Motors Avtovaz, J.V. between GM, Russian vehicle producers Avtovaz and the EBRD to produce a small sports utility vehicle derived from the Niva, and sold under the Chevrolet brand (decision taken in 2001)

Sources: CCFA, Répertoire mondial des activités de production et d'assemblage de véhicules automobiles, December 2001, Paris.

brands. All in all, with its previous internationalization-related learning experiences, GM would seem to better than Ford at adapting to local environments, and in developing partnerships with indigenous firms. This also applies in continent-sized emerging market countries.

With their large populations, and given the (sometimes contradictory) signs that their economies are about to take off, continent-sized countries such as China, India and Russia may well become extremely important markets for the world's automobile firms. For this to occur, economic growth would first need to consolidate, then subsequently generate an expansion of the middle class – the dynamics of motorization are such that this socio-economic group is the prime catalyst behind the demand for automobiles.

In terms of the facilities it currently maintains in these continent-sized countries, General Motors' ability to adapt to local environments, and above all to manage partnerships through the incorporation of relational learning processes, gives it an advantage over Ford in both Russia and China. Following the 1998 rouble crisis, GM postponed, modified and even abandoned three projects to which it had committed itself in the former CIS member states. Its plans to assemble 25,000 cars in the Ukraine (as part of a joint venture with Avotzaz and Daewoo) have definitely been dropped, and its partnership with Yelaz in the Tartar Republic has been mothballed (this was supposed to be a new plant whose initial annual production of 50,000 Chevrolet Blazers and Opel Vectras was due to rise over the medium term to 300,000 units). There has also been a shift in GM's agreement with Russia's main automaker (Avtovaz) relating to the assembly of 150,000 Opel Astras in the Togliatti plant, which is now to be used primarily for the production of a locally designed vehicle (derived from the Lada Niva and sold under the Chevrolet brand as part of a joint venture between GM (41.5%), Avtovaz (41.5%) and the European Bank for Reconstruction and Development (17%). Having adapted to the constraints of the local market (lower purchasing power means that vehicles have to be inexpensive, and that demand will remain highly variable) and to the limitations of the institutional environment (political uncertainty, problematic technological transfers), GM's projects have taken on a definite local colour – whereas Ford has been pursuing its standard approach, and trying to produce a European model in Russia. Towards this end, Ford has created a joint venture near St. Petersburg, an assembly plant due to have an annual production of 25,000 units (soon rising to 100,000) of its Focus model.

GM is also the first American manufacturer to have assembled a passenger car (the Shanghai) in China, where it has a 50% stake in a joint venture with the Shanghai Automotive Industrial Corp. GM should eventually resolve the problems it experienced with Jimbei, its first joint venture in China, and this project was relaunched in 2001. A third joint venture was being negotiated with Wuling Automotive, and by the end of 2001 this was intended to lead to the production of minivans and mini-trucks. Ford, on the other hand, in 1997 took a 30% stake in JMC (Jiangling Motors Corporation), a firm that assembles a range of different vehicles, including Ford Europe's Transit van (the target here being 60,000 units per year). In 2001, Ford finally found the way to enter China's passenger car market. This involved a joint venture with Changan Automobile, a Chinese vehicle producer, relating to the production of a small hatchback (the Ikon) derived from the Fiesta platform that had initially been designed for the Indian market.

In India, Ford was quicker than GM to benefit from the new conditions that the country has been offering to foreign investors. The failure of its Indian operations, run as a joint venture with Mahindra and Mahindra and intended to serve as an assembly site for its European Escort model, induced Ford to reposition itself in this country by creating its own subsidiary (Ford India) and developing the Ikon. As for GM, it began to adapt to the changing circumstances in India in 1994 when it took 50% of a joint venture called GM India (together with its local partner Hindustan Motors, that took the remaining 50%). This entity was intended as a site for assembling a hatchback version of the Opel Astra. Later, in 1999, the American firm took total control of this subsidiary.

Ford may have pioneered the idea of integrating the spaces bordering a given site into a new form of vertical (and therefore hierarchized) regional division of labour, but GM has been better at dealing with more complex local realities and at negotiating collaborative arrangements. Nevertheless, these nuances should not mask the fact that the two US firms have displayed highly imitative behaviour, both with regard to their decision to open up to new geographic areas, and in terms of the way in which they have reorganized the older entities they run in the other parts of the world.

The reorganization of older developmental areas

In addition to Ford's and GM's actions in countries that are new to them, and because of the way in which emerging country power in general rose during the 1990s (Humphrey *et al.*, 2000), the two American firms have been remodelling their facilities thoroughly in their older peripheral areas (such as South America and Asia-Pacific).

The two groups' South American presence has largely been predicated upon the activities of their European subsidiaries, Opel and Ford Europe, especially with respect to the products they offer in this part of the world. Large-cylinder North American vehicles have been unsuccessful commercially in this region – the Brazilian automobile market's expansion during the 1990s was a result of the advent of the 'people's car'. These small cars, equipped with engines of less than one litre, represent two-thirds of all sales at the start of the twenty-first century (Norberto and Uri, 2000). For automakers who maintain a presence in South America, small-sized European cars such as the Opel Corsa (sold under the name of Chevrolet) or the Ford Ka and/or Fiesta constitute the basic model. The creation and consolidation of Mercosur has also created greater similarity between the South American and European situations. In certain respects, this regional integration process replicates the European (common market) trajectory, and thus works to the advantage of European teams, who can share their experiences with their South American counterparts. A vertical regional division of labour is also being organized among the various Mercosur member states, above all between Argentinian and Brazilian factories. Yet the two US firms' strategies in this part of the world should not be analysed as a simple replication of solutions that have already been used in Europe. Their South American strategies are based on the introduction of a number of organizational innovations that over the long run will probably affect Ford's and GM's productive systems everywhere.

In order to produce and assemble in South America, locally adapted versions of models that were initially designed and developed in Europe, the two US firms began quasi-simultaneously to experiment with modular production. With GM's 'Blue Macaw' and Ford's 'Amazon' projects, the two American companies have been trying to implement a small-car assembly system in which first-tier component makers are given the responsiblity for designing, producing and assembling modules and sub-systems. Their experiments with such innovative forms of organization have been taking place in Brazil's more recently industrialized regions, at newly built greenfield assembly sites where component makers not only participate in the initial investment programmes themselves, but also locate their own facilities on site (or at least in the immediate vicinity). On occasion, suppliers even get directly involved in assembly line operations. At GM's Gravatai plant, which opened in 2000, sixteen component makers are working on the manufacturing site itself, delivering modules for a derivative version of the Opel Corsa (a three-door hatchback version going under the name of the Chevrolet Celta). For example, door assembly operators employed by Lear, an American component maker, work standing alongside GM employees. And with Ford's project in the Salvador de Bahia province, scheduled to go on-line by the end of 2002, American and European automakers' Brazilian experimentation with modular production will be further reinforced (Lung *et al.*, 1999).

Although they have been present in the Asia-Pacific region for as long as they have in South America, the two big American groups have suffered in this part of the world from the closure of national borders (that is, Japan in 1933) and, later on, from the full-blown onslaught of Japanese followed by Korean automakers. In reality, Ford and GM have fallen behind in Asia-Pacific, relinquishing market leadership to firms such as Toyota, Mitsubishi and Hyundai – and they have been trying progressively to reorganize their presence in this part of the world by developing strategic alliances with Asian automakers. Ford took a stake in Mazda in 1979, and this Japanese firm subsequently became the focal point for all its activities in the Asia-Pacific region. In fact, in Japan, South East Asia and Australia (where Ford also sells the Maverick), most of the vehicles being sold under the Ford brand name are in fact rebuilt Mazda models, such as the 323 and the 626. The offices of Ford's Asia-Pacific regional division have also been localized in Japan, attesting to Mazda's dominant role in terms of products and techniques. Now, it is true that in the world as a whole, integration has previously been a generally slow process (relatively rapid in North America but non-existent in South America and only anecdotal in Europe). However, with Ford effectively assuming total control over Mazda in 1996, the ever-greater degree of co-operation in South East Asia (Thailand, the Philippines, Taiwan) should enable global integration to move to a higher level.

GM has been following the same type of approach in the Asia-Pacific region, where it has been seeking shelter in partnerships with Japanese firms such as Suzuki, Fuji Heavy Industries and Isuzu (see above). By integrating these partners into its own organization, GM can access their competencies with regard to small-sized city cars and vans, and diesel-fuelled vehicles. However, this integration could in the long run become a difficult one to manage, as it implies a cohabitation within the GM group of a number of firms that sometimes offer similar resources. In some ways, Opel and Suzuki are rivals, particularly with respect to small-car design and development. For the present, like Ford with Mazda, GM has been leaving high-volume vehicles to one side and concentrating primarily on niche vehicle collaborative arrangements with its partners in Japan (that is, for the Agila model).

In South Korea, the two American groups each began by allying themselves with a local manufacturer – Kia for Ford and Daewoo for GM. These alliances, settled in the 1970s and 1980s, have now been dissolved. Yet it had once seemed that both of the American companies were going to get involved in the launch of an inexpensive small world car: the Kia Pride/Ford Festiva; and even before that, GM's 'world car', the Opel and Vauxhall Kadett (which was also marketed under the Daewoo and Chevrolet brand names). In the late 1990s, the Korean automobile industry went through a major crisis. As a result, Ford separated in 1998 from Kia (Hyundai having in the meantime taken a stake in this company). Subsequently, the two American firms vied with one another to take over Daewoo – Korea's last independent car company after the alliances that had been concluded between Samsung and Renault(-Nissan) and between Hyundai and DaimlerChrysler(-Mitsubishi). Despite its high level of debt, Daewoo remained an attractive proposition. It offered direct access to the South Korean market, to the many different emerging countries where it had already set up operations, and to the industrialized countries' bottom-of-the-range small city car segment. Ford was ahead after the first round of the Daewoo take-over negotiations, but later decided to drop out of the race, even though the acquisition would have enabled the company to return to its original ideal of being able to offer a universal, standardized, solid and inexpensive car. Finally, GM and Daewoo announced in September 2001 that the US firm would acquire the Korean automaker. However, negotiations are still continuing at the time of writing, without any guarantee that the announced deal will be concluded. If this is the case, the GM–Fiat–Daewoo group will represent around 25% of total world vehicle production (see Appendix Table A3.1).

Redefining the automobile groups' perimeter of activities

In recent times, industrial firms (and first and foremost North American groups) have been working very hard to refocus their productive activities on those areas that they see as being their core business. In the automobile business, this has meant the design, assembly and commercialization of vehicles (passenger cars or vans). The pressure to refocus on core businesses and to seek out new profit opportunities has forced firms to make a number of new choices. Once again, Ford and GM find themselves in a similar situation. They have had to abandon any conglomerate-like diversification strategies; withdraw from the component-making sector (first by converting their parts manufacturing entities into subsidiaries and then floating them on the stock market); and devise strategies that are new, and which focus on the services that are associated with automobiles.

The abandonment of diversification strategies

Little by little, the two groups have been selling off activities that they see as being marginal in terms of their 'core business'. In certain cases (that is, concentric diversification), GM and Ford have been letting go of activities that were considered to be distinct from the automobile business. These are investments whose original justification had resided in their economic opportunity (high profitability), or else in their fulfilment of a strategy that had stressed the need to seek out activities whose business cycle ran counter to the automobile industry's, and which therefore stabilized overall income. In other examples, the two Americans have been withdrawing from activities that at one time had been more or less close to their core business – affecting what is conventionally defined as their corporate 'border'.

Ford and GM thus began during the 1980s to drop out of certain businesses whose operational technologies had once seemed to offer potential synergies. One example was their production of heavy trucks, tractors or major public works construction equipment. GM withdrew a long time ago from all heavy truck production. Ford sold its interest in this area to Freightliner in 1997. Despite Henry Ford I's affection for tractor production, in 1990 Ford sold to Fiat all the agricultural and public works equipment production activities it had been hoping to consolidate when it had acquired the New Holland company. That same year, Ford also separated from its Ford Aerospace subsidiary (whose position in the group had seemed to be reinforced because of other recent acquisitions) and sold it to Loral. During the 1980s, the Big Three (including Chrysler) were operating under the illusion that synergies existed between aerospace and automobile manufacturing, and they therefore became involved in the former market. In the 1990s, however, these illusions slowly began to fade. One conclusion we can draw is that firms restrict the technological perimeter of their core activities by getting rid of those activities they deem to be more or less marginal. High-tech activities require considerable investment in new product development, but more often than not, once people have exploited the outcome of these various R&D-related investments, in the end they feel disappointed. The sectors discussed above all seemed to turn on shared technologies (that is, mechanics or electronics), but contrary to appearances, there was little overlap in the specific competencies and types of capabilites being mobilized. There was too much of the economic and financial risk that is associated with technological uncertainty, and bureaucratic and organizational costs were too high. Moreover, as we discuss below, by the spin-offs of their component-making subsidiaries, the firms were also able to increase their overall focus on their core automobile production activities.

Another generic reason for a diversification strategy is that firms often hunt for activities that are either barely linked to, or else totally disconnected from, their main line of business (automobiles, in our example). This type of diversification enables them to generate financial surpluses that can offset insufficient and/or excessively volatile profit rates in their core business. This is clearly the case with automobile production, where profit rates have generally been low for a long period of time, and where massive cyclical fluctuations in North American sales weighs on returns. GM, with its long tradition of conglomerate-like industrial diversification (that is, its foray into Frigidaire brands) has organized an extremely diverse set of activities – many of which have been totally unrelated to the automobile business. Since the mid-1990s, however, GM has in the main disposed of the high-tech subsidiaries it acquired during the previous decade. In 1995, it sold Electronic Data System (EDS), a world leader in information systems. In 1997, it sold Hughes Aircraft's defence activities to Raytheon. Whereas one in four employees in the GM Group worked outside the automobile sector in 1994–5, this percentage dropped to below 5% in 1997–8.[3] At the time of writing, GM's industrial presence outside the automobile sector has truly shrunk – although there remain a few traces of former diversification initiatives, such as heavy-duty transmissions (Allison Transmissions) and railway transport (GM Locomotive Division). Above all, GM still has Hughes Electronic Corp., which has been very active in new multimedia service packages (such as DirecTV). Yet even this space (satellite) and communications subsidiary has been refocusing on its own core business. It has been concentrating on interactive television; increasing its co-operation with AOL; selling its satellite building business to Boeing; and in January 2000 withdraw from its positions in the mobile and local telephone markets. As of early 2002, GM seems to be looking for a way to sell Hughes.

Whereas GM, ever since its foundation by W. C. Durant in the early twentieth century, has tended to work as a conglomerate-like structure, Ford has traditionally been more focused on the automobile business. The ambition of Donald Petersen, chairman of Ford from 1985 to 1990, was to equip the group with a second line of business in order to reduce its exposure to short-term cyclical fluctuations, such as those that had almost caused the parent company to become bankrupt in 1980–2 (Bordenave, 1998b). Petersen tried to commit Ford to the finance sector, which had previously been a regular source of profit (see Table 3.4). He committed resources to the acquisition of several major financial institutions (The Associates, Meritor Credit Corp., U.S. Leasing) and acquired several deeply troubled S&L's in an effort to build up a major network that could be centred around the First Nationwide Financial Corp. Petersen was clearly a visionary – between 1985 and 1999, finance generated half of Ford's profits. Moreover, this profitability was unconnected to its other activities' business cycles (Froud *et al.*, 2000). Nevertheless, none of these investments would turn out to be as successful as the resale of The Associates (which generated a capital gain of US$16 billion when it was sold off in 1999) – and at the time of writing Ford has withdrawn totally from those financial activities that are unrelated to its automobile business. On the other hand, it has maintained the financial activities that are related to its core business. The Ford Automotive Credit subsidiary, for example, which finances new and used car sales, generates high profits.

Table 3.4   Ford's withdrawal from financial activities unrelated to its core automobile business

1985	First Nationwide Financial Corp. (US$493 million) acquired
	Network extended through acquisition of a number of S&Ls
1986	State Savings (Ohio), Citizens Home Savings (Ohio), St Louis Federal (Mo), Lincoln Federal (Ky), Capital Savings (Ariz)
1988	Uptown Federal (Ill), Lincoln Fed (NJ), Bloomfield Savings (Mich), First Dearborn Fed. (Mich), Columbia Savings (Colo), Mile High Federal (Colo), Pathway Financial F.A. (Ill), Cardinal Federal (Ohio)
	Sold 1994
1987	US Leasing International Inc. (US$512 million)
	Resold 1997 (capital gain of US$1 billion)
1989	Meritor Credit Corp. (US$1.4 billion)
1989	The Associates (US$3.4 billion)
	Resold 1998 (capital gain of US$16 billion)
1990	Mellon Financial Services Corp. (US$75 million), Transamerican Fleet Leasing Corp.
	Marine Midland Automotive Financial (US$300 million)

Separating from component-making subsidiaries

In the early 1980s, and because of their major involvement in component manufacture, General Motors and Ford were the most integrated automobile firms in the world, and particularly in North America. Their automobile component production activities put them in first and third place respectively in that sector's world-wide rankings. And yet this intense vertical integration both groups shared was the result of distinct historical trajectories. On the one hand, there was the deliberate internalization strategy Henry Ford had started to pursue during the 1920s (manifested in the design of the *Rivière Rouge* integrated industrial complex). And on the other, there was W. C. Durant, whose dispersed efforts when GM was first constituted led to the purchase of a wide variety of activities – followed by A. Sloan, who tried to create strategic and structural coherency through the establishment of a multi-divisional organization (Chandler, 1962). The two US automakers' schemes of vertical integration were strengthened by the agreements they had negotiated with the UAW labour union as part of the Fordian compromise that was consolidated in the immediate aftermath of the Second World War. During the Western economies' boom years, firms felt that they would be able to derive competitive advantage from vertical integration. By the final quarter of the twentieth century, however, and as a result of all of the structural changes that were caused by the global confrontations which marked this era, vertical integration had become a handicap. US firms were producing more than 50% of a car's value internally – but for the Japanese groups, this figure was only 15% to 20%. Indeed, the late twentieth century coincided with the rise of what came to be known as the 'Japanese model of management', one basic component of which was the use of a pyramid of sub-contractors in an effort to achieve an efficient and flexible management of vertical relationships.

From the 1980s onwards, Ford and GM began systematically to rationalize their component production activities, by making their groups' own plants compete with external suppliers. They also began to move out of non-strategic business sectors, and tried to focus on those activities where they could benefit from size-related advantages. These rationalization efforts were accompanied by the reorganization of their components divisions, which housed all their component-making activities (GM and Ford organized these into business lines). During the latter half of the 1990s, these divisions became autonomous subsidiaries, named Delphi (GM) and Visteon (Ford). This step-by-step withdrawal was completed by the dissolution of all financial links between the parent companies and the subsidiaries they ultimately spun off. In 1999, for example, Delphi was separated from GM through an exchange of shares, and it became completely autonomous (at least financially). The following year, Ford did the same with Visteon (see Table 3.5). Moreover, the trend is not necessarily over – both American firms have been externalizing a number of motorization activities they no long consider to be central to their core automaking business. By setting up its transmissions factories as joint ventures with German specialists (ZF for Batavia in the USA, and Getrag for its European plants), Ford has shown clearly its opinion that gearboxes no longer fit within the perimeter of its basic competencies. And possessing few internal competencies in the field of diesel motors, the two American automakers seem prepared to resort to external competencies, with Ford turning to Peugeot in Europe, and GM to Isuzu (or Fiat).

Delphi has become deeply involved in the design and production of pre-assembled modules and integrated systems. This implies a clear departure from the special relationship that had previously existed between the component-making subsidiaries and their parent companies. Firms must be able to supply a diversified clientele (one that includes rival automakers) if they are to benefit from a scale of production that is high enough to allow them to spread out the heavy costs they have to assume in developing new components systems (Salerno and Dias, 2000). Global competition in the component-making industry has eaten away at profit margins at the same time that the reinforcement of non-price competition has required ever-greater

Table 3.5   Ford and GM's former component-making subsidiaries

Component-making firm	Total sales year 2000 (US$ bn)	World-wide ranking
Delphi Automotive Systems	26.5	1st
Visteon Automotive Systems	18.6	2nd

Source: *Automotive News*.

investments in R&D (Sadler, 1999). With the rise of electronics and other types of new technologies (materials-related and so on), these activities have become increasingly capital-intensive. Irreversible sunk investments having become increasingly onerous – and the various activities of the component-making sector have tended to become more autonomous (in that they now involve businesses that rely on extremely specific competencies and knowledge bases). There are few synergies in research and development terms, and even though the necessarily vertical nature of the co-ordination procedures presupposes the existence of co-design mechanisms, profitability is tenuous and risks are high. All these factors explain GM and Ford's sudden withdrawal from vehicle manufacturing as well as their externalization of upstream activities – and why their ambitions have subsequently moved downstream, towards the service sector.

Rent-seeking in the service sector

Given the reduced outlook for profits in the manufacturing sphere, the two American groups have positioned themselves to be leaders in 'automobile-related production and services'. This strategic positioning, which they have openly espoused, is based on several observations. First of all, financial activities, notably subsidiaries such as GMAC and Ford Credit specializing in financing car sales, have long been a source of regular profits for the two groups. On average, over the period between 1983 and 1999, financial activities accounted for 40% (GM) and 50% (Ford) of net income. Second, a car's commercialization represents a large portion (25% to 30%) of its price. Rationalizing automobile distribution systems can create substantial savings. Finally, new car purchases are only part of the motorization outlays of households (less than 25%). It is therefore important to have a presence in those spending categories where, by introducing industrial knowledge, the firm can rationalize its business lines – and at the same time offer a product–service tandem that is capable of generating increased profits.

This has been the main issue at stake in the distribution network restructuring that has started to take place in North America and Europe. Ford has made major changes in this area, but GM has been somewhat more cautious (Jullien, 1998). Ford has been trying to assume direct control of its distribution activities, even as it has been developing alliances with its partner distributors. In the United States, the rise of publicly quoted distribution companies has become a threat for independent distributors. Following the example of companies such as Carmax and AutoNation, Ford has started to merge its sales points into larger distribution platforms (that is, superstores) in an effort to possess enough competent staff and improved equipment to allow it offer a whole range of standardized services relating to new and used car sales, associated services (financing, insurance, vehicle repurchase agreements), maintenance and repairs. These platforms (the Ford Retail Network) are joint ventures in which the car manufacturer holds a 49% stake, the rest being held by distributor groups that are already active in a given commercial area. The development of e-commerce has further accentuated the pressure on traditional networks. Ford's sudden change of direction has provoked relatively hostile reactions, notably from the independent distributors with which the firm has to negotiate. Ford's reaction has been to announce that it will not unilaterally be managing its own web-based sales – that is, that it will be calling upon its network to help implement Internet-based forms of commercialization, and it will finally be abandoning its platforms strategy in the USA. In Europe it will be easier to reinforce the company's direct control of its retail network (Jullien, ch. 4 in this volume).

GM had also tried to develop its own commercial structure, but ultimately decided to come to an agreement with its network of distributors and develop joint ventures to be responsible for selling these sorts of products and services. Although its approach has been more pragmatic than Ford's, GM basically faces the same types of problems. To cut down on the number of sales points it runs, GM started in 1997 to set up large vehicle sales centres (GM Malls) and tried to associate its distributors with this initiative, but their unfavourable reaction caused a freezing of this experiment. The same types of initiatives have taken place in Europe, where the automotive groups have had to restructure their sales networks in light of the dismantling foreseen for the year 2002 of Europe's current exceptional regime of automobile distribution. Ford also seems ahead of the game in this part of the world, having merged its European distribution points into the local alliances it maintains with partners such as the Jardine Group in England. On the other hand, GM's German dealers, by negotiating a new distribution policy, have forced this latter company to revisit its initial plans.

By positioning themselves in service activities revolving around the various ways in which automobile products are used, GM and Ford are looking to explore systematically different potential sources of profits. Ford, for example, in addition to its car rental business (Hertz) has been investing in new forms of activities, including rapid repair or vehicle maintenance (acquisition of Kwik-Fit in Europe, Master Service in Mexico and B-Quik in Thailand). It has also been getting involved in the used product (vehicles and parts) and recycling markets, particularly in the United States. The creation of the Ford Automotive Services Group manifests the firm's desire to strengthen automobile-related service activities so that they become as important as manufacturing activities – just as the creation of Ford Financial Services Group had attested to its desire during the 1980s to become involved in Finance. Nevertheless, J. Nasser's departure in late 2001 (he was replaced by W. C. Ford as head of the company) led to a major turnaround in orientations, with Ford having decided to sell its non-core activities (Kwik-Fit in Europe, recycling and used parts activities in the USA). The new types of services with which the two groups have become involved are also tied into automobiles' new electronic functionalities: with OnStar, GM has been striving to become a leader in on-board navigation services. All in all, whereas both firms' core manufacturing businesses have shrunk considerably, their service activities have been experiencing exponential growth. This trend might have encountered its limits with Nasser's dismissal, and with Ford's new top management team's 'back to basics' drive. The desire to become a leader in automotive services and in the new Internet economy has caused Ford to face up to its products' quality-related problems (design, reliability and so on) and to re-focus its activities on the firm's automotive core competencies.

Conclusion

In recent years, Ford and GM have become involved in new areas (through their exploration of new countries and regions – that is, emerging markets) and in new activities. Both of these novelties imply that they are going to have to restructure global organizations that have been clearly drawn along regional lines. Their repeated efforts to unify markets and to organize a planet-wide division of labour, first manifested themselves in the 'world car' strategy of the 1970s, have not always proved conclusive, and in words as well as in deeds, both firms have been very cautious and hesitant in implementing their global platforms. And even though both have been trying to create some convergence between the high-volume models that each produces for the European and North American markets, they have recently had to reaffirm the authority and autonomy of their European subsidiaries (Ford Europe and Opel/GM Europe) within a transregional type of configuration involving a clear return to regional platforms for high-volume products.

In addition to problems relating to the way in which the firms' two dominant regions are linked, they have also encountered difficulties with the alliances they have been trying to set up, and with their mergers and acquisitions strategies. Alliances are usually positioned in such a way as to complement a firm's historical productive bases, but we can anticipate that Ford and GM will soon be organizing painful competitive battles between their own internal departments (in North America or in Europe) and their new allies, whether in Europe (Fiat, Volvo, Land Rover) or in Asia (Mazda, Isuzu, Suzuki, and even Daewoo).

All in all, globalization has been characterized by tremendous heterogeneity, both with respect to consumer demand patterns (note the difficulties experienced in creating transatlantic platforms, developing specific emerging country models and so on) and with respect to the automobile firms themselves – especially since they now need to make allowance for their new allies in whatever calculations they make. Above and beyond the frequently ambitious speeches that can be heard on the topic of globalization (analyses stressing the savings that can be made thanks to potentially higher volumes), Ford and GM have been trying to act pragmatically, and implement configurations that mesh well with their product policies:

- World-wide strategies for the top-of-the-range and niche vehicles that (following the Ford Premier Automotive Group's example) will be produced in a single region and sold in all markets;
- Purely regional strategies where products that have been designed and manufactured locally will only be targeting a specific regional market (that is, most light trucks in North America and high-volume passenger cars) – with exportation being a marginal activity at best; and
- Transregional strategies, with two modalities: (i) the derivation of specific models using one regional platform (for example, products for emerging countries); and (ii) the sharing of mechanical and electronic modules on several vehicles. Global modular and technology sharing strategies are to replace global platform strategies.

With their reticular configurations, Ford and GM possess a vast portfolio of diversified competencies. Moreover, this portfolio can be widened furthered through alliances and mergers and/or acquisitions. The articulation and integration of these resources remains a major challenge for both groups, and they will have to try to develop innovative modes of organization if they want to come to terms with the internal as well as the external heterogeneity of the automotive world. The trend towards financialization and immaterial activities also seems to have been reversed, as the complexity of designing and producing vehicles remain a strong nexus of competencies – and one that should not be dispersed.

Translated by Alan Sitkin

Statistical Appendix, GM and Ford

Table A3.1 The internationalization of Ford and GM's automobile production, number of vehicles produced in 2000 (thousands of units)

	North America (NAFTA)	Europe (EU)	Japan	Other countries	World
Ford[a]	4,694	2,229		400	7,323
Mazda	68	10	779	70	927
Ford network	4,762	2,239	779	470	8,250
As a percentage of Ford network's total global production	*57.7%*	*27.1%*	*9.4%*	*5.7%*	*100.0%*
Ford network's percentage of total local production	*26.9%*	*13.1%*	*7.7%*	*3.5%*	*14.2%*
General Motors[b]	5,630	1,858		645	8,133
Isuzu, Fuji-Heavy & Suzuki	227	34	1,638	679	2,578
GM network	5,857	1,892	1,638	1,324	10,711
As a percentage of GM network's total global production	*54.7%*	*17.7%*	*15.3%*	*12.4%*	*100.0%*
GM network's percentage of total local production	*33.1%*	*11.0%*	*16.1%*	*9.9%*	*18.4%*
Fiat Auto		1,696		945	2,641
Daewoo				717	717
GM–Fiat–Daewoo	5,857	3,588	1,638	2,986	14,069
As a percentage of GM–Fiat–Daewoo total global production	*41.6%*	*25.5%*	*11.6%*	*21.2%*	*100.0%*
GM–Fiat–Daewoo percentage of total local production	*33.1%*	*20.9%*	*16.1%*	*22.4%*	*24.1%*
Total local production	**17,699**	**17,142**	**10,144**	**13,311**	**58,296**

Notes
(a) Ford, Mercury, Lincoln, Jaguar, Aston Martin, Volvo Car, Land Rover;
(b) Chevrolet, Buick, Oldsmobile, Pontiac, Cadillac, Saturn, Opel, Vauxhall, Saab.

Source: CCFA.

Table A3.2 Ford Motor Company historical data, 1987–2001

Year	World-wide Ford					Geographical data						
	Total company	Automotive sector			Financial services	North America		United States		Europe		
	Employment	Vehicle sales	Turnover	Net income/(loss)	Net income/(loss)	Vehicle sales	Net income/(loss)	Net income/(loss)	Employment	Vehicle sales	Employment	Net income/(loss)
	Thousands	Units in thousands	US$ millions	US$ millions	US$ millions	Units in thousands	US$ millions	US$ millions	Thousands	Units in thousands	Thousands	US$ millions
	(a)	(b)	(c)	(d)	(e)	(f)	(g)	(h)	(i)	(j)	(k)	(l)
1987	350	6,171	71,797	3,767	858	4,040	2,842	2,723	181	1,655	109	989
1988	359	6,662	82,193	4,609	691	4,313	2,678	2,474	186	1,799	111	1,459
1989	367	6,608	82,879	3,175	660	4,131	1,285	1,099	188	1,879	115	1,190
1990	370	6,023	81,844	99	761	3,632	50	(17)	180	1,816	126	145
1991	332	5,623	72,051	(3,186)	928	3,212	(2,284)	(2,215)	156	1,887	118	(1,079)
1992	325	5,940	84,407	(8,628)	1,243	3,693	n.a.	(405)	158	1,722	109	(647)
1993	322	6,184	91,568	1,008	1,521	4,131	n.a.	1,482	167	1,493	100	(873)
1994	338	6,853	107,137	3,913	1,395	4,591	n.a.	3,002	181	1,709	103	128
1995	347	6,606	110,496	2,056	2,083	4,279	n.a.	1,843	186	1,709	n.a.	116
1996	372	6,653	118,023	1,655	2,791	4,222	2,255	2,007	190	1,820	106	(291)
1997	364	6,947	122,935	4,714	2,206	4,432	4,434	3,706	190	1,800	104	272
1998	345	6,823	119,083	4,752	17,319	4,370	4,612	n.a.	174	1,850	105	193
1999	374	7,220	136,973	5,721	1,516	4,787	6,137	n.a.	173	1,960	135	26
2000	346	7,424	141,230	3,624	1,786	4,933	4,886	n.a.	163	1,962	132	(1,130)
2001	n.a.	6,991	131,528	(6,267)	814	4,292	n.a.	n.a.	n.a.	2,161	n.a.	n.a.

Notes

(a), (i), (k) Average employment in all Ford's activities.

(b), (f), (j) Cars and trucks (tractors sales until 1991 are not included); including all Ford Motor Company's units and vehicles manufactured by Ford and sold to other manufacturers. Jaguar and Volvo cars are included from 1989 and 1999, respectively.

(c), (h), (d), (g), (l) Visteon included until 1999.

(d) Including: exceptional provision of US$6,883 million for post-retirement health-care benefits in 1992; loss of US$2,252 million on spin-off of Visteon in 2000. Ford lost US$784 million in 2001 when excluding unusual charges and other items.

(e) Including: gain of US$15,955 million on spin-off of The Associates in 1998.

Source: Ford reports.

Table A3.3 General Motors historical data, 1986–2001

Year	World-wide GM								Geographical data		
	All activities	Automotive activities			Financial and insurance	North America automotive activities			Europe		
	Total Employment	Vehicle sales	Turnover	Net income/(loss)	Net income/(loss)	Vehicle sales	Net income/(loss)	Employment	Vehicle sales	Net income/(loss)	Employment
	Thousands	Units in thousands	US$ billions	US$ billions	US$ billions	Units in thousands	US$ billions	Thousands	Units in thousands	US$ billions	Thousands
	(a)	(b)	(c)	(d)	(e)	(f)	(g)	(h)	(i)	(j)	(k)
1986	877	8,376	90,210	1,435	1,184	6,356	2,003	633	1,268	(0,343)	123
1987	813	7,497	89,610	1,707	1,486	5,555	(0,169)	583	1,301	1,255	118
1988	766	8,108	97,440	2,992	1,477	6,122	0,318	538	1,340	1,810	112
1989	775	7,907	99,110	2,796	1,069	5,655	0,132	531	1,464	1,830	118
1990	761	7,454	96,910	(3,109)	0,769	5,420	(5,524)	503	1,608	1,915	130
1991	756	7,404	94,610	(6,795)	1,038	4,794	(8,264)	486	1,615	1,763	133
1992	750	7,827	102,810	(4,152)	1,219	4,975	(5,588)	478	1,665/1,806	1,333	141
1993	711	7,851	107,910	0,243	0,918	5,198	(0,872)	448	1,622	0,605	131
1994	647	8,381	123,250	2,272	0,920	5,587	0,690	433	1,705	1,337	126
1995	745	8,320	132,160	4,032	1,031	5,328	2,388	437/255	1,725	1,579	129
1996	647	8,263	133,170	2,337	1,241	5,142	1,672	424/245	1,795	0,778	79
1997	608	8,776	139,140	0,449	1,318	5,549	0,203	237	1,850	(0,170)	79
1998	594	8,024	131,840	1,634	1,422	5,071	1,542	226	1,882	0,419	94
1999	398	8,786	142,190	4,981	1,534	5,874	4,857	217	1,968	0,423	91
2000	388	8,746	143,770	2,291	1,161	5,775	3,174	212	1,879	(0,676)	89
2001	362	8,022	n.a.	0,367	1,177	5,136	1,270	202	1,760	(0,765)	73

Notes
(a) Total employment in all GM activities (automotive, and other) on 31 December (including Delphi until 1998).
(b), (f) Production in 1986 and 1987.
(g) Including component activities, Delphi until 1998.
(h) Total GM in the USA until 1996 (left); GM North America Automotive since 1995 (right).
(i) Sales in Western Europe until 1992 (CCFA). Including Central and Eastern Europe since 1992.
(k) GM Europe – including Saab employees since 1998.

Source: GM reports.

Notes

1 In Appendix Table A3.1, the two firms' global production is broken down by selected consolidation parameters.
2 As such, this is a truly global model. However, we shall not be delving any further into it in this chapter, given that we are focusing here on the breakdown of business between North America and Europe. Note that a similar situation exists with the Corsa and the Vectra, European models that are intended to be developed on the Gamma and Epsilon platforms.
3 Source: GM activity reports.

References

Bardou, J. P., Chanaron, J. J., Fridenson, P. and Laux, J. M. (1977) *La révolution automobile*, Paris: Albin Michel.

Bélis-Bergouignan, M. C., Bordenave, G. and Lung, Y. (2000) 'Global Strategies in the Automobile Industry', *Regional Studies*, vol. 34, no. 1.

Bordenave, G. (1998a) 'Le premier demi-siècle de Ford en Europe: la résistance opiniâtre d'un espace à l'universalisme proclamé d'un modèle d'organisation productive', *Le mouvement social*, no. 185, October–December.

Bordenave, G. (1998b) 'Globalization at the Heart of Organizational Change: Crisis and Recovery at the Ford Motor Company', in M. Freyssenet, A. Mair, K. Shimizu and G. Volpato (eds), *One Best Way? Automobile Firms Trajectories and the New Industrial Models*, Oxford/New York: Oxford University Press.

Bordenave, G. (2000) 'Globalisation et partage des plates-formes', *La Lettre du GERPISA*, no. 146, November.

Boyer, R. and Freyssenet, M. (2000, 2002) *Les modèles productifs*, Paris: La Découverte; Revised English edition: *Productive Models: The Conditions of Profitability*, London/New York: Palgrave, 2002.

Carrillo, J. and Hualde, A. (1997) 'Maquiladoras de tercera generacion. El caso de Delphi-General Motors', *Commercio Exterior* (Mexico), vol. 47, no. 9, September.

Carrillo, J. and Montiel, Y. (1998) 'Ford's Hermosillo Plant: The Trajectory of Development of a Hybrid Model', in R. Boyer, E. Charron, I. Jürgens and S. Tolliday (eds), *Between Imitation and Innovation: The Transfer and Hybridization of Productive Models in the International Automobile Industry*, Oxford/New York: Oxford University Press.

Chandler, A. D. Jr (1962) *Strategy and Structure*, Cambridge, Mass.: MIT Press.

Dassbach, C. H. A. (1989) *Global Enterprises and the World Economy: Ford, General Motors and IBM, the Emergence of the Transnational Enterprise*, New York: Garland.

Dosi, G. and Teece, D. (1998) 'Organizational Competencies and the Boundaries of the Firm', in R. Arena and C. Longhi (eds) *Markets and Organization*, Heidelberg/New York: Springer.

Flynn, M. S. (1998) 'The General Motors Trajectory: Strategic Shift or Tactical Drift?', in M. Freyssenet, A. Mair, K. Shimizu and G. Volpato (eds), *One Best Way? Trajectories and Industrial Models of the World's Automobile Producers*, Oxford/New York: Oxford University Press.

Freyssenet, M. and Lung, Y. (2000) 'Between Globalization and Regionalization: What Is the Future of the Automobile Industry?', in J. Humphrey, Y. Lecler and M. Salerno (eds), *Global Strategies and Local Realities: The Auto Industry in Emerging Markets*, London: Macmillan/New York: St. Martin's Press.

Freyssenet, M., Mair, A., Shimizu, K. and Volpato, G. (eds) (1998) *One Best Way? Trajectories and Industrial Models of the World's Automobile Producers*, Oxford/New York: Oxford University Press.

Froud, J., Haslam, C., Johal, S. and Williams, K. (2000) 'Ford's New Strategy: A Business Analysis of Financialisation', in M. Freyssenet, and Y. Lung (eds), *The World that Changed the Machine: The Future of the Auto Industry for the 21st Century?*, Proceedings of the Eighth International Colloquium of GERPISA, Paris.

Hounshell, D. A. (1984) *From the American System to Mass Production 1800–1932*, Baltimore, Md: Johns Hopkins University Press.

Humphrey, J., Lecler, Y. and Salerno, M. (eds) (2000) *Global Strategies and Local Realities: The Auto Industry in Emerging Markets*, London: Macmillan/New York: St. Martin's Press.

Jullien, B. (1998) 'Les constructeurs face aux nécessaires mutations de la distribution: quelles leçons tirer des évolutions rapides en cours aux Etats-Unis?', in Y. Lung (ed.), *Du côté du marché. Actes du GERPISA*, no. 23.

Jürgens, U. (1998) 'Implanting Change: The Role of "Indigenous Transplants" in Transforming the German Productive Model', in R. Boyer, E. Charron, U. Jürgens and S. Tolliday, *Between Imitation and Innovation: The Transfer and Hybridization of Productive Models in the International Automobile Industry*, Oxford/New York: Oxford University Press.

Laux, J. M. (1992) *The European Automobile Industry*, New York: Twayne.

Layan, J. B. (2000) 'The Integration of Peripheral Markets: A Comparison of Spain and Mexico', in J. Humphrey, Y. Lecler and M. Salerno (eds), *Global Strategies and Local Realities: The Auto Industry in Emerging Markets*, London: Macmillan.

Lung, Y. (1991) 'Stratégie industrielle et structuration de l'espace d'une firme multi-nationale. L'"économie-monde" de la Ford Motor Company', *Revue d'économie régionale et urbaine*, no. 1.

Lung, Y., Salerno, M. S., Zilbovicius, M. and Carneiro Dias, A. (1999) 'Flexibility through Modularity: Experimentations with Fractal Production in Brazil and in Europe', in Y. Lung, J. J. Chanaron, T. Fujimoto and D. Raff (eds), *Coping with Variety: Flexible Productive Systems for Product Variety in the Auto Industry*, Aldershot: Ashgate.

Madsen, A. (1999) *The Deal Maker: How William C. Durant Made General Motors*, New York: John Wiley.

Norberto, E. and Uri, D. (2000) 'La révolution des petites cylindrées. Le nouveau marché des voitures populaires au Brésil', in J. B. Layan (ed.), *Firmes multinationales et nouveaux pays automobile. Actes du GERPISA*, no. 29.

Pointet, J. M. (1997) 'Pour une conceptualisation du mimétisme de produit: mimétisme volontaire et mimétisme contraint', *Economie Appliquée*, vol. L, no. 1.

Porter, M. (1986) 'Competition in Global Industries: A Conceptual Framework', in M. E. Porter (ed.), *Competition in Global Industries*, Boston, Mass.: Harvard Business School Press.

Raff, D. M. G. (1999) 'G.M. and the Evolving Industrial Organization of American Automobile Manufacturing in the Interwar Years', in Y. Lung, J. J. Chanaron, T. Fujimoto and D. Raff (eds), *Coping with Variety: Flexible Productive Systems for Product Variety in the Auto Industry*, Aldershot: Ashgate.

Sadler, D. (1999) 'Internationalization and Specialization in the European Automotive Components Sector', *Regional Studies*, vol. 33, no. 2.

Salerno, M. and Dias, A. (2000) 'Product Design Modularity, Modular Production, Modular Organization: The Evolution of Modular Concepts', in M. Freyssenet and Y. Lung (eds), *The World that Changed the Machine: The Future of the Auto Industry for the 21st Century?*, Proceedings of Eighth International Colloquium of GERPISA, Paris.

Tolliday, S. (1998) 'Transferring Fordism: The First Phase of the Overseas Diffusion and Adaptation of Ford Methods 1911–1939', in R. Boyer, E. Charron, U. Jürgens and S. Tolliday (eds), *Transfer and Hybridization: The Genesis and Diffusion of New Models of Production in the Automobile Industry*, Oxford/New York: Oxford University Press.

Volpato, G. (2003) 'Fiat Auto: From 'forced' internationalization towards intentional globalization', in M. Freyssenet, K. Shimizu and G. Volpato (eds), *Globalization or Regionalization of the European Car Industry?* London/New York: Palgrave Macmillan.

Wilkins, M. and Hill, F. E. (1964) *American Business Abroad, Ford on Six Continents*, Detroit: Wayne State University Press.

4
The Internationalization of American Automobile Service Companies and Changes in Distribution
Bernard Jullien

Introduction

Analysts who do not have a great deal of time at their disposal find it difficult to draw any clear-cut conclusions from the various ways in which the European and American automobile distribution landscape has been restructured since 1995. Concepts that are initially seen as unassailable truths or as forms of received wisdom are often quickly replaced by ideas that are diametrically opposed in nature. It is tempting to say that, after five years of experimentation by all the actors involved in these searches for new methods of dealing with downstream issues, we are less rather than more sure about what the future holds. Whereas in the mid-1990s it was possible to draw inferences from the economic and commercial shortcomings of the traditional configurations we were accustomed to using, our former understanding has been undermined both by a series of major changes that deviate from a direction that once seemed capable of opening up a wide range of new possibilities; and also by the problems that existing firms and new entrants have encountered during their attempts to fill this vacuum.

This being the case, analysts with a particular interest in the changes affecting automobile distribution and service sectors have witnessed the emergence of a new theme for a new century – the internationalization of distribution. Viewed in the late 1990s as something that was highly unlikely, relatively untimely and/or necessarily indirect (Jullien, 1999), internationalization now seems to correspond to an increasingly tangible reality. It has two main dimensions: the first being European; and the second, which constitutes the object of this chapter, transatlantic.

At the European level, we have seen the intensification of new (and even more so of used) vehicle flows. There has also been a clear-cut, albeit marginal, internationalization of actors involved in repair and distribution activities. Given the sizes of the corresponding European markets and the persistent disparities in 'national vehicle utilisation systems' (Jullien, 2001), it stands to reason that this situation might offer an opportunity to open up the various markets – after all, by taking advantage of decoupled current economic situations, inventory management can be organized at a pan-European level; and the volatility in group performances can be reduced. Nevertheless, a gap exists in this area between the perception of opportunities and the desire to exploit them; that is, by designing profitable operational organizations. This gap is usually forgotten whenever, as claimed in the business models of a certain number of new entrants in Europe and the United States (Chanaron and Jullien, 1999), firms have tried 'to exploit sources of economies of scale' or 'to apply methods used in the retail sector to the automobile business'. It can only be filled through the development of competencies, but these are known to be subject to a high degree of uncertainty. Moreover, such learning is very time-consuming (and therefore requires a major long-term financial commitment).

In so far as operators in Europe are having to learn about this 'regional' style of management while experimenting at the same time with methods once considered to be a possible embodiment of the two other types of opportunity (Volpato and Buzzavo, 2003), the outcome and the very survival of this orientation remain deeply uncertain. However, it is essential that they face up to such issues, given that the internationalization movement in question encompasses certain highly conflictual aspects. After all, as demonstrated by the 2001 European public debate on exemptions in the automobile distribution system, the parties involved are playing for very high stakes (that is, the way in which value is to be shared, market power and so on). These are paramount concerns for the main categories of operators, actors who are doing battle with one another in a number of different areas: manufacturers, car rental companies and financing companies vying with one another over used-car flow management; manufacturers, component makers and insurers fighting over the spare parts and repairs markets and so on.

The issues are clearly complex, and therefore need to be handled with great care. It remains that the prime challenges facing automakers and users are so important that they cannot be avoided. It thus seems timely to broach the topic of the internationalization of automobile distribution and services via its second, transatlantic, dimension. Although this dimension may seem to be far less dramatic than its purely European counterpart, the initiatives the American firms have undertaken in Europe in the late 1990s and beyond are meaningful at a number of different levels:

1. Contrary to the old cliché about American leadership, for the operators concerned it is much less a question of coming to Europe to apply tried and trusted recipes from back home than an attempt to exploit European specificities. In so far as Europe still features a high degree of national

heterogeneity in terms of its automobile distribution, service and utilization modes, the very decision to set up operations in Europe is a meaningful one in and of itself. The American operators' internationalization drive therefore provides us with a wealth of information on the European system.

2. A corollary to this is the interest that the American firms have manifested for Europe, and the way in which this reveals the limitations of the business models they have been attempting to deploy. Above and beyond the characteristics of the American configuration to which this refers, such companies' internationalization efforts reflect elements that relate to the conditions in which the organizations and commercial concepts they are trying to promote become sustainable. Two essential aspects emerge from this perspective: one that is legal in nature; and the other financial.

3. Given the many different operators involved in the transatlantic internationalization of the distribution sector, any analysis thereof should follow a systematic approach to the automobile and to its modes of utilization. Such an approach invites us to renew our understanding of the automobile phenomenon (Jullien, 2002), opening it up to include the varying uses a population makes of one and the same product. When seen in this light, the restructuring of the automobile distribution sector (and the procrastinations that have been associated with this drive) are issues that are seemingly related to firms' basic difficulties in dealing with the way in which the poorer sections of a population use the product.

We shall be developing these three main ideas in succession, focusing primarily on the major distribution groups and putting forward for each of them an analysis of the strategies being followed by the leading figures from the other operator categories.

American operators' transatlantic operations: the imposition of a model or an exploitation of differences?

In Europe, the economic and business press, as it has done with many other sectors, has often taken as its starting point for discussions on automobile distribution an allegedly American model, one that is reputed to be (neo-)liberal and modern. Surprisingly, this fantasy also arose during the recent debate on exemption, with the press having evoked the possibility that European supermarkets might soon be selling new cars, 'just like they do in the United States'. At the same time, in the USA, the trade press spoke of the European debate in the following terms: 'If it weren't such nightmare for the auto industry in Europe, you might think it was laughable – but it isn't. There is a real fear that the EC will disband the franchise system entirely.' An editorial in *Automotive News* even concluded that 'it just shows that maybe relationships in the United States aren't that bad after all'.[1]

This is a clear signal that American operators did not wait for the European system to become as (neo-)liberal as their own before moving to

Europe to apply recipes they had already experimented with back home, where such a framework supposedly does exist. In a certain number of cases the opposite occurred, and the example of Ford between 1998 and 2001 is highly significant in this respect. This does not mean that the American operators were motivated only by the desire to take advantage of differences in relative bargaining strengths and legal frameworks. Disparities in market structures and economic prospects have also constituted a pole of attraction.

American automakers: from the exporting of a model to the exploitation of European opportunities

Partially as a reaction to these new entrants, and in part because this was an old plan whose implementation had always been postponed because operators did not want to force their dealers into open rebellion (with all the commercially damaging effects this would have had in the short run), in 1998 Ford began to consolidate its networks in the United States. After founding a legal entity that was first named 'Auto Collection' and later 'Ford Retail Networks', it created two experimental sites (in Tulsa and Salt Lake City). These entities were supposed to undertake co-ordinated management of all the representations of the group's marques within a given geographical region. They were also meant to centralize back office functions, advertising budgets and a number of after-sales operations, to achieve major cost savings and increased commercial efficiency. Towards this end, it was necessary that a certain number of franchised dealers would agree to sell their business to the entity. Ford offered to take a significant, albeit minority, stake in the new company, leaving the majority shareholding to the franchisees it selected.

At first Ford manifested a relatively conservative and defensive attitude towards the major automobile distribution groups, companies that first began to solidify in 1998 (once they had overcome their earlier problems in developing superstores specialized in the mass marketing of more recent used cars). However, it later decided to rely on these groups, accompanying their consolidation drive as best as possible with a view towards controlling this move (Jullien, 1998).

The consolidation concept had already spread to a number of regions when it began to run into some major difficulties during its implementation in Tulsa. In fact, this was the only region where a *modus operandi* of this ilk could be experimented with fully – but by 1999 serious commercial and financial problems were already beginning to arise, and in 2000 Ford started to pull out. This transpired even before the regulatory and legal counterattack that the dealers were later to organize; a long time before J. Nasser was forced to leave the company; and before the abandonment of the Ford Motor Company's transformation strategy.[2]

What is important for the purposes of this chapter is the extremely rapid decision that was made to develop this consolidation strategy in Europe. In the great Fordian tradition, this first took place in the United Kingdom, starting in

London in late 1999 via a publicly traded distribution group called Pendragon. With Ford's 2000 take-over of the English auto repair chain Kwik-Fit (which had long been the owner of the Speedy rapid repairs chain on the European continent), the hub policy also reached into mainland Europe.

After four years of denials and turnarounds, Ford began to reverse direction in the United States, while sending increasingly frequent signals to its franchised dealers in an attempt to reassure them about their future. Even the certification programme that had been launched in 2001 with a view towards standardizing and controlling the sales and repair services being developed under the umbrella of the group's marques was no longer extended on a voluntary basis. For four years, the company's network renewal operations had performed relatively poorly. Conversely, even though Bill Ford's back-to-basics strategy lead the company to resell Kwik-Fit (which had never been entirely integrated into its strategy), the consolidation operations continued in Europe as part of a policy that (even if it was being pursued more discretely than had been the case in the United States) would directly cause Ford to carry out a partial integration of its distribution function; to reduce drastically the number of investors in its pool; and to make a much more global effort to 'Taylorize' the activities of its European dealers (Jullien, 2000).

GM, the other main American automaker to maintain a presence in Europe (and whose difficulties in developing a distribution rationalization policy in the United States are studied below), seems to have been provoked into making the same kinds of decisions. GM acted a little less overtly than did Ford, and decided not to pressure its networks into making improvements in areas such as after-sales or used vehicles. Nevertheless, in the United States its new aspirations involved little more than offering its networks new/used-car certification programmes; or else new repair chains (such as Goodwrench). In Europe, on the other hand, GM launched a much more centralized policy, convincing Opel in 2002 to abandon its 900 dealership contracts in Germany and to sign only 470 new ones, thus reducing the number of points-of-sale from 2,200 to 1,750. As such, the American automakers were able to accomplish things in Europe that they did not seem able to do back home.[3]

Other American operators' European automobile sales and after-sales operations

In a December 2000 article on automobile distribution in Europe entitled 'After the Block Exemption', a reporter from *Automotive News Europe* predicted for the year 2006 that 'the American chain AutoNation has joined with UK dealer groups Pendragon to seize opportunities in continental Europe. These big groups have bought up hundreds of franchised dealerships, and now exert tremendous influence on carmakers. They now have a big voice in dictating what kind of products the carmakers produce, and the prices they sell those products at.' In February 2002, the American distribution group UAG (United Auto Group), the fourth largest in the United States in the year 2000, acquired the English Sytner Group PLC (owner of forty dealership contracts corresponding to forty-eight franchised points-of-sale) for US$155 million. UAG's chairman, Penske, stated: 'We want the Sytner team to focus on the UK, but their expertise will be called upon as we look for the opportunities on the Continent.'[4] Starting in 2000, Autobytel, which sells automobiles via the Internet, started its European operations up in the United Kingdom, and rapidly extended them to the Continent. During the same period, General Electric Capital continued to expand its credit, leasing and automobile rental operations in Europe; Mannheim Auctions, the re-marketing giant, set up shop in the UK and then in France; and the two big American component makers, Visteon, and especially Delphi, announced development plans for the European after-sales markets.

From all these examples, we get the impression that, even though the media's recurring fantasy as expressed by the *Automotive News Europe* reporter is more ungrounded in 2002, and that the European competition authorities' have continued to grant manufacturers the right to organize their distribution activities on a selective basis, the presence of American actors in the automobile distribution and service sectors still constitutes one of the stronger trends of the early 2000s. Clearly, depending on the specific activity, the approach taken by US firms to internationalization differs quite significantly among these actors. It is none the less generally true that, even though it may not have been what was planned initially, these firms are seeking to exploit opportunities in Europe that do not exist in the USA, as opposed to applying successful US business models in a European context. The legal changes to be introduced in 2002 in Europe are likely to reinforce this tendency.

The most exemplary case in this respect is probably UAG, whose decision to establish operations in Europe was taken at the same time as the European Competition Commission's publication of its latest regulatory plans. Above and beyond opportunities offered by the British configuration (where the fact that the groups involved are publicly traded companies makes it possible to acquire a wealth of franchises in one fell swoop), articles in the press indicate that 'the law seems to be on Penske's side'. Three arguments have been advanced to sustain this thesis:

(i) the possibilities offered by multi-branding constitutes an opportunity. This is pervasive in the United States, where even though such opportunities are generally limited to brands belonging to one and the same constellation, it is possible for distribution groups to limit their risks and to maximize returns on the capital being used;

(ii) the automakers' choice between exclusivity and selectivity will cause them to seek partnerships with groups that are large in size and capable of making investments; and

(iii) the deregulation of the spare parts and after-sales markets, and the manufacturers' loss of power in this area, will also offer new opportunities.

In addition to these arguments, UAG may well be hoping to use Europe
to stave off one of the main impediments to the major American distribution groups' efficiency – that is, the fact that it is (legally) impossible for
them to obtain volume-based discounts from manufacturers (EIU, 2000).
The other limitation on the expansion of a group such as UAG in the United
States is the relative dearth of opportunities to acquire profitable businesses,
particularly in those upscale segments that UAG would like to focus on
because of the higher margins they generate and because they involve
greater customer loyalty towards all the services a franchise can offer. These
mega-distribution groups thus eventually find themselves holding a relatively small market share each, and consequently may not necessarily view
North American expansion alone as a sufficient means of achieving their
expansion drives – although most of them have remained relatively cir-
cumspect about the outlook for further development in Europe.

The other main category of operators that seems determined to place
expected changes in European regulations at the heart of its planning
process is undoubtedly the American components makers. Freed from the
feudal domination of Ford and GM, and better integrated into initial assembly co-development projects (where they work together with European
automakers), Visteon and Delphi are also counting on their after-sales divisions to develop their activity in Europe. Towards this end, Delphi in particular is relying on acquisitions (it has bought Lucas, a repair network that
specializes in diesel motoring systems), and its representatives have been
working very hard to influence European regulatory discussions in an effort
to undermine the 'natural link', trying to ensure that technical information
is communicated to the independent repair shops and that the concept of
original parts is eventually redefined (AutoPolis, 2000). For these two firms,
who are also trying their hardest to optimize the shape of the American market, Europe offers major opportunities. This relates primarily to the size of
the profit margins that the manufacturers have been capturing on spare
parts in Europe (something that allows them to envisage a favourable positioning in pricing terms) – but it is also a question of market share. This latter factor is already a significant one, and for those networks the marques
have been putting together in recent years in this area it has become even
more so. Note, for example, that in Europe marque networks have been able
to keep 40% of the after-sales market, versus 20% in the United States.[5] If
there has been no further deterioration in this market share, it is because of
the products' increasingly technical nature and complexity. This is the result
of the work that is being carried out on behalf of manufacturers by the component makers (who derive little advantage from this). For Delphi, as with
Bosch or Valéo, the main issue is the dissemination of technical information

and the development of in-house networks. This would enable these companies to share whatever rents do exist with the manufacturers and their networks. Once again, Europe offers in this respect opportunities that are highly improbable in the American landscape.

As such, and contrary to the conclusions that many people might have come to during the latter half of the 1990s, the real reason why many American operators turned to Europe is the failure (or in any event, the mediocrity) of the initiatives that had been taken in the United States in attempts to rationalize and/or to exploit automobile modernization or import opportunities through an application of recipes that had been tested in other mature sectors. To better understand and assess the chances of success of such transatlantic internationalization initiatives, we should try to identify the obstacles they have had to face in the United States, thus establishing if (and under what conditions) these can be overcome in Europe.

Are the conditions allowing the sustainability of these new distribution and service concepts absent in the United States and present in Europe?

Distribution innovations versus two fundamental uncertainties

In its 2000 report on automobile distribution in the United States, the Economist Intelligence Unit notes: 'Despite billions of dollars in investment and the entrance of proven movers and shakers from other industries, the retailing revolution continues to teeter on the brink of happening.' The following developments are particularly noteworthy: the closure or transformation into points-of-sale of the new vehicle franchises located inside AutoNation's superstores (and the resale of certain dealerships in 2001); Ford's abandonment of Ford Retail Networks and resale of its Tulsa dealerships to UAG; GM's decision not to pursue its dealership acquisition programme; Autobytel's very mediocre performances; and the comfortable earnings of groups such as Lithia or Sonic, which 'look more like the existing private dealer chains than like any new model' (EIU, 2000). Given this chain of events, the dominant feeling is one of inertia.

To understand why formulae that seemed highly convincing on paper have not been able to materialize despite four or five years of hard work, we should first take a look at the double uncertainty that weighs upon any model of productive organization (Boyer and Freyssenet, 2000), whether this involves distribution and services or another field of activity: productive or technological uncertainty; and market uncertainty. Superstores constitute a typical form in this respect. They create problems of economic reliability (sourcing of more recent used vehicles, cost control, reliability of 'industrialized' systems of vehicle renovation and so on) as well as problems of commercial reliability when compared with the three existing systems: dealership sales, sales via independent traders, and sales between private individuals. Where the groups involved in such policies were able to find the necessary funding, they learnt through trial and error how to adjust their strategies and modes of management in such a way as to overcome such problems. Nevertheless, few have survived and only CarMax (with support from the group to which it belongs, a derivative of Circuit City, the electronic goods mass retailer) continues to defend this concept in 2002 – albeit apparently not unsuccessfully. Similarly, the difficulties that Ford and GM have both encountered in the United States in organizing their distribution and after-sales activities on an extended geographic basis do not tell us whether intrinsically this constitutes an example of an idea that is good but wrong, in that it relies on hypotheses that are ungrounded since they focus on the existence of latent economies of scale and on an improvable type of geographic and commercial segmentation. Indeed, by 2000, such policies, which had been launched rather cautiously in 1998, were increasingly subject to criticism.

As such, we can consider that the uncertainty still exists, and that in the United States the problem is basically located upstream – that is, before the learning that is needed to overcome such obstacles can take place. The reasons underlying the rapid abandonment of these policies are both legal and financial in nature. The former category relates mainly to the American environment – but the latter is also present in Europe.

The law: a hindrance in the United States; a catalyst for change in Europe

As an automobile manufacturing country, the United States is marked by its two legal and competition-related traditions: common law and federalism. Only a certain number of American states engage in automobile manufacturing. Those that do not are, as is the case in Europe, less inclined to allow their judges (and therefore their jurisprudence and law) to provide comfort to the manufacturers. In the courtrooms of these latter states an influential and territorially well-organized lobby, the NADA, orchestrates a tireless defence of its dealer constituents against the manufacturers and their 'abusiveness'. The end result is that in the United States manufacturers find it truly difficult to control their networks, with any attempt to discipline network practices being construed as a failure to respect the integrity of the contracts each marque has signed.

For this reason, new marques (that is, Saturn or Lexus) or new entrants are the only actors with any real freedom to experiment with new modes of governance – for example, by linking remuneration to customer satisfaction indexes. Still, and even for these firms, in many American states a manufacturer's desire to own some of its own points-of-sale is countermanded by the fact that this form of integration is purely and simply prohibited. In certain states (such as Virginia), even a minority manufacturer stake is not allowed in an entity where dealers have a majority shareholding.

The same applies with contracts that cannot be abrogated, even if notice is given, without consent from the dealer. The only possibility then is a take-over by another firm or even by the manufacturer itself – as long as the purpose is to conduct a resale or else to close the point-of-sale. It stands to reason here that consolidation can only take place progressively; that it has never been possible to satisfy all of the different actors' intentions in this area; and that American automakers have come to the conclusion relatively quickly that it is basically preferable to build up large publicly traded groups. Nevertheless, even for these groups, the legal protection the traditional dealers have been granted still weighs heavily in the equation. Superstore chains are the only actors who can bid to purchase the 'buy-back' options the manufacturers own, and for this reason they are the ones who have been acquiring dealerships since 1997 (with certain states having moved to prohibit them from controlling entire geographic regions). Above all, the manufacturers are not allowed to offer them any special deals (that is, preferential pricing), and they are therefore deprived of the essential competitive advantage they could have derived from their size.

This means that the highly aggressive posturing that had characterized the early stances taken by the supporters of this new way of looking at the automobile distribution business changed within a relatively short period of time. A similar thing happened to the manufacturers when they ran into identical obstacles. In fact, the manufacturers ultimately aligned themselves with the dealers, despite the fact that ostensibly they have few interests in common. For example, Wayne Huizenga, the very media-friendly and dynamic chairman of AutoNation, while trying to build up a national distributor brand (and more generally to develop a strategy focused on a 'maximisation of the repeat sales that occur over the lifetime of each vehicle that AutoNation has initially purchased from a manufacturer'), changed gear from 1999 onwards, first delegating operational management to a former Mercedes executive who quickly set up a 'back-to-basics' strategy, before simply closing his superstores in the year 2000 to concentrate on traditional distribution.

On the one hand, legal texts can change from one state to another, but on the other, in the common law tradition, judges (who are elected) influence the rule-making process more than do legislators. The jurisprudential framework for manufacturers, new entrants or 'consolidators' is therefore highly complex whenever anyone undertakes a 'nationwide' initiative that can be attacked in each state and therefore involves judgements that are variable in nature and subject to appeal. This problem covers a multitude of phenomena: the powerfulness of each state's dealer lobby; the absence of any distribution policy; the fact that the objectives being followed by each of the parties involved may be lacking in clarity. In a system that is in any event derogation-orientated (after all, for more than a century people have accepted practices that contravene the tenets of common law competition ideals), competitive casuistry and rhetoric relating to the defence of consumer interests are in fact little more than illusions. If no alternatives to the prevailing system are clearly identified, if innovations in this area do not perform brilliantly from the very outset, and if no new lobby is able to offset the power that the two existing lobbies wield – then the legal framework underpinning the American automobile distribution sector will constitute a major impediment to change.

Curiously, even though the 'American benchmark' dominated the headlines during the 1990s, the European configuration is quite different on this score. Despite the obvious differences in sensitivity that have been cropping up more and more frequently between those European countries that have no manufacturers and those (such as Germany, France or Italy) that go to Brussels regularly to communicate their wish list, automobile distribution in Europe is subjected to Community regulations that are applicable throughout the EU. Up to 2002, this clear framework was largely influenced by the manufacturers who, despite restrictions introduced in 1995, have been much freer in this area (and more confident of their rights) than is the case the United States. Moreover, the rights that were granted to the automobile manufacturers have enabled them from the very outset to organize the European territory into a more densely woven type of commercial network, one that via the after-sales market offers a modicum of profitability to even those points-of-sale that only commercialize a few vehicles. Similarly, consolidation (when it is considered desirable) can take place at a much more rapid pace. If this is the case, it is primarily because automakers in Europe, unlike the situation in the United States, are given the right to integrate their distribution function. And indeed this is what they do: DaimlerChrysler threw itself headfirst into this policy starting in late 2000; and Renault (which traditionally distributed part of its product line via its 'branch' network) accentuated this orientation and used it as a means of organizing the consolidation of its European networks into its Renault Europe Automobile subsidiary – which is planning to distribute more than 400,000 vehicles in 2002, a volume that is approximately equal to that which the world's leading automobile distribution group, AutoNation, achieves in United States.

The rejuvenated regulatory framework within which the automobile distribution and service sector will be operating in Europe from 2002 onwards is obviously going to be less beneficial to the manufacturers. Still, it will be less of a handicap for them than a problem for their traditional networks. This is because, unlike events in American courtrooms, the dealers were not the main drivers behind the negotiation of new regulations in 2000 and 2001. Instead, the prime catalysts were the component makers and their allies from the repair and independent distribution sectors. The net outcome has been that the most notable developments in this field relate to the separation between sales and after-sales; and to the concept of original parts. As we have seen, for a group like UAG (and for other American component makers), this appears to be an opportunity to take advantage of in Europe. On the other hand, for those American manufacturers (and for other automakers) who are already present in Europe, it will constitute more of a threat, inasmuch as they are being deprived of a rent they used to share with their networks to ensure a modicum of profitability for the latter (Jullien, 2001). It stands to reason, however, that these changes will tend to bring the European configuration closer to the American one (where sales and after-sales only represent 12% of dealer revenues versus 25% in Europe), and that Opel and Ford, which, as we have seen, have already consolidated their European networks, will no longer find it so difficult to cope with the new configuration.

All in all, inasmuch as different parties have been involved in the various legal negotiation processes (Kirat, 2000), and because the corresponding process itself is based on common law in one case and on state law in the other, the European automobile distribution system appears to be more permeable to innovations, some of which are welcomed by the manufacturers, but others are greeted with less enthusiasm.

In addition, in the US case, legal rules stem from a continuous and splintered type of process, whereas, in Europe, they have to involve negotiations (if they are to become durable). This seems to have two advantages:

(i) operators benefit from relative legal security once the rule has been established; and
(ii) the regulatory sphere in Europe is able to play a role whereby it catalyses strategic thinking – something it cannot do in the USA.

The financial constraints weighing upon the reconfigurations of the American and European distribution sectors

Neglected far too often and for far too long in analyses of automobile distribution and services, financial considerations deserve our attention for at least five reasons:

(i) the motivations underlying the granting of distribution and after-sales activities to the operators to whom the automakers have delegated responsibility for such functions are primarily financial in nature;
(ii) the very ability to innovate in distribution matters seems to require long-term financial commitments whose absence largely explains the relative failure of the initiatives that have taken place in the United States;
(iii) the motivations that UAG publicized to explain its take-over of Sytner stressed this factor;
(iv) the consolidation that manufacturers desire in both Europe and the United States essentially refers to issues of this sort; and
(v) the strategy that certain European automakers have been emphasizing in order to discourage new entrants into the distribution market has consisted of trying to cut margins on new vehicle sales, something that contradicts investors' aims.

To understand the nature of this constraint and how it interferes with the American operators' transatlantic strategies (and before trying to ascertain the European configuration at this level), once again we can try to show the effect it has had on the developments that have been observed in the United States since the mid-1990s.

As demonstrated by the after-sales markets, essentially the only real vectors of change are new entrants into the market. This is the case because, for reasons that are essentially legal in nature, manufacturers in the United States can neither get their networks to adopt the behaviour and innovations they desire, nor can they partially integrate them in such a way as to be able to provide their dealers with proof of why they should be adopting the innovations that are deemed to be desirable. For a short period of time, the superstore chains played this role, relying to a large extent on stock-market-related strategies that, as part of the euphoria accompanying the advent of the 'New Economy' in the United States, enabled them at least for a time to support the very heavy investments and large operating losses that were inevitable during the first few years following the application of their revolutionary concepts. This strategy meant convincing investors of the value of their business models and showing a rate of expansion that could justify such losses while giving the impression that it would be unreasonable not to believe in the initiative's ultimate success. The result was oversubscribed IPOs and exceptionally high stock prices. As such, whenever these groups felt the need to acquire a dealership, they were able to do so cheaply by offering the seller shares instead of cash. In much the same way, during this period of time they were also able to engage the competencies of managers who had gained experience working for the major manufacturers. This led both to a sense of participation in their 'success story' and to a distribution of lucrative stock options.

It remains that this process was an eminently reversible one that first began to come under fire in 1999 when stock prices dropped. At the same time there was increased incredulity regarding the 'sustainability' of the accompanying expansion policies. Publicly traded automobile distribution groups were asked to display, on a quarterly basis, rapid improvements either in their earnings or in their profitability standards. Investors began to focus less on revenues and more on earnings. This led to a very rapid drop in stock prices. For example, CarMax plummeted from US$20 a share in 1998 to US$20 in 2000. Of course, above and beyond the drastic revision in developmental plans and business models that was necessitated by this chain of events, previously unrestrained acquisition policies could no longer be fulfilled with the same rhythm and/or by using the same methods. Cash had to be found, along with bank funding. Many firms adopted a strategy of offering guarantees to the market and to the manufacturers, giving up on costly innovations to focus on acquisitions and restructuring programmes that hitherto would have involved traditional dealer activities alone. Thanks to some judicious decisions that were made about which businesses should be acquired, and because of the implementation of tight management standards, new vehicle distribution activities were able to generate profits that were above average for the sector. The publicly traded groups used these profits as a springboard for further expansion, even though their stock prices (especially in 2000) stayed in the doldrums. The groups that seemed to manifest the greatest dynamism were those that had been built on the foundations of a regrouping of traditional businesses, and which had never ventured into superstores or tried to develop a national distributor brand. Four operators who had been relatively unknown in the late 1990s suddenly replaced AutoNation and CarMax as the figureheads of the automobile business: Lithia Motors, Sonic Automotive Group, Group1 Automotive and UnitedAuto Group. CarMax alone remained focused on a superstore policy.

To fund this 'consolidator' mission, the few groups in question in the United States relied heavily on manufacturers and importers. Not only did these two categories begin to overcome the initial mistrust they had felt for these distributor groups (agreeing to systematic changes in the ownership of the contracts by which they were bound), but beginning in 2000 they started to finance the operations discussed above via their own captive firms. For example, in August 2000, Sonic Automotive (the second-largest American group that year) made sure that the credit line of US$350 million that Ford Credit had already extended to it to fund its own acquisitions was replaced by a US$500 million syndicated loans to be shared by Ford Credit and DaimlerChrysler Financial. Similarly, in 2001 Chrysler Financial Company LLC and Toyota Motor Credit Co. collaborated in lending UAG US$831 million.[6]

Given the difficulties these groups had encountered in their attempts to raise capital on the stock market and to obtain financing from the mainstream banks, the captive firms began to assume a greater role at the very time that the groups' direct acquisition policies were starting to run out of steam. More generally, the manufacturers seemed to use their captive firms to extend to the 'mega-dealers' those advantages that the manufacturers themselves no longer had the right to grant to them as part of a product sale. In other words, they began to provide increasingly open support to the distributor groups in question, apparently considering that this constituted a prerequisite for any future restructuring of their own distribution activities.

This is quite understandable in light of the various difficulties the manufacturers had faced in 1999 and 2000 during their efforts to implement changes in their own distribution and service functions. Nevertheless, such policies remained relatively ambiguous and risky. After all, during this period, the distribution groups' very survival, and their ability to pursue their 'consolidator' mission, seemed to be predicated on whether or not they could receive support from the manufacturers. Moreover, the manufacturers did appear to be more capable than previously of controlling the strategies, magnitude and longevity of the support they were providing. Yet, by helping the distributor groups to stay healthy, they were also helping them to regain a modicum of strategic freedom. For example, in the latter half of 2001 the New York stock prices of the groups in question recovered strongly, and at the same time several of them (particularly AutoNation) returned to a much more aggressive type of positioning. Above and beyond renewed attempts to build up distributor brands capable of attracting consumers' attention (such as the brands of the manufacturer whose products the company is distributing), AutoNation's executives, who were able to avoid having to rely on support from manufacturers' captive firms, stressed that they themselves were able to negotiate advantageous terms and conditions with banks, and used their own captive firm, AutoNation Financial Services, to reinforce group profitability.

In general, AutoNation, along with all the mega-dealers, can be expected to pursue highly selective expansion strategies from now on. Their aim is to emphasize the most profitable brands – with these usually being the brands that the importers offer. They also want only to invest in growth businesses and regions. Conversely, they will be disinvesting (as AutoNation began to do in 2001) in areas where the outlook is less promising and which do not help to increase the price of the dealership contracts they will be acquiring. For example, UAG justifies its transatlantic investment policies with the argument that the businesses it takes over are on average 25% cheaper in Europe than in the United States. This seems to indicate that the distributor firms will only be able to fulfil their 'consolidator' role to a partial extent, and that in the meantime (until the manufacturers begin to take a close look at the question of margins) they will have to be satisfied with whatever market share they already own.

Several of the new vehicle distribution disinvestment operations being observed in Europe indicate something that has been admitted implicitly by manufacturers such as Renault or DaimlerChrysler (whose direct investments mesh well with distributors' reintegration policies) – namely that the same issue exists in Europe.[7] Of course, the fact that automakers are allowed to initiate a much more directive type of distribution policy alters the terms of the debate. Nevertheless, and inasmuch as it is difficult to generalize this reintegration solution, financial constraints necessarily weigh upon consolidation initiatives and on manufacturers' delegation of their distribution activities to operators who have become increasingly solid at a financial and managerial level.

It remains that, if the solution to this problem has been (and in all likelihood will continue to be) postponed for a few years, it is as a result of three main factors:

(i) the manufacturers do not depend solely on new entrants to take consolidation measures, inasmuch as they can achieve this simply by de-referencing distributors; by regaining control of certain points-of-sale;

or by ensuring that they are acquired by family-run firms that are relatively less demanding in profitability terms;

(ii) the most promising businesses have not yet been selected or acquired,
something that will allow American or local distribution groups to
continue to expand and prosper; and

(iii) even though it has long been under attack in Europe, the after-sales rent
remains substantial, and the new regulations will be slow to take this
advantage away from the manufacturers and their networks.

For all these reasons, it is easy to understand why, for a group such as
UAG, entry into the European market is a strategy that appears to be just
as sustainable as seeking to expand in the United States (especially since
the exit costs involved are very unlikely to be excessive). Thus, and just like
the American and other component makers who will be participating in this
attack on the after-sales rent, it is highly probably that other American distribution groups will also try to gain a foothold in Europe (even if they do
not understand this at present).

All in all, there seem to be profound differences between the American
and European configurations of the automobile distribution and service
landscape. If so, it is not because restructuring programmes are 'less
advanced' in Europe than in the United States. Instead, it is because of reasons that basically relate to the relative negotiating strengths of manufacturers and traditional distributors. Even though the legal and financial
landscapes are changing, they reflect this asymmetry, and it would appear
to be for this reason that the European automobile distribution and service
sector continues to attract American investors.

Conclusion: from distribution-related financial issues to the economics of the whole branch – the problem with utilization systems and how operators account for them

The differences that have been observed between the financial and legal
environments in which innovative (or potentially innovative) firms in the
automobile distribution sector operate reveal that the learning that needs to
take place to overcome the two fundamental uncertainties we have highlighted has barely had the chance to develop in an American configuration
that singularly limits manufacturers' ability to manage this learning (and to
profit from it). In addition, this configuration makes it very difficult for new
entrants who are subjected to the constraints of shareholder value management to develop such learning. Conversely, the European configuration has
up to now expressed an implicit choice that consists of leaving it up to the
manufacturers to manage the branch (and its changes) in a systemic manner, hence to experiment and rationalize. In the reconfiguration that is
beginning to take shape in the early 2000s, it would appear that there has

been an attempt to orchestrate some sharing of this power, and that various American operators have interpreted this as an area of new opportunities.

Although this analysis accounts effectively for the lion's share of the strategic initiatives that the main operator categories have been undertaking in the United States and in Europe, it nevertheless leaves untouched a very wide swath of the world of automobile distribution and services. In fact, the initiatives we are dealing with here essentially relate to the traditional activities that are being carried out in the manufacturers' networks – and to the elements of change that affect them directly. As certain studies have demonstrated (Froud *et al.*, 2000; Jullien, 2002), this activity has, up to the time of writing, focused mainly on new vehicle sales. Yet this only affects a minority of driver households, and therefore only a small proportion of a population's total automobile-related spending. This raises the question of whether, and how, the elements that make up these restructuring and internationalization drives are also linked to the subliminal constituents of the underlying utilization systems. What seems to have transpired is that the innovations and exacerbated competitive pressures that have arisen (whose impetus lies in the American operators' transatlantic internationalization drives) basically only involve the small percentage of total automobile spending in which the manufacturers themselves are directly involved. As such, the analysis does not delve into an area that, albeit not entirely unknown, remains relatively untouched in Europe. In so far as it is essentially in this area that current and upcoming regulatory changes will be paving the way for new competition, it is here that most of the branch's future will be played out over the next few years.

Dissimilar and interdependent utilization systems

Analysis of a configuration such as the one that can be found in France shows that most automobile spending targets operators other than the manufacturers or their networks. For example, French households devoted only 30% of their motorization spending in 1995 to new car purchases, corresponding to the acquisition of 1.6 million new vehicles. In the same year, they bought almost 3 million used cars. In Britain, the equivalent figures were 920,000 and 5.6 million, respectively.

Based in this observation, it stands to reason that different populations feature different types of automobile consumption (which we can call 'utilization systems') that not only coexist but also depend on one another. The structure of such interdependencies is particularly complex. At an initial level, we can be satisfied with a 'demographic' type of evidence and focus on the rotation of parks of vehicles. Here manufacturers appear to have a role to play, consisting of providing the system with new vehicles that escape progressively from their control as they are fed into somewhat diverging types of utilization systems (which sometimes only depend to a small extent on the products that the manufacturers and their networks offer). Used vehicle markets cover a vehicle's mode of circulation throughout its entire lifetime. This is the source of the very specific nature of the durable good that is an automobile – unlike the situation observed with washing machines or cell phones, those who purchase a new good in the auto market are less likely to be thinking about its utilization costs.

Thus, at a secondary level, it is the structure of the automobile offer itself that is in question. This offer system entertains a twofold relationship with the utilization systems and their interdependencies:

(i)   product suppliers draw meaning from the structuring of the product's utilizations, and from the market and profit opportunities they face; and

(ii) through the services they offer and their pricing practices, they help to structure the utilization systems that the various household categories invent in order to manage their own motorization needs.

From both these points of view, an analysis of emerging automobile distribution and service-related innovation and internationalization drives shows clearly that they focus mainly on opportunities that are found during the first few years of the vehicles' life. A priori, they are therefore aimed at smaller, better-off population groups.

A type of innovation and internationalization that has concentrated on the core concerns of manufacturers and their networks

Apart from the changes taking place in Europe with regard to spare parts and after-sales services, manufacturers and new entrants in both the United States and in Europe have been deploying most of their efforts in such a way as to learn how better to handle (or at least how not to mishandle) purchasers of new or more recent used cars – a market that throughout the world has traditionally constituted the prime target for manufacturers and brand networks. In this market, as is the case with Ford, for example, the various actors' strategic impulses have involved trying to take a serious look at the issue of what kinds of services should be offered to those consumers who do not buy new vehicles. Such impulses have generally been the ones to bring about the strategic reorientations that have actually taken place.

Once again, AutoNation has been a figurehead in this area. Initially, the operator was not even thinking about selling new vehicles. Instead it wanted to develop two superstore chains: one (AutoNation) dedicated to more recent used vehicles that are still under warranty, and the other (Super Value) focusing on less recent vehicles – ones that are at least five years old and no longer under warranty. The latter chain was the first to close (in late 1998) and the former was abandoned in 2000. In the meantime, it is worth remembering, AutoNation had embarked on a policy involving a massive acquisition of franchised dealers and the principal activity of the world's number one in this sector will, in fact, be traditional distribution.

Similarly, if we observe the development of used-vehicle Internet auction sites, we can see that these are basically service providers for networks that use them as a way of listing their inventories online. Yet most of the used car market is made up of vehicles that are more than five years old, sales of which are negotiated more or less everywhere between private individuals or via specialized small companies. The sites that have been developed to deal with these types of markets have never really been able to discover who should be paying, and in general the only ones that have survived are those that are linked to private sales newspapers, for whom they represent an additional cost.

What remains are after-sales and spare parts activities. In these areas we have seen manufacturers fighting back against any erosion of their market share. Some have tried to preserve in-house a greater share of the repairs and maintenance operations being carried out on the (new or used) vehicles that their networks have sold. They do this by improving the quality of the services and/or by forcing customers to visit only the brand's own after-sales services. With varying degrees of success, manufacturer networks have tried to limit the success of rapid repair specialists and to develop their own services in this field (dispensing with the need to make an appointment, and offering all-in-one pricing and guarantees). Above all, in both the United States and in Europe the extension of warranties on new and used vehicles has become a generalized practice, and this tends to turn customers into captive clients. All these concepts make it easier to deal with the traditional customer bases of a brand's networks. On the other hand, they do not make it any easier to attract households who prefer buying from other private parties or from older used-car specialists, financing their purchases through independent credit organizations and getting their cars repaired by independent garages or by specialized franchisee chains.

Once again, we have seen (and will continue to see) a number of initiatives wherein manufacturers are trying to bring home some of the spending that in many cases they have missed out on for years. This was the reason for Ford's acquisition of Kwik-Fit and Fiat's takeover of Midas, for example. It has also been the motivation for the development of multi-brand repair chains such as Renault (with Carlife in Europe) or GM (with Goodwrench in the United States). None the less, in these cases we have also seen that the automobile groups seem to be at best partially committed to this path; simultaneously they are preparing their exit from it.

All in all, the innovation and/or internationalization drives that have accompanied the sector's sales (and associated after-sales) operations rarely appear to be capable of really freeing themselves from their existing focus on new vehicle sales. More specifically, even though efforts have patently been made to improve the handling of used-vehicle-related operations (that is, repairs, financing and insurance), this has mainly been directed at the same type of clientele. Inversely, the few efforts that some actors have undertaken in the older used-vehicle markets have been very cautious in nature. Moreover, they have apparently struggled to generate the expected profitability.

Towards new forms of integration for users who have been neglected by the European automobile system

At the time of writing, in the early 2000s, there is still a major difference between the relationship that prevails in the USA or in Europe between automobile utilization or product offer systems. As we have seen, the proportion of after-sales operations that brand networks handle in Europe is twice what it is in the USA, with the end result that the new-vehicle sales system in Europe is financially much more dependent on after-sales and on spare parts sales. It is as if automakers in the United States have given up *de facto* on a large part of their potential customers, entire population categories that neither their dealers nor their captive firms (nor, for the most part, their spare-part sales departments) target, either directly or indirectly. This is not the case in Europe, for reasons that relate mainly to the structures and regulations that continue to apply to spare parts (because of what has been called the 'natural link' between sales and after-sales). Little by little, regulatory discussions in Brussels in 2001 began to focus on this issue. The main legal innovations to take place from October 2002 will come from a weakening of this link.

Up to now, around 50% of all parts sold in Europe (called original parts) could only be sold by the manufacturers themselves (EIU, 2000), working through their own in-house networks. This has been the case even for the 50% of these parts that were made for the manufacturers by the component makers. It is this reality that the new legal texts will be addressing, considering in general that there is a distinction between sales and after-sales, and that there is no reason to prevent the makers of the parts from being involved directly in the distribution of their own products. In addition, manufacturers are going to be forced to disseminate technical information on their products, and to open up their training programmes to the independents who repair them.

Even when this was only a working hypothesis, Louis Schweitzer, the president of Renault, stated in *Automotive News*: 'I'm worried. The parts are where the margins are.' Accurate and reliable information is hard to find on this subject. Nevertheless, looking at the numbers provided in this same article by the executive of a components making company, we can understand why Schweitzer is so concerned. According to this source, a part that a component maker sells to a manufacturer for US$110 is sold on to the dealer for US$250 and to the consumer for US$500.[8]

As such, in the early 2000s, the central interdependency between the different utilization systems for purchasers of new and guaranteed vehicles, or else for buyers of used vehicles, is a fact in Europe – even though the latter category currently only manifests itself when it needs a vehicle repair. Used vehicle purchasers try to avoid dealing directly with brand networks, but for a whole range of operations their garage is reselling them a part that was bought from the brand network, thus subsidizing the efforts that the manufacturers have been making to display and to sell their products. This is what caused Louis Schweitzer to comment that with the upcoming European regulation there is a little chance that his new vehicle prices will be any lower.

This regulatory development is the fruit of joint efforts by independent parts distributors (who often are also the managers of independent repair chains) and by component makers. Undeniably, it constitutes a source of change, of innovation, and provides a reason for American investors to put their money into Europe. There are two related reasons for this:

(i) it deeply destabilizes the fragile equilibrium between the branch's downstream operations and the overall economics of this downstream area. In particular, for the first time in Europe it raises questions about the funding of new vehicles' brand representation; and

(ii) it attracts investors (and innovators, including certain manufacturers) to markets that have hitherto remained outside the activities that are carried out by the key players in the US and European automobile systems – actors who account for the automobile spending of most of the households in the developed Western countries; that is, consumers who up to now have never dealt directly with a manufacturer's original product offer.

Translated by Alan Sitkin

Notes

1 *Automotive News*, 30 July 2001.
2 This strategy was summarized in 2000 by a Ford executive as follows: 'Not long ago Ford's strategy was to become the leading automobile manufacturer in the world. Our vision today is to deliver superior shareholder returns by being the world's leading consumer company for automotive products and services.'
3 *Financial Times*, 25 February 2002.
4 *Automotive News*, 18 February 2002.
5 *Auto-Infos*, 31 October 2001.
6 *Automotive News*, 29 January 2001.
7 CICA is France's second-largest distribution group. Hong Kong's Jardine Motors bought it from the Pinault Printemps La Redoute group in 1993 and sold it to PGA Motors in early 2002.
8 *Automotive News*, 22 October 2001.

References

Autopolis (2000) *The Natural Link between Sales and Service – An Investigation for the Competition Directorate-General of the European Commission*, http://europa.eu.int/comm/competition/car_sector/distribution/eval_reg_1475_95/studies/sales_and_service.pdf. (November).

Boyer, R. and Freyssenet, M. (2000, 2002) *Les modèles productifs*, Paris: La Découverte, 2000; Revised English edition: *Productive Models: The Conditions of Profitability*, London/New York: Palgrave, 2002.

Boyer, R. and Freyssenet, M. (2001) 'The World that Changed the Machine – Synthesis of GERPISA Research Programs 1993–1999', *Actes du GERPISA*, no. 31, April.

Chanaron, J. J. and Jullien, B. (1999) 'Production and Distribution: Toward New Coherences and New Competencies', in Y. Lung, J. J. Chanaron, T. Fujimoto and D. Raff (eds) *Coping with Variety: Flexible Productive Systems for Product Variety in the Auto Industry*, Aldershot: Ashgate.

EIU (Economist Intelligence Unit) (2000) *EIU Global Automotive Retailing*: Economist Intelligence Unit.

European Commission (2000) *Report on the Evaluation of Reguation No 1475/95 on the Application of Article 85 (now 81) of the Treaty to Certain Categories of Motor Vehicle Distribution and Servicing Agreements*, http://europa.eu.int/comm/competition/car_sector/distribution, (November).

Freyssenet, M., Mair, A., Shimizu, K. and Volpato, G. (eds) (1998) *One Best Way? The Trajectories and Industrial Models of World Automobile Producers*, Oxford/New York: Oxford University Press.

Froud, J., Haslam, C., Johal, S., Jullien, B. and Williams, K. (2000) 'Les dépenses de motorisation comme facteur d'accentuation des inégalités et comme frein au développement des entreprises automobiles: une comparaison franco-anglaise', in G. Dupuy and F. Bost (eds), *L'automobile et son monde*, Paris: L'Aube.

Jullien, B. (1998) 'Les constructeurs face aux nécessaires mutations de la distribution: quelles leçons tirer des évolutions rapides en cours aux Etats-Unis?', in Y. Lung (ed.), *Du côté du marché, Actes du GERPISA*, no. 23.

Jullien, B. (1999) 'Les restructurations majeures de la distribution automobile passent-elles par une internationalisation des opérateurs?', in M. Freyssenet and Y. Lung, (eds), *Internationalization: Confrontation of Firms Trajectories and Automobile Areas*, Proceedings of the Seventh International Colloquium of GERPISA, Paris.

Jullien, B. (2000) 'La distribution automobile en 2000: vers le partenariat ou la Taylorisation', in M. Freyssenet and Y. Lung (eds), *The World That Changed the Machine: The Future of the Auto Industry for the 21st Century*, Proceedings of Eighth International Colloquium of GERPISA, Paris.

Jullien, B. (2001) 'Systèmes d'utilisation, systèmes de production et de prestation auto-mobiles: dynamiques et cohérences économiques', in Y. Lung (ed.), *Reconfiguring the Auto Industry: Mergers, Acquisitions, Alliance and Exit*, Proceedings of Ninth International Colloquium of GERPISA, Paris.

Jullien, B. (2002) 'Consumer v. manufacturer or consumer v. consumer? The implications of a usage analysis of automobiile systems', *Competition and Change*, no. 1.

Kirat, T. (2000) *Economie du Droit*, Paris: La Découverte.

Volpato, G. and Buzzaro, L. (2003) 'European automotive distribution: the battle for selectivity and exclusivity is not over', in M. Freyssenet, K. Shimizu and G. Volpato, *Globalization or Regionalization of the European Car Industry?*, London/New York: Palgrave Macmillan.

Part II

The Diversity of Internationalization Trajectories and the Local Hybridization of Japanese and Korean Automobile Firms

5
A Maverick in the Age of Mega-mergers? Toyota's Global Strategies

Koichi Shimizu

In 2000, Toyota, the number three automaker (by sales volume) in the world, sold 1.772 million vehicles in Japan through 308 dealers, and 3.383 million overseas through 170 distributors deploying around 5,400 outlets in some 160 countries. So, at the start of the new century, Toyota's sales network was already fairly globalized, with the markets in the East European countries showing potential for expansion. As for its overseas production, Toyota assembled 1.468 million vehicles in twenty-six firms (subsidiaries and joint ventures) based in twenty-three countries. In Japan, Toyota produced 3.429 million vehicles, of which 1.706 million were exported. Toyota, then, seems to be well on the way to globalizing its production network at the time of writing, but its globalization of production is very recent.

Although in general the internationalization process passes through four phases: export strategy, strategic alliances and shareholding investments, foreign direct investments, and globalization (Laigle, 1997), the internationalization trajectory of Toyota follows another way, analysed in the studies of multinational firms during the 1970s and 1980s (Delapierre *et al.*, 1983, for example). The successful export strategies of firms have encountered protectionist policies by importing countries because of growing trade deficits, effects on local firms and so on. So, the firms are forced to manufacture their products there to avoid protectionist barriers – quotas, prohibitive import taxes and so on. Localized production will then take the place of exports. Toyota's globalization process has followed this route, except for some marginal cases. The fact that its overseas production essentially began to replace exports from 1985 shows that its internationalization strategy changed from an export-centred strategy to a localization of production during the first half of the 1980s. Toyota's internationalization trajectory arose, at least in the mind of Toyota's management, from the specificity of the Toyota production system (TPS). Through the necessity of coping with trade conflicts and claims of local governments, Toyota was forced to localize production. Having changed course in such a defensive way, Toyota decided to deploy a global production network. Can Toyota carry out by itself such a globalization strategy in the age where international mega-merger or mega-fusion between automakers looks an obliged path through which they could survive and win the fierce market competition?

General tendency

Toyota Motor Sales (TMS) began exporting in 1952, just after being separated from Toyota Motor Corporation (TMC) because of the financial crisis of this latter. The real take-off of its exports was marked during the second half of the 1960s as Figure 5.1 shows. From then to 1985, its exports expanded. They were only interrupted by short sluggish terms as those in 1973, 1978–9, and 1981–4. These decelerations in exports were caused by different circumstances. The decrease in 1973 was apparently provoked by the first oil crisis. If we break down the exports by region, it however becomes evident that this decrease was the result of only the rapid shrink of sales on the North American markets (decrease of 40,000 vehicles). The 1978–9 decrease, apparently due to the second oil crisis, came in fact from three regions, South East Asia and Oceania, Middle East Asia, and Africa. In the same way the

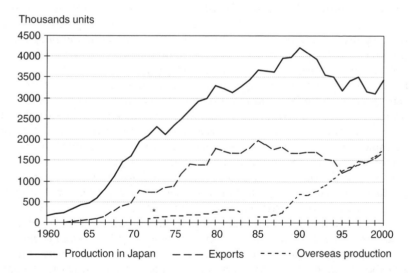

Figure 5.1 Domestic production, overseas production and exports, Toyota, 1960–2000

Notes: The graph with asterisk represents the volume of KD sets exported, which was not included in the data of exports until 1988. After that, they were treated as a part of exports.

Sources: Toyota (1987), Toyota (2001) (annual data).

deceleration of exports in 1981–4 came from Latin America and Africa (see Appendix Table A5.1). Toyota's production in Japan continued to expand until 1985 thanks to the growing domestic market and the increase in its exports especially towards the North America.

This second tendency was reversed from then because of the increase in overseas production, especially in the USA. Nevertheless the production of Toyota in Japan continued to grow until 1990 thanks to an economic boom fuelled by the 'financial bubble' of 1987–90 (see Figure 5.1). Toyota's overseas production increased rapidly from 136,300 units in 1985 to 1.7514 million in 2000. NUMMI, a Toyota/GM joint venture, began to produce in December 1984. Toyota Motor Manufacturing Kentucky (TMMK) and TMM Canada (TMMC) launched their car production in 1988, and TMM Indiana (TMMI) began to produce in 1998. In consequence, Toyota's production in North America increased from 64,000 vehicles in 1985 to 1.104 million in 2000, and over 60% of vehicles sold in the North America have been produced there since 1995.

Of course, this inversion of export trend does not mean the decrease of overseas sales. In fact, the latter continued to grow from 2.107 million vehicles in 1989 to 3.383 million in 2000 (see Table 5.1). Even the fall of sales in South East Asia in 1998 because of the economic crisis of the ASEAN countries was compensated for by the increase in sales in the North America and Europe. These markets have been absorbing more than half of its overseas sales since 1970 (1.766 million vehicles in 2000), whereas the Asian markets share in its overseas sales remained at the level of about 20% until in 1996, and fell to 10% after the Asian financial crisis (see Table 5.1). Moreover, Toyota's domestic production suffered from the slowdown of domestic demand and the increase in overseas production. As for the turnover, Toyota realized 8,935.5 billion yen in Japan, 3,949.5 billion in the North America and 1,858 billion in the others in 1997 (accounting year), 9,204.6 billion in Japan, 4,737.3 billion

Table 5.1 Sales per region, 1989–2000 (in thousands of units)

	1989	1990	1991	1992	1993	1994	1995	1996	1997	1998	1999	2000
NA	1,056	1,168	1,122	1,125	1,116	1,174	1,169	1,252	1,357	1,516	1,631	1,766
SA	43	50	65	80	90	79	96	82	115	120	100	106
E	436	451	450	423	394	389	384	412	471	541	592	656
SEA	180	271	292	325	386	414	433	445	418	230	253	339
O	145	161	138	135	147	153	145	144	148	177	172	177
MA	121	135	155	200	185	159	133	152	185	212	187	217
Af	126	135	133	124	122	114	136	136	144	130	123	122
Total	2,107	2,371	2,354	2,412	2,440	2,482	2,496	2,622	2,838	2,930	3,058	3,383
Japan	2,309	2,504	2,355	2,229	2,066	2,041	2,060	2,135	2,006	1,711	1,664	1,772

Notes: NA, North America; SA, South America; E, Europe; SEA, South East Asia; O, Oceania; MA, Middle East Asia; Af, Africa.

Source: Toyota, 1999 (annual data).

in North America, 1,204.9 billion in Europe, 905 billion in other countries in 1998. It is then obvious that the North American markets have an overwhelming weight in Toyota's globalization strategy. So, it is natural that Toyota established its global strategy mainly taking account of American political and industrial situations, at least in 1980s and 1990s.

This overview of the internationalization of Toyota clearly shows two phases: the first can be characterized by an export-centred phase, and the second by a localization phase of production that began to replace exports since 1985. The rate of overseas production with respect to overseas sales, has been continuously increasing from about 22% in 1989 to over 50% in 2000, though fluctuations according to the regions (see Appendix Table A5.1). The localization rate in three regions, South East Asia, Oceania and Africa, also surpassed the 50% level. The rate is low as for Europe, South America, and Middle East Asia. But the construction of an assembly plant in France (the Yaris is produced from 31 January 2001) and the assembly of passenger cars (the Corolla) in Brazil started in 1998 must increase in the long run the rate in the first two regions. Production operations are also prepared in the China and in the Czech (joint venture with Peugeot SA). Consequently, Toyota's globalization of production will still progress.

In short, if the 1960s and 1970s are the period of expanding its commercial network worldwide, the 1980s and 1990s (also in the first decade of the twenty-first century) are therefore regarded as the period of expanding a global production network. The next two sections analyse the circumstances of these two processes.

The era of export-centred strategy: 1951–80

Having a conviction that exports should be necessary to develop a mass production, TMS (Toyota Motor Sales) set up an Export Department just after its foundation in 1950. TMS tried to export Toyota's commercial vehicles, mainly the Land Cruiser (four-wheel drive) from 1954, towards the niche markets or market segments where advanced Western carmakers still had not their strong presence. Countries in South America, Asia and Oceania were its preferred markets because the Land Cruiser met there only the Land Rover and the American Jeep as its competitors. TMS was then going to carry out 'aggressive sales activities' (Toyota, 1988) in Latin America (Colombia, Peru, Bolivia, El Salvador, Costa Rica) and the Caribbean (Puerto Rico, Dominican Republic) at the beginning of the 1960s. Its exports to Taiwan, Thailand, Australia and some countries in the Middle East Asia (Saudi Arabia, Kuwait, Jordan and UAE) and in Africa (Ethiopia, South Africa and so on) also began in this period. Already some of these countries had prohibited the import of completely build-up vehicles. TMS was obliged to export KD sets to be assembled locally. But these exports even in small volume and the small production of vehicles were surely reckless.

KD assembly of the Crown in Mexico, started in 1960, was a complete failure, because of a bad preparation of KD sets and finally because Toyota's local partner was arrested for the sake of political affairs. So TMS abandoned this market in 1964. As just after the Mexican government prohibited the imports of vehicles, Toyota has completely withdrawn from Mexican market. Toyota itself says about this period: 'in a sense, TMS began exporting almost blindfold' (Toyota, 1987, 1988). Lessons learned from the experiences in Mexico and others were the 'importance of properly preparing its knock down system and also of selecting local partners' (Toyota, 1987, 1988).

Toyota would meet with two other severe difficulties around 1970. In Korea, Shin Jin Motor had been assembling around 20,000 of Toyota's CKD from 1969, but this company chose GM as its partner in 1972 to found a joint venture. So, Toyota has lost the production base in Korea. In Taiwan, as the government restricted the import of vehicles, production cooperation began between Toyota and Lu Ho AIC. However, the latter was finally controlled by Ford in 1973 after failure in negotiation between Toyota and Lu Ho under changing political situations (political relations between Japan and Taiwan became worse after the Japanese prime minister had visited China). Toyota could not construct its production base in Taiwan until 1985. Localized production of the Land Cruiser in Brazil since 1958 had been also suffering of chronic deficits until the beginning of the 1970s.

In addition, there was a quality problem: the vehicles exported were not suitable to local conditions: too small engine, abnormal body vibrations and other problems. The turning point in Toyota's export strategy might be the failure in 1958 of its export of passenger cars (the Crown) to the USA. Recognizing the too low quality of the Crown exported, TMS completely stopped its exports for four years. Admitting the importance to develop cars suited to local conditions, TMC then intensively studied the technical problems of its vehicles by comparing them with Americans'. The 1964 model of Corona and the 1968 model of Corolla were acceptable and marketable in American market and other major markets. From such experiences, Toyota learned the importance to develop vehicles suited to local conditions, and also that of after-sales service. Toyota also revised its exports system: TMS established Export Headquarters in 1962, whereas TMC set up its Export Department in 1963. By organizing the Joint Export Conference, two companies build up a cooperation system in order to develop a coherent export strategy.

Though Toyota encountered difficulties in selling in Great Britain, France, Italy and the Federal Republic of Germany with their own automakers' tight sales network, its exports to Europe rapidly grew from 13 units in 1960 to 59,000 units in 1970. In sum, Toyota organized twenty-six new distributors in twenty-four countries during the 1960s against seventeen distributors in sixteen countries in the 1950s, whereas fourteen new distributors in fourteen countries would be organized in the 1970s. In Europe, Toyota's marketing strategy has been in having one distributor in each country.

During the 1970s, and especially after the first oil crisis of 1973–4, Toyota's exports rose remarkably, from 482,000 units in 1969 to 1.785 million in 1980. A regional breakdown shows that North American, European and Middle East Asian markets absorbed a large part of this increase, that is 1.124 million units (see Appendix Table A5.1). North America has constituted Toyota's prime overseas market since 1968, which absorbed over half of its exports from 1970 to the end of 1980s. Toyota's exports to this region amounted to 762,000 units in 1980 against 245,000 in 1969. Europe has become Toyota's second overseas market since 1972 and came to import over 300,000 units in 1980. After that followed the Middle East Asia that imported about 280,000 units in 1980 against 15,000 in 1969. The US market has become the market which would then determine its policy about overseas operations during the 1980s and 1990s.

This rapid growth of its exports towards North America and Europe means not only that quadrupling of oil price led Western users to buy compact and sub-compact cars that consumed less combustion, but also that high quality of Japanese cars began to be recognized by them. Japanese automakers arrived to produce the vehicles that consumed less energy with high quality and low price (Freyssenet *et al.*, 1998).

Until around 1980, Toyota's internationalization strategy was centred on exports. Toyota's management had been thinking that exports were more profitable than localized production because overseas production operations could not run as well as those at its domestic assembly plants.

In fact, the Toyota production system (TPS) was based on an intensive regional division of labour between Toyota and its major suppliers in and around Toyota City and on the 'mutual trust' between the management and the union. *Kaizen* (continuous improvement) has been contributing to increase the quality of products and the productivity. Work process has been designed and organized by the group leaders (*kumi-cho*) who have been also fixing the standardized work of their group in collaboration with their chief leaders (*ko-cho*). These characteristics giving high performance to the TPS were considered, by its management itself for a long time, unique even in Japan and difficult to be transferred abroad where industrial relations and carmaker-supplier relations were quite different from those of Toyota (about the detail, see Shimizu, 1999).

In consequence, the management had no mind until 1980 to transfer its production to any country even if Toyota could sell its vehicles in large quantities, except the countries that have prohibited the import of completely built-up vehicles. However trade conflicts between Japan and the USA obliged Toyota to produce there. So, 1980–5 period became the first turning point in Toyota's globalization strategy.

The era of the globalization of production: from 1980

Strategic modification under an agreement regime of voluntary restraint

Facing the trade conflicts and the growing claim of local governments for the substitution of imports by localized production at the dawn of the 1980s, Toyota had to change its strategy.

The protectionist pressure in the USA obliged the Japanese government to set up in 1981 the voluntary restraint of Japanese passenger car exports towards the USA (1.680 million cars a year until 1983, 1.850 million in 1984, 2.300 million in 1985–91, 1.650 million in 1992–3). Under this quota regime, Toyota would firstly make limited exports more profitable: increase of exported commercial vehicles (the Hilux) excluded from the quota, and switching exported passenger cars from low range to high range (the Celica, the Supra and the Camry). By founding a transport logistic company (1981) and a financial company (1982), Toyota then strengthened its marketing. As a consequence, and despite the quota regime in the USA and Canada, Toyota's exports to North America increased from 723,000 units in 1980 to 1.115 million in 1986, the peak year of its exports to this region. After that Toyota launched a series of new luxury cars from 1987, the Celsior (LS400), the Windom (ES300) and the Aristo (GS300) sold under the new brand Lexus.

Toyota met the same situation in Europe. The EC Committee demanded the Japanese government for slowing down its growing exports. Some countries had been restricting imports of Japanese vehicles so as to protect local automobile industry – France, Italy especially. Consequently, exports to Europe grew slowly: increasing by 40% over the ten years 1980–90.

In addition to these protectionist policies, Toyota had to cope with rapid appreciation of the yen from 1985. So, Toyota had no choice other than to promote overseas production. Toyota was then going to construct transplants in the North America and Europe and to organize a global production network. This new strategy was clearly presented in Toyota's 'New Global Business Plan' for 1995–8.

Construction of transplants in North America and the UK

As mentioned above, Toyota could not believe in successful transplantation of its production system. For this reason, it negotiated the foundation of a joint venture with Ford at the beginning of the 1980s. They could not reach a conclusion because of their disaccord about the model to produce. In such a situation, GM proposed Toyota to create a joint venture from which GM could learn the TPS and procure sub-compact cars it would build. Toyota could organize production as it wanted by the help of GM. This joint venture, NUMMI (New United Motor Manufacturing), started producing the Nova for GM in December 1984, and the Corolla FX for Toyota in 1986. These models have been replaced respectively by the Prism and the Corolla sedan in 1988 because of their disappointing sales. NUMMI also assembles 285T trucks (Tacoma) from 1994.

Surely timid at the beginning, but through its experiences in this joint venture, Toyota came to convince itself of the transferability of the TPS to American industrial situations, and then decided to construct by itself its own transplants in the North America. So, TMM USA in Kentucky (TMMK) started assembling the Avalon, the Camry and the Sienna in 1988, and the TMMC (Canada) producing the Corolla from the same year. In order to increase its production capacity up to 1.45 million vehicles a year by 2003, a new assembly plant of utility vehicles (UV and SUV) was constructed in Indiana (TMMI) for producing the Sequoia and the Tundra from 2000 (see Appendix Table A5.2). Toyota has also four production facilities of engines and parts in the North America.

These transplants in North America have recorded better performance than had been expected (see Toyota (1987, 1988), also Besser (1996) and Mishina (1998) regarding TMMK, and Adler *et al.* (1988) regarding NUMMI). The quality and productivity of the vehicles they have been producing were comparable with those of their mother plants in Japan (Takaoka for NUMMI, Tsutsumi for the other transplants). The TPS then proved its transferability even into countries where industrial and business relations were very different from those in its home country. However, this did not mean that all of the TPS components have been set into place at these transplants.

Detailed studies of these transplants remark that some production organization techniques were modeled directly on Toyota's. So, *kanban*, *heijunka* (levelling the production volume over several months), *kaizen*, visual control by the *andon* system with line stop system, *poka-yoke* (error-proofing devices), team concept, standardized work were settled there. Toyota also was making efforts to construct the 'mutual trust' between management and workers as well as between transplant and suppliers. These studies also emphasized that Toyota's human resource management and industrial relations were hybridized there. For instance, though Toyota's production allowance was not adopted there, because of the wage system in the transplants following the norm of the UAW, a functional equivalent ('performance improvement plan sharing' at NUMMI, bonus at TMMK) to the production allowance was introduced. It is also the case of the 'growing-in' period of wage rate for the new hired workers, which is regarded as the functional equivalent of Toyota's grade system (Besser, 1996; Adler *et al.*, 1998; Mishina, 1998).

However, the production system implemented in transplants remained static. In fact, the dynamics of the TPS resides in the way in which Toyota is carrying out cost reduction in improving quality and productivity (Shimizu, 1999). The main actors of *kaizen* for improving production efficiency, quality and security on the shop floor at Toyota in Japan are group leaders, chief leaders and engineers assigned to the plant, who are doing those activities as one of their functions under the efficiency management. Of course, team members engage in *kaizen* through the suggestion system as well as a QC circle, but the management does not demand them an effective cost reduction or an increase in production efficiency. In the transplants, on the contrary, *kaizen* was carried out only by team members through suggestion system and/or QC circles.

This is for several reasons. First, in spite of their experiences of over than ten years, American team and group leaders were not still on the level of their Japanese colleagues' competence. At Toyota, such a competence was historically accumulated and succeeded by shop floor managers and engineers, whereas American team and group leaders just began, we can say, to learn know-how by doing their functions in day-to-day operations and model changes. Second, their Japanese colleagues had experienced the jobs of their team or group more than ten years before being promoted to team leader. So they had sufficient know-how about working process and could behave as the leader of team or group members in good fellowships. By contrast, if *kaizen* conceived by team leader or group leader was imposed to workers, it would be rejected by them in the American context. In fact, *kaizen* was often regarded as intensifying work. So, making *kaizen* by workers themselves was favorable for training their *kaizen* mind about quality and efficiency, and creating a fellowship among team members in the case of QC circle so far as their employment is assured (however, delicate problems were surely occurring – see Adler *et al.*, 1998).

In this domain, Toyota's general policy is to try at first to set into place Japanese-style management, and if employees do not accept it, to search for another acceptable way or a functional equivalent to adapt the TPS to local industrial relations. In fact, Toyota's basic policy about human resource management is first of all in creating a mutual trust between the company and its employees, between managers and workers, among managers as well as team members. 'Teamwork' in Toyota's jargon represents inter-individual cooperation on the basis of such a mutual trust. So 'teamwork' does not means only working on team in workshops but also cooperation between managers and workers, between teams, groups, sections, and divisions. Toyota has been thinking that the TPS can run and develop on the basis of such a 'teamwork'. Until the end of 1990s, Toyota succeeded in settling this 'teamwork' in its transplants in North America. Of course, Toyota recognizes that long time is still necessary so that employee's competence at transplants catches up that of Japanese. Until then, the know-how accumulated and used in Japanese plants continues to be mobilized to the transplants in order to improve their productivity and product quality without of course neglecting the contribution of their workers. It is also the case of suppliers of transplants. Long term relationships and mutual trust are the first requirements for the cooperation between transplant and its suppliers aiming at improving quality and reducing costs of parts supplied.

In Europe, a Portuguese company, Salvador Caetano LMVT, began assembling Toyota's trucks in small quantity from 1968. This operation remains minor producing about 4,518 vehicles a year (Dyna, Hiace and Optimo) with 1,038 employees even in 2000. Therefore, Toyota's real production in Europe began with the construction of Toyota Motor Manufacturing in the UK (TMUK), and the production of the Carina E in 1992. This model had not sold as expected, then was replaced by the Avensis in 1997. TMUK also began assembling the Corolla by constructing the second assembly line in 1998. Its production volume came close to the level of 200,000 cars. The main reason for this localization of production in the UK was apparently the construction of the EU that would make difficult the exports towards the European markets protected.

TMUK resembled in assembly line to that of its mother plant, Tsutsumi assembly plant, however adopting a different approach from that in its American transplants to the management of industrial relations and the purchase. According to the collective agreement between TMUK and AEU (Amalgamated Engineering Union) in 1991, they put into place the TMAB (Toyota Members Advisory Board), consisted of members of top management and employees' representatives nominated by vote. TMAB has been regularly discussing the issues concerning two parties: wage, working conditions, company policies that influenced the employees. TMUK applied the annual salary even for the blue-collar workers following after the Nissan UK, which then has been revised every year based upon the progress of worker's skill and company's performance. Its production system is of course based upon the TPS, but had the same problems of *kaizen* activities as in TMMK. At the beginning then, the persons dispatched from Tsutsumi plant was taking care of *kaizen* of production process. As for the purchase of parts, Toyota gave the priority to the procurement from European suppliers (160 firms with half from UK in 1994). As in the USA, TMUK organized a technical support team in order to help its suppliers to improve the quality of their products under the long-term relationship with them. Then, here also, the just-in-time supply has not been applied as in Japan. Is confirmed then the adaptation of TPS to the local industrial and business conditions.

Localization of production in other countries up to the mid-1990s

Toyota's main assembly plants outside of the North America and Europe are found in Australia, South Africa and ASEAN countries (Indonesia, Thailand and Malaysia). In Australia, where Toyota had exported vehicles from 1959 and begun KD assembling from 1963, it had to satisfy the Australian government that demanded for increasing the local content rate up to 85% of vehicle price. So, Toyota reorganized, in 1977, Olbaly Trading (Toyota having 90% of its equity) into TMA (Toyota Manufacturing Australia) for producing passenger cars and created an engine plant. Toyota also took 50% equity of AMI (Australian Motor Industries) in 1972, which has since been producing Toyota's utility vehicles. Purchasing parts and engines also from an Australian subsidiary of GM, and constructing a press plant in 1981, the local content rate of produced vehicles has been over 85% of their price since 1980. However, these two subsidiaries remained unprofitable because of inefficient production organization. So, Toyota implemented the TPS there in 1982 by realizing two shift works, standardized work, and short time die change system in order to increase their productivity. Then, TMA and AMI became the first plants to which Toyota applied the TPS in foreign countries. By the way, Toyota founded in 1988 a joint venture with GM, UAAI (United Australian Automotive Industries, the Australian version of NUMMI), that absorbed TMA and AMI. UAAI produced Toyota's Corolla and Camry and GM's Comodor, in order to reply to the Australian government encouraging the development of national automobile industry. As the government policy became less constraint, and perhaps because of the divergence in their strategy GM and Toyota dissolved this joint venture in 1996. Toyota sold all its shares to UAAI that has become the complete subsidiary of GM (GMHI), whereas the production facilities for Toyota has been reorganized into TMCA (Toyota Motor Corporation Australia), a subsidiary of Toyota Motor Sales Australia (TMSA). With 4,103 employees, TMCA produced in 2000 92,422 units of the Corolla and the Camry and supplied at the same time the Nova and the Apollo for GMHI.

In South Africa, TSAM (Toyota South Africa Motors), a marketing company founded in 1961, began assembling CKD sets of the Stout in 1962 and the Corona in 1964. Responding to the local government's demand for increasing the local content rate, TSAM constructed in 1969 an engine plant. So the local content rate of Toyota vehicles reached 55% in weight. Toyota's relation with South Africa was kept even during the period where its apartheid regime internationally became critical after 1985, though Toyota 'adopted a more prudent policy in 1988' in its exports (Toyota, 1987, 1988). Not withdrawing from South Africa, Toyota could reinforce the production of TSAM after the collapse of the apartheid regime. By localizing production, TSAM then arrived to produce over 79,000 vehicles with 7,085 employees in 2000. Toyota has also a small production base in Kenya from 1977, assembling about 500 KD sets a year with 286 employees in 2000.

Among the ASEAN countries, Thailand, Malaysia and Indonesia were the countries Toyota preferred. In Thailand the government applied a reduction by 50% of the duties on vehicles produced at local KD assembly from 1962. So TMT (Toyota Motor Thailand) founded by Toyota and TMS (Toyota Motor Sales) began to assemble KD sets. For the same reason in Malaysia, Bolneo Motor, renamed Assembly Services Sdn. Bhd., started KD assembly in 1968. In Indonesia, the government prohibited the import of vehicles in 1970. P.T. Toyota-Astra Motor, a joint venture of Toyota and P.T. Astra International, began assembling KD sets of the Corona. Gaya Motor also commenced KD assembly of the Land Cruiser and trucks. Over time, and especially after the

ASEAN's requirement for BBC (brand to brand complementation) among ASEAN countries, Toyota had to found parts companies – Toyota Auto Body Thailand in 1979, Siam Toyota Manufacturing in 1989 in Thailand, and T&K Autoparts Sdn. Bhd. in 1992 in Malaysia.

'A new global business plan' 1995–8: the second turning point in Toyota's globalization strategy

In 1995, the trade conflicts between Japan and USA was at the peak. On 16 May, Michael Kantor of USTR (United States Trade Representative) declared the imposition of duties of 100% for price on Japanese high range cars imported. In such a situation, Toyota set forth the 'New Global Business Plan' for the years 1995–8 in order to alleviate the conflicts. This plan consisted of promoting localization of production, increasing local procurement of parts, materials and equipment, and augmenting imports from abroad and exports from overseas plants to other countries.

Localization of production

Its objective was to increase overseas production in three regions – North America, Europe and Asia-Oceania – from 1.216 million units in 1994 to 1.900 million in 1998. Then the share of overseas production in overseas sales had to rise from 48% to 65% (see Table 5.2). This objective was not

Table 5.2 New global business plan, Toyota

	1994	1995	1996	1997	1998	Objective 1998
Production/sales	48%	58%	60%	n.d.	53%	65%
Production (thousands)						
North America	735	824	900	838	1,010	1,250
TMMK	285	380*	386*	432	480	500
TMMC	86	90		109	170	200
NUMMI	364	354*	365*	358*	400	400
Europe (TMUK)	85	88	100	108	170	220
Asia and Oceania	396	450	440	454	280	640
Taiwan	65	n.d.	n.d.	68	73	110
The Philippines	30	n.d.	n.d.	31	11	60
Thailand	110	n.d.	n.d.	96	35	200
Indonesia	80	n.d.	n.d.	100	17	150
China	n.d.	n.d.	n.d.	17	n.d.	n.d.
Vietnam	n.d.	n.d.	n.d.	1	2	n.d.
Total	1,216	1,253	1,346	1,379	1,380	1,900
Increase from 1994		37	130	163	164	684

Note: Data with asterisk come from JAMA (1999).

Source: Toyota Internet Drive (1999).

attained because of the economic crisis of ASEAN countries in 1998. However, the production capacity of its transplants in the North America was reinforced up to 1.250 million units in 1999 after the construction of TMMI which could produce 150,000 utility vehicles (Tundra T100). The production volume in 1998 of these transplants was 1.010 million, including those of NUMMI and TMMK. In Europe, by constructing the second assembly line in 1998, TMUK expanded its capacity up to 200,000 units. In Asia, though the objective for this region was to produce 640,000 units in 1998, its production volume shrank from 454,000 vehicles in 1997 to 280,000 in 1998 (from 246,700 in 1997 to 124,800 in 1998 if we take account only of the vehicles of which local content rate surpasses 40% of the total value of the parts in the vehicle). As a result, the total production volume of these regions in 1998 remained 1.380 million units in contrast with 1.900 million in the 'Plan'. Concerning the share of overseas production in overseas sales, Toyota seems to have renounced fixing objective since the objective was difficult to attain because of change in market conditions. In fact, this share in 1998 remained about 58% according to Toyota – a regional decomposition of the share in 1997 gives about 60% in North America, 25% in Europe and Asia, and 50% in Oceania (see Table 5.3). However, we have to remark that by promoting this 'Global Business Plan', Toyota succeeded in largely expanding its global production capacity, under the policy of 'produce where demand exists'.

Table 5.3 Localization rate per region, 1989–2000 (%)

	North America	South America	Europe	South East Asia	Oceania	Middle East Asia	Africa	Total
1989	23.87	11.52	0.66	40.70	37.30	0.99	66.32	22.39
1990	32.73	10.26	1.57	50.15	36.71	3.34	61.98	28.59
1991	32.91	10.49	2.16	50.44	35.88	2.00	63.48	28.46
1992	43.52	3.89	2.76	43.25	36.57	1.00	54.85	31.70
1993	47.72	2.88	12.57	41.91	39.90	1.14	66.64	36.42
1994	49.51	4.69	24.02	53.83	44.89	3.01	67.40	42.36
1995	62.43	3.85	24.86	59.82	37.31	17.55	64.39	50.21
1996	62.56	3.89	30.20	57.35	46.88	18.26	62.80	51.34
1997	61.79	3.30	23.09	59.03	52.36	12.86	63.51	48.99
1998	63.51	12.79	32.48	54.38	56.88	6.78	57.13	50.09
1999	65.10	16.82	30.64	72.00	52.97	5.04	55.52	52.68
2000	62.50	18.56	26.43	79.52	52.29	6.77	63.63	51.78

Note: The localization rate means the ratio of regional production volume over regional sales volume.
Source: Toyota, 2001 (annual data).

Local procurement policy of parts, materials and equipment

The American government as well as other local governments had demanded increasing export of parts from their countries and local content rate of localized production operations. Mainly under pressure of the USA, Toyota changed its procurement policy from the well-known closed policy – '*keiretsu* transaction relations' – to 'open door policy' by setting in place 'Toyota Global Optimized Purchase System', supported by 'Supplier Improvement Support Programme'. If potential suppliers can propose competitive cost in respecting quality, delivery time as well as committing themselves to continuous improvement, Toyota was ready to conclude purchasing contracts with them. Promoting the BBC in ASEAN and localizing parts production by construction of parts companies or plants, Toyota has been making efforts to increase local content rates and the level of local production integration. In 2000, 89% of vehicles produced abroad have the local content rate over 40% of the total value of parts in the vehicle, evaluated with their F.O.B. price.

Sales of imported cars to Japan

Toyota also tried to sell more imported cars of other automakers through its distribution networks. Already in 1992, Toyota organized the DUO network for selling VW/Audi cars according to the agreement concluded with VW, that produced Toyota's pickups in its Hanover plant. The sales volume of VW/Audi cars by the DUO chain was 19,000 units in 1994, 34,000 in 1997 but to 28,000 in 1998 because of the Japanese economic stagnation. Toyota also began to sell in Japan the Cavalier produced by GM (7,000 units in 1998, but their import has ceased in 2000 because of their unpopularity), and the Avalon produced by TMMK (4,000 units in 1998).

Exports from transplants

In order to satisfy local governments claim as well as to obtain economies of scale, Toyota has been promoting exports from its transplants. TMUK began export its automobiles towards the outside of the Europe from 1996, and engine blocks to Japan. The BBC was organized in ASEAN countries: production of power steering units and lower ball joints in Malaysia, of constant velocity universal joints in Philippines, and of engine blocks in Thailand, for example. In 2000, about 400,000 vehicles were exported from its transplants: TMMC (138,668 units), TMUK (138,326 units) the three plants in the USA (41,574 units) and TMCA (45,613 units).

Implementing the 'New Global Business Plan', Toyota wanted, as the No.1 Japanese automobile producer, to cool down the trade conflicts with USA and Europe. However, it didn't remain inactive in other regions.

In South America, Toyota had assembled mainly CKD vehicles in small quantity in Brazil from 1959, in Venezuela from 1981 and in Colombia from 1992. In total, they had built only thousands vehicles until 1997. The market potential of the Mercosur led Toyota to construct a new assembly plant in Argentina, which began to produce the Hilux in 1997, and another with annual capacity of 150,000 units in Brazil, in 1998. So, the volume of vehicles produced of which local content rate attained over 40% of the total value of the parts in the vehicle (FOB base) has surpassed 15,000 units from 1998, and 19,700 thousand in 2000.

In the Middle East and South Asia, Toyota assembled CKD vehicles in Bangladesh from 1982 and in Pakistan from 1993. It began the production of the Corolla in Turkey at the end of 1994 by Toyota Sabanci Motor Manufacturing Turkey Inc. (TSMT). It also produced in India the Toyota Qualis, multipurpose vehicles developed for local market, by founding Toyota Kirloskar Motor (TKM) from 1997.

Facing the age of world oligopolistic competition from 1999

At the end of the twentieth century, the merger of Daimler-Benz and Chrysler, the absorption of several 'specialist' automakers by 'generalists', and the alliance of Renault and Nissan, of GM and Fiat have created a world oligopolistic competition. In addition, investment in R&D for developing ecological vehicles is urgent and necessitates more and more important financial resources. Can Toyota pursue its 'maverick' internal growth strategy in such a situation? So, we see in this section the offensive localization of Toyota since 1999, its financial resources for its globalization strategy, the internationalization of product development, the impact of globalization upon its home industrial organization and finally its partial alliance strategy to develop new ecological car technologies.

The offensive localization of Toyota since 1999

The instability of the pound sterling penalized the exports of the cars produced in the UK. Toyota decided to construct in France an assembly plant to supply small cars well adapted to the European market. Founding Toyota Motor Manufacturing France (TMMF), Toyota started the production of the Yaris (Vitz in Japan) near Valenciennes from 31 January 2001. That is not all. Toyota decided in 2001 to construct in Czech a joint venture with Peugeot SA, which will produce small cars, co-developed by two firms and to be sold by Toyota, Peugeot and Citroën from 2005. This joint venture has to become an European version of NUMMI.

In China, Toyota had difficulty to enter there for a long time. Shenyang Jimbei Passenger Vehicle Manufacturing Co. (SJPVM) produces Toyota's light trucks (Hiace) since 1991 with Toyota's technical assistance, but these vehicles had not been sold as Toyota's ones bearing a Chinese brand name, Jimbei (Golden Cup). Betting on the big potential of Chinese markets now beginning to rapidly growth, Toyota negotiated as a late comer with the Chinese government over the construction of its own assembly plant which would produce vehicles with Toyota's badge, and the production of the Platz by Tianjin Automotive Xiali Co. Ltd (TAX), producer of the Daihatsu's Charade. These two projects were authorized by the government in 1999, so the Tianjian Toyota Motor Co. Ltd (TTMC) was founded in 2000 in Tianjin City to produce a new compact car, based on the same platform as Vitz and Platz, from 2002. In addition, Sichuan Toyota Motor Co. Ltd (SCTM) began the production of the Coaster, a light truck, in April 2001, whereas TAX began to produce the Platz in December 2001. Doing so, Toyota seems finally well prepared for catching up its precursors in China, VW, GM, Suzuki and Honda.

Although Eastern Europe, especially the Russian region, remains the untouched land for Toyota, its production network is going to covers almost all mains regions – not only the Triad regions (North America, Western Europe and Asia), but also Mercosur, South Africa and Central Europe – in order to 'produce where demand exists'.

Toyota is famous for its debt-free management from the mid-1970s. However, Toyota chose to finance its productive investments by emission of bonds profiting from low interest rates, in Japan, and to reinforce its financial assets. Consequently, Toyota has disposable financial resources enough to carry out by itself the globalization strategy, including worldwide competition for ecological car development.

About the management of transplants, Toyota seems giving a special status to the North American subsidiaries. NUMMI was a fifty-fifty joint venture of GM and Toyota, TMMC being wholly owned subsidiary of Toyota, whereas the capital of TMMK was financed of 80% by Toyota Motor Sales USA (TMS USA) and of 20% by Toyota. This is because Toyota wanted to localize TMM USA by TMS USA's reinvesting profits gained there. This localization policy in the USA led to found a holding company in the USA, Toyota Motor North America (TMNA), and a company controlling Toyota's American facilities, Toyota Motor Manufacturing North America, in 1996. From then, TMNA has owned of 100% TMMK, TMMI, TABC, TMM West Virginia, and of 87% Bodine Aluminum. Toyota also has its holding company in Germany, Finland and Sweden, Norway and South Africa, which however concerns the distribution companies. Its overseas transplants outside of the USA were owned of 100% by Toyota (TMC in Japan) and then controlled directly by Toyota. In general, their president being a Japanese, other Japanese staff dispatched from Toyota strongly support locally employed managers as general managers or advisors of them. Honda has a tendency to manage its transplants by Japanese staff, whereas Nissan has delegated transplant's management to local managers. Toyota is found between them about the management personnel policy (Suzuki, 1991; Tabata, 1995). As for the other production facilities, Toyota shared their capital with local companies because of local government policy (see Appendix Table A5.2).

The internationalization of product development

Toyota decides the product policy of its overseas production facilities, centralizing the product development into the Product Engineering Design

Department at Toyota City. Local market informations are sent to Toyota by its foreign subsidiaries. Toyota decides the new model to produce and launch for the local markets. Toyota's engineers travel to meet the engineers of foreign subsidiaries in order to perfect the design of parts. Or, as in the case of the development of TUV (basic utility vehicles: Kijan and Zace), local engineers come to participate in the product development at Toyota. This character of centralized product development will not change in the near future, but the design of body feature is different.

Toyota has three design centres: Design Centre in its Tokyo Head Office, Calty Design Research in the USA (since 1973) and N.V. Toyota Motor Europe in Belgium (from 1990), which was moved to the south of France (Côte d'Azur), and renamed Toyota Europe Design Development in 1998. So, when a new car development is planned, a design competition is organized amongst these three design centers. For example, the body shape of the Prius was designed by an engineer at Calty Design Research after their competition, that of the Yaris (Vitz) by a designer at N.V. Toyota Motor Europe. These centers are of course founded to develop the car designs suited to the local markets, but also to realize innovative car designs their Japanese homologous can not conceive as in the case of Prius and Vitz.

However, it is not probable in the foreseeable future that these overseas design centers have a competence to develop product designs. In Japan Toyota group has three product designs centers: that of Toyota, that of Toyota Auto Body (utility vehicles, trucks and minivans), and that of Kanto Auto Works (sedans and minivans), without mentioning Hino Motors (trucks and bus) and Daihatsu (mini-cars, low range cars). This means that a competitive incentive exists among the firms in the Toyota Group giving a certain dynamics to the product designs.

The impact of globalization on Toyota's home industrial organization

As we saw above, Toyota's global business looks running well. However, foreign localization of production is actually posing two problems, aggravated by the long stagnation of Japanese economy.

First, though in Japan, Toyota has to maintain the production at the level of more than 3 million vehicles in order to keep its employees (about 70,000), it seems difficult to follow this policy in the long run. In fact, production of many plants, including those of its body makers such as Kanto Auto works, has been getting down. Hino, a truck maker of Toyota group, decided to reduce about thousand employees. Kanto Auto Works announced the shutdown of one of its assembly plants producing passenger cars. Even at Toyota, the 'tact time' at Motomachi and Tsutsumi plants became two times longer in 1998 than had been in the 1980s because of shrink of production volume. The situation is more serious as to its Japanese suppliers. Toyota's purchasing from them has a tendency to reduce, because not only of 'delocalization' of production, but also of Toyota's 'Global Optimized

Purchase System'. Though Toyota is recommending them a diversification of their products outside the automobile industry, it is difficult for weak suppliers especially under second-tier suppliers to redeploy their business.

Second, facing international mergers and cooperation between automakers, Toyota decided to reinforce the ties among its group companies:

- Five vice-presidents were dispatched to Denso, Aishin, Toyota Automatic Loom, Toyota Auto Body and Toyota Finance in 1999. A holding company seems to be founded in order to reinforce the control over its group companies, especially over Denso that has been less dependent on Toyota (only 45% of its products were sold to Toyota) deploying its own strategy that sometimes compromised Toyota's interests. For example, without the agreement of Toyota, Denso sold to Fuji Heavy Industry a new engine control technology (VVT-i) that Denso had developed in collaboration with Toyota for four years from 1991 (*Asahi Shinbun* (Asahi newspaper), 29 April 1999). With holding company and direct control by dispatched person, Toyota at least could supervise its group companies so to prevent them from transferring new high technology to its rival companies, because the advanced high technology is regarded as a main weapon in fierce market competition.
- Because of over capacity, emerged from the 'delocalization' on the one hand and market stagnation on the other, Toyota revised its relations with Daihatsu and Hino by increasing its shareholding. Though assembling Toyota's low range vehicles (Corolla, Townace, and so on) from 1968 and with managers dispatched from Toyota, Daihatsu kept its own commercial strategy by developing its own vehicles in mini-cars and low range cars that often competed with Toyota's ones. Toyota increasing its shareholding up to 51.19% from 33.4% (15.4% before 1995) in 1998, Daihatsu became now Toyota's subsidiary that produces mini-cars Toyota does not produce (Daihatsu supplies to Toyota two small cars, the Duet and the Cami, from 1999 and a small SUV, the Sparky, from 2000). In addition, the overseas operations Daihatsu deployed might be under the control of Toyota (see Figure 5.2). As to Hino, a heavy truck and bus maker, that had been assembling Toyota's Hilux and so on from 1968, Toyota increased its shareholding up to 20.1% from 11.0% in 1998 (36.6% in 2001), so that Hino was also integrated in the division of labour in the Toyota Group. From 1999, it seems that Hino definitely became the Toyota Group's heavy truck and bus maker.

Partial alliance strategy

After the commercialization of the Prius by Toyota, the first 'hybrid car' in the world, development of ecological car became the focal point in the world-wide competition among automakers. On the stagnant market, winners would be

137

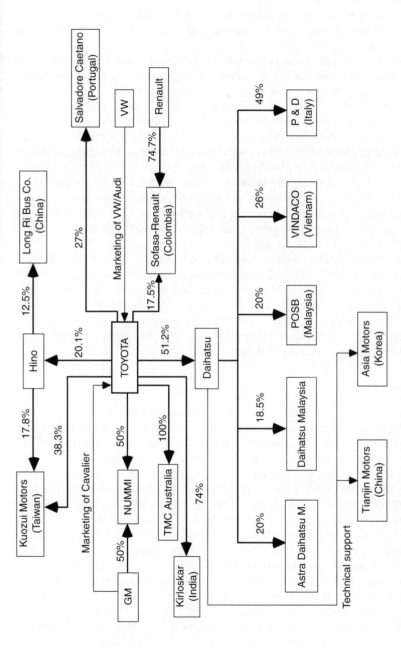

Figure 5.2 Strategic alliances and shareholding investments, Toyota, 1998

those who launch brand new and salable cars without gasoline engine before its rivals by setting its technology as de fact standard. However, the development of such a brand new technology demands a huge financial resources and time.

Toyota considers the development of ecological technology as one of the essential conditions for winning the fierce global competition at the twenty-first century. It founded a joint venture with Matsushita, Panasonic EV Energy, in 1996 in order to develop a new battery (fuel cell) for the Prius, which has been supplied to Honda from 1999 for its hybrid car. The success of the Prius constitutes a trigger for the others. Toyota itself does not believe the hybrid system of the Prius could be a final version. These circumstances augment financial and human resources to be invested in R&D, and necessitate a technological co-operation among various firms concerned. In order to develop de facto standard technologies of ecological cars, Toyota concluded a technological cooperation with GM in April 1999, into which Honda would participate after concluding a mutual supply agreement of engines with GM in December 1999.

In others fields, Toyota has also concluded alliances with other automakers: with VW about co-operation in environment technology, including recycling, navigation system and telematics from 1998; with DaimlerChrysler, Renault and Ford about the Automotive Multimedia Interface Consortium, established in 1998. Of course, all these technological alliances of Toyota remain partial, because Toyota does not search any merger or fusion with those firms.

Conclusion

Internationalization strategy of Toyota changed during the first half of the 1980s from export-centered one to the localization strategy of production, excepting for early KD assembly in several countries and localized small production in Brazil, forced by local governments' protectionist policy. This change was imposed to Toyota, though it preferred the exports to the overseas production for the sake of its TPS, considered untransferable. The trade conflicts from the end of the 1970s, the voluntary restraint of exports towards the USA were the main reasons for Toyota's decision to produce in the USA. The rapid appreciation of yen from 1985, but also the experience of transferability of the TPS led Toyota to expand overseas production operations for substituting its exports with products of its transplants. This tendency was reinforced when Toyota established its 'New Global Business Plan' in order to alleviate the trade conflicts with the USA in 1995. From then, 'produce where demand exists' became Toyota's globalization strategy. Remark that this globalization of production has been deployed on the basis of its international sales network created during the 1960s and 1970s. Then, Toyota does not carry out its overseas productions where the demand has to be searched yet. Also, it is out of question for Toyota to merge with any foreign automaker, because its industrial model is too specific to do it. Moreover, Toyota has financial assets enough to conduct this strategy and invest in the R&D of ecological vehicles, as it was shown by the launch of the Prius. Toyota seems capable to compete on the world automobile market where the zero sum game is played.

However, this does not mean that its industrial model remains unchanged. Reinforcement of the ties of its group companies, move towards the foundation of its holding company, 'delocalization' of production, increasing parts procurement from abroad suggest a reorganization on going of its industrial organization in Japan. Is Toyota aiming to become a global company? On the other hand, Toyota changed its product policy. Now, Toyota gives its priority to product innovation in order to take the initiative in developing future vehicles like as the Prius or in giving a new concept to cars like as Vitz (Yaris), as if the development of such cars prior to the others constituted the best card to compete on the zero sum game market. In any way, Toyota's industrial model seems moving from 'continuous reduction of costs at constant volume' (Freyssenet *et al.*, 1998) into 'innovation and continuous reduction of costs at constant volume'.

Statistical appendix, Toyota

Table A5.1 Toyota's globalization, statistical data, 1960–2000 (thousands of units)

Year	Domestic production	Exports	Overseas production	Exports per region					
				NA	SA	E	SEA/O	MA	Af
1960	154.8	6.4		0.5	2.1	0.01	2.9	0.4	0.09
1961	210.9	11.7		0.4	5.2	0.06	5.1	0.6	0.2
1962	230.4	11.2		1.1	2.3	0.1	6.0	0.7	1.0
1963	318.5	24.4		1.2	2.4	0.6	14.7	1.4	4.2
1964	425.8	42.8		3.8	3.8	2.3	23.6	1.6	7.6
1965	477.6	63.5		13.2	5.0	5.9	28.7	3.2	7.5
1966	587.5	105.1		27.5	9.0	12.3	38.0	6.7	11.6
1967	832.1	157.9		42.7	14.1	18.1	55.2	8.5	19.3
1968	1097.4	279.1		107.4	21.5	25.7	86.4	12.8	25.4
1969	1471.2	395.1		180.1	25.8	41.2	89.4	15.5	43.1
1970	1609.2	481.9		245.1	28.5	59.0	86.6	19.0	43.7
1971	1955.0	786.3		462.0	43.6	87.7	106.9	19.5	66.5
1972	2087.1	724.6	*102.2	359.4	38.8	162.8	98.9	24.2	40.4
1973	2308.1	720.6	*123.9	310.5	38.5	163.1	124.1	30.0	54.3
1974	2115.0	856.3	*138.4	370.4	49.8	138.4	161.8	60.6	75.3
1975	2336.1	868.4	*154.2	318.7	43.8	185.7	149.8	102.8	67.5
1976	2487.9	1177.3	*160.7	475.7	61.1	228.8	184.5	161.4	65.9
1977	2720.8	1413.2	*176.9	597.1	91.4	234.1	213.6	209.3	67.8
1978	2929.2	1382.2	*200.0	598.2	66.1	214.7	206.4	221.6	75.2
1979	2996.2	1383.6	*209.4	636.1	65.1	255.3	167	198.1	62.1

Table A5.1 continued

Year	Domestic production	Exports	Overseas production	Exports per region					
				NA	SA	E	SEA/O	MA	Af
1980	3293.3	1785.4	*261.2	762.8	106.2	318.7	223.6	279.5	94.6
1981	3220.4	1717.5	*298.4	764.5	91.6	269.8	221.6	254.7	114.3
1982	3144.6	1665.8	*301.8	735.4	81.0	271.9	196.6	323.9	57.0
1983	3272.3	1664.4	*269.6	769.2	69.8	312.3	201.6	279.8	31.7
1984	3429.2	1800.9		900.9	77.9	302.6	253.5	229.9	36.1
1985	3665.6	1979.9	136.3	1017.3	79.4	347.7	281.4	221.2	32.9
1986	3660.1	1875.8	152.5	1115.1	81.6	415.0	139.6	91.4	33.1
1987	3638.3	1770.9	192.3	992.9	68.0	422.6	127.5	118.9	41.0
1988	3968.7	1815.7	244.4	947.8	61.1	429.8	181.3	111.5	84.2
1989	3976.0	1669.1	471.6	814.0	51.2	441.5	202.9	112.8	46.8
1990	4212.4	1677.1	677.7	780.2	60.1	446.6	207.7	134.6	47.9
1991	4085.1	1703.6	669.9	768.2	79.4	436.0	211.7	155.9	52.4
1992	3931.3	1698.2	764.5	684.3	99.9	406.8	237.0	215.8	54.4
1993	3561.8	1539.0	888.7	603.0	96.6	347.6	270.4	181.6	39.8
1994	3508.5	1504.5	1051.3	653.5	89.2	334.9	244.9	144.8	37.0
1995	3171.3	1202.4	1253.3	454.4	110.9	263.3	225.0	97.8	51.0
1996	3410.1	1276.7	1346.0	456.3	86.2	304.8	254.5	124.2	50.6
1997	3502.0	1494.3	1390.1	526.5	119.6	401.4	245.9	146.8	54.0
1998	3165.8	1462.8	1467.6	584.3	110.3	369.7	170.2	172.0	56.2
1999	3118.2	1548.0	1611.0	667.7	71.4	447.2	182.8	128.2	50.7
2000	3429.2	1706.2	1751.4	725.6	86.1	488.3	218.8	143.1	44.4

Notes: The numbers with asterisks represent overseas assembly volume of KD. NA, North America; SA, South America; E, Europe; SEA, South East Asia; O, Oceania; MA, Middle East Asia; Af, Africa.

Source: Annual data (Toyota, 1987; Toyota, 1999, 2000, 2001).

Table A5.2 Toyota overseas assembly plants, 2000

Region	Country	Name	Share (%)	Start of production	Production	Employees	Products
North America	Canada	TMMC	100	Nov. 1988	184,410	2,440	Corolla, Camry Spolara
	USA	TMMK	TMNA 100	May 1988	495,490	7,759	Avalon, Camry, Sienna
		TMMI	TMNA 100	Dec. 1998	129,724	2,460	Tundra, Sequoia
		NUMMI	50	Dec. 1984	294,361	4,844	Corolla, Tacoma
South America	Argentina	TA	99	Mar. 1997	17,333	725	Hilux
	Brazil	TDB	99.99	May 1959	18,815	1,024	LC, Corolla
	Colombia	FDA	17.50	Mar. 1992	6,577	827	Hilux, LC
	Venezuela	TVCA	90	Nov. 1981	12,234	904	Corolla, Dyna, LC
Europe	France	TMMF	100	Jan. 2001	–	1,038	Yaris (Vitz)
	Portugal	SC	27	Aug. 1968	4,518	2,024	Dyna, Hiace, Optimo
	UK	TMUK	100	Dec. 1992	171,368	3,104	Avensis, Corolla
Africa	Kenya	AVA		Aug. 1977	494	286	Dyna, Hilux, LC, Hiace
	South Africa	TSAM	27.80	June 1962	79,561	7,085	Camry, Corolla Dyna, Hiace, Hilux, LC, TUV
Asia	China	SJPVM		Nov. 1991	54,016	6,500	Hiace
	Indonesia	PTTAM	49	May 1970	89,932	4,704	Crown,Camry, Corolla, Soluna, Dyna, LC, TUV
	Malaysia	AS Sdn	UMW 100	Feb. 1968	19,611	1,146	Camry, Corolla, Dyna, Hiace, TUV, Liteace, Hilux, LC

Table A5.2 continued

Region	Country	Name	Share (%)	Start of production	Production	Employees	Products
	Philippines	TMP	95	Feb. 1989	18,658	1,446	Camry, Corolla, TUV
	Taiwan	KM	47 (Hino 10)	Jan. 1986	81,511	2,361	Corona, Tercel, TUV, Hiace
	Thailand	HMT		Aug. 1972	409	893	Dyna
		TMT	69.60	Feb. 1964	69,401	3,738	Camry, Corona, Corolla, Hilux, Soluna
	Vietnam	TMV	70	Aug. 1996	4,688	358	Corolla, Hiace, Camry, LC, TUV
Oceania	Australia	TMCA	100	Apr. 1963	92,422	4,103	Camry, Corolla
Middle East and South Asia	Bangladesh	AA		July 1982	271	110	LC
	India	TKM	88.9	Dec. 1999	21,422	1,439	Qualis
	Pakistan	IMC	12.50	Mar. 1993	10,259	693	Corolla, Hilux
	Turkey	TSMT	50	Sept. 1994	14,640	670	Corolla
Total	23 countries	26 firms			1,892,125	62,681	

Source: Toyota (2001), Toyota Internet Drive.

References

Adler, P. S., Goldoftas, B. and Levine, D. I. (1998) 'Stability and Change at NUMMI', in R. Boyer, E. Charron, U. Jürgens and S. Tolliday (eds), *Between Imitation and Innovation*, Oxford/New York: Oxford University Press.

Besser, T. L. (1996) *Team Toyota. Transplanting the Toyota Culture to the Camry Plant in Kentucky*, New York: State University of New York Press.

Delapierre, M., Madeuf, B., Michalet, Ch.-A. and Ominami, C. (1983) *Nationalisations et internationalisation*, Paris: La Découverte.

Freyssenet, M., Mair, A., Shimizu, K. and Volpato, G. (eds) (1998) *One Best Way? Trajectories and Industrial Models of the World's Automobile Producers*, Oxford/New York: Oxford University Press.

Inoue, T. (1995) 'Jidosha-Sangyo no Genjyo' (Status Quo and Problems of the Automobile Industry), in Faculty of Commerce at the University of Waseda, and Public Communication Centre on Economics (eds), *Global Strategy in the Japanese Automobile Industry*, Chuo-Keizai-Sha (in Japanese).

Laigle, L. (1997) Stratégies et trajectoire d'internationalisation des firmes asiatiques et européennes, *Actes du GERPISA*, no. 22, February.

Mishina, K. (1998) 'Making Toyota in America: Evidence from the Kentucky Transplant, 1986–1994', in R. Boyer, E. Charron, U. Jürgens and S. Tolliday (eds), *Between Imitation and Innovation*, Oxford/New York: Oxford University Press.

Nikkan Jidosha Shinbun (1998) *Handbook on the Automobile Industry* (in Japanese).

Shimizu, K. (1998) 'A New Toyotaism?', in M. Freyssenet, A. Mair, K. Shimizu and G. Volpato (eds) (1998) *One Best Way? Trajectories and Industrial Models of the World's Automobile Producers*, Oxford/New York: Oxford University Press.

Shimizu, K. (1999) *Le Toyotisme*, Paris: La Découverte.

Suzuki, N. (1991) *Amerika Shakai no nakano Nikkei-Kigyo* (Japanese firms in American society), Tokyo: Toyo Keizai Shipo-sha (in Japanese).

Takahashi, Y. (1997) *Nihon Jidosha Kigyo no Gurobaru Keiei* (Management of localized plants of Japanese automobile firms), Nihon Keizai Hyoron Sha (in Japanese).

Tabata, T. (1995) 'Kaigai Business Globalization', in Faculty of Commerce at the University of Waseda, and Public Communication Centre on Economics (eds), *Global Strategy in the Japanese Automobile Industry* (in Japanese).

Toyota (1987, 1988) *A History of the First 50 Years*. Published in both Japanese and English.

Toyota, *Annual Report* (annually from 1974).

Toyota (1999, 2000, 2001) *Toyota no Gaikyo* (Toyota Outlook), Toyota Internet Drive.

6
Nissan: From a Precocious Export Policy to a Strategic Alliance with Renault

Hiroshi Kumon

Nissan Motor took an aggressive approach to exports and overseas production, especially in the 1980s, when it adopted a bold strategy for internationalization. This expansion of export and overseas production supported Nissan's growth and it succeeded in transferring its production system overseas and forming a global network. However, Nissan revealed weaknesses in product development and marketing in the 1990s. It was unable to respond effectively to the decreasing domestic market and chose to survive as a global maker by forming a capital alliance with Renault. Several explanations, related to the loss of its market share at home, have been given for the path that Nissan followed. These explanations included labour relations in which the labour union interfered with management prerogatives (Kamii, 1994; Saga and Hanada, 1999), weak marketing and sales functions (Shimokawa, 1994), the classical profit strategy of 'volume and diversity' (Freyssenet, 1998), and a lack of integrated management (Ghosn and Nakagawa, 2001). This chapter investigates the process through which Nissan Motor internationalized and the effects of this. The internationalization process involved exports, overseas production, transfer of the production system to foreign plants, and the capital alliance with Renault. The salient questions to ask are: Why did Nissan pursue an aggressive internationalization strategy? How did it transfer the production system? Why did it fall into financial crisis and choose a strategic alliance with Renault? How do they construct a strategy for survival?

Exports and KD production, encouraged by the MITI: 1957–79

Export strategy

Nissan put a great effort into exports under Katsuji Kawamata, who promoted an export strategy after becoming president in 1957. The major banks with which Nissan Motor did business were the Fuji Bank and The Industrial Bank of Japan Ltd, and Nissan's management was closely intertwined with the political world. Its efforts to be strong in exports related to the policies of MITI (the Ministry of International Trade and Industry), which encouraged manufacturing firms to export. At the same time, Nissan adopted Total Quality Control methods to increase productivity and quality. Nissan's export volume increased from 73,157 in 1965 to 884,861 in 1975, and 1,465,827 in 1980 (Nissan, 1975, 1985). Although it lagged behind Toyota in the domestic market from the latter half of the 1960s, its export volume was almost the same as that of Toyota. Exports were another important means of maintaining production volume. Nissan had advantages in technology that it gained from Britain's Austin Motors through a technical tie-up. Nissan combined the technology acquired from Austin Motors through licensed production with its own technology. Nissan completely redesigned its models, including engines and all other parts. As a result, Nissan surpassed Toyota in production volume of passenger cars from 1960 to 1962, and acquired a reputation for superior technology. This successful experience exerted a dominating influence on Nissan's behaviour for a long time.

Nissan was able to increase its export volume by including the Bluebird among its range of export products, and surpassed Toyota in export volume from 1960 to 1965. However, Toyota overtook Nissan in market competition by improving its R&D and by introducing innovations in its manufacturing process. Toyota recognized its shortcomings in product quality and decided to introduce its own total quality control system, as well as implement the so-called '*kanban*' system throughout the company. It introduced manufacturing innovations during the first half of the 1960s, and developed a moderately priced car to meet the needs of a newly 'motorized society', which enabled it to surpass Nissan in sales volume. Nissan also fell behind Toyota in the timing of the introduction of popular new models in step with the progress of motorization. Although Toyota invested much effort in manufacturing technology and continuous improvement on the shopfloor, Nissan prioritized equipment modernization and factory automation. The labour unions of the two companies also responded to management policy differently. Neither union was adversarial, adopting instead a cooperative policy with management. However, Nissan's union remained firm in its position against a productivity increase movement initiated by managers, fearing that it would increase their workload. When there was a major strike in 1953, one group of employees, which regarded company survival as the most important issue, organized a new union. This new union took over leadership of the labour movement within the company and exerted a strong influence upon management. A labour agreement concluded in 1955 made specific reference to matters including personnel and other management prerogatives. The labour union sometimes interfered in management responsibilities, thus hindering flexible decision-making by management.

Export by region: USA rapidly became the company's largest export market

Nissan had exported vehicles to the Asian market before the Second World War, and resumed exporting to this area in 1949, particularly to Korea, Thailand and India, followed by Indonesia, Burma and the Philippines. Although volume was very limited until 1957, Nissan decided to commit itself to exports in 1958, announcing that it would seek new export markets, mainly in Asia. There are two forms of export to developing countries – namely, the export of completed vehicles and that of KD sets. Nissan entered a technical tie-up with Yue Long Motor of Taiwan in 1957 and with the Indian government in 1960. Yue Long Motor was the first KD production base for Nissan. Also, Nissan began to export KD sets to Thailand in 1962, and completed Nissan vehicles to Hong Kong, Singapore, Malaysia and Pakistan by 1961, thus covering the main Asian countries. As exports increased all over the world, the rate of exports to Asia gradually decreased. The export volume in 1980 was 48,639 passenger automobiles and 43,729 commercial vehicles, totalling 92,378 units, or 6.3% of the total export volume of 1,465,827 units.[1]

Nissan planned to export vehicles to North America in 1957, and exhibited a new model at the motor show for imports in Los Angeles in 1958. Nissan Motor Corp. USA was established in 1960 and shouldered complete responsibility for importing all Nissan brand vehicles. The president was Takashi Ishihara, who was later appointed president of Nissan Motor. Exports to North America increased rapidly from 1965, and the USA became the company's largest export market. Although the volume was only 1,330 units in 1960, it had reached 652,903 units by 1980, accounting for 44.5% of Nissan's entire exports. However, voluntary export restraints were enacted in 1981, after which the export volume gradually decreased. Exports to Canada began in 1960 and a sales company, Nissan Canada Inc., was set up in 1965.

Exporting to Europe was not easy for Japanese automakers, as they entered the market later than they had in North America. Nissan chose the EFTA region as its first export market, only later exporting to the EEC region. Since there were few major automakers in the EFTA region, Nissan was able to enter the market more easily there. Nissan delivered a sample model to Norway in 1959 and started exporting in 1962. Though Nissan then tried to increase its exports to Scandinavian countries, sales there were not easy. Nissan selected Belgium as its first export country in the EEC region, setting up a Brussels office in 1964 and exhibiting a model at an international motor show. Nissan began exporting to Belgium and the Netherlands in 1966, the first time in the EEC region. Nissan then expanded its export markets, entering England and France in 1968. Exports to Europe totalled 336,975 units, accounting for 23% of the company's exports in 1980.

Nissan's presence was the highest among the Japanese automakers, with a 3.3% share of the European market in 1997.

Nissan has invested a great deal of effort into Central and South America for a long time because of the many Japanese immigrants who live there. First, Nissan started exporting trucks to Brazil in 1951. It has continued exporting cars to this area since 1958. As many countries adopted import substitution industrialization policies, Nissan exported both complete vehicles and KD sets. It invested heavily in Mexico, and in 1959 exported complete vehicles to that country for the first time. When the Mexican government declared a ban on auto imports the following year, Nissan decided to produce vehicles there. It established Nissan Mexicana S.A. de C.V. in 1961, to which it exported KD sets, consigning vehicle assembly to a local plant. When the Mexican government raised the local content requirement to 60% in 1964, Nissan decided to construct a manufacturing plant, and production of vehicles began in 1966. Although Toyota withdrew from Mexico, Nissan expanded its production capacity there. The Mexican manufacturing plant has close ties with the American plant, and exports vehicles to both South and North America. Nissan also chose to export KD sets to other countries, and started KD assembly in countries such as Chile in 1962 and Peru in 1966. It also elected to consign assembly operations in Venezuela in 1963 and Ecuador in 1987. At the time of writing, however, KD sets are assembled only in Ecuador. The export volume to the Central and South American market reached 79,860 units in 1980, accounting for 5.4% of Nissan's exports.

Shipments to the Oceanian market began with exports to Australia in 1958, and to New Zealand in 1962. When the Australian government adopted a policy to support domestic production, Nissan subcontracted assembly to a local automaker in 1966. In response to a change of government policy in 1975, Nissan bought up the local company to assemble cars at its own plant. Although Nissan expanded the production capacity of the engine manufacturing plant, the Australian government again changed its automobile industry policy from one of protection to an open market policy by reducing tariff rates in 1991. Nissan therefore switched from local production to imports from Japan, thus exploiting the lower tariff rate. Nissan began local assembly in New Zealand in 1963, but the government adopted a similar industrial policy to that in Australia, prompting Nissan to change its policy from local production to importing.

Nissan decided to export to South Africa in 1958, its first exports to the African market. Thereafter, Nissan expanded exports to include Sudan, Ethiopia, Angola, Ghana and Zimbabwe, and exported KD sets to South Africa, Kenya and Zimbabwe. Exports (and their share of the total export markets) in 1980 amounted to 48,585 units (3.3%) to Oceania, and 103,325 units (7.0%) to Africa.

Aggressive overseas settlement with the aim of moving from a domestic to a global market: 1980–98

Overseas production strategy

Nissan adopted an aggressive strategy for globalization in 1980, primarily because of the policies of Ishihara, who became president of Nissan in 1977. While Kawamata, the previous president of Nissan, who had adopted an export strategy, hailed from the Industrial Bank of Japan, Ishihara had served his entire career with Nissan. Since Nissan's market share fell during the 1970s, while Toyota's increased continuously, Ishihara was compelled to devise a new competitive strategy. His was a mission to gain a new competitive edge over Toyota, and he therefore adopted a globalization strategy with the aim of shifting from the domestic to the global market. He prioritized product development, domestic sales and overseas operations (Nissan Motor, 1985), and set up an independent overseas operations department in 1980, formerly a part of the export department. Toyota, on the other hand, was forced to shift to overseas production as a result of trade friction and the appreciation of the yen, despite a reluctance to engage in overseas operations and an aversion to the pioneer risk. In the case of Nissan, such environmental factors were secondary to the primary motivation of the president's choice of strategy.

Ishihara also initiated reforms in the labour relations he inherited from Kawamata. The labour union, which had been established during the 1953 strike, interfered in management issues, especially those concerning personnel. Ishihara believed that labour relation reforms would boost productivity and improve product quality. One of the issues involving labour relations was the decision to build a manufacturing plant in England. After his retirement, management and labour concluded a new agreement in 1986, which specified that management had authority over personnel issues. The labour – management council was also defined as a consultative system and not a decision-making system (Kamii, 1994).

Production and specific modalities by regions

Nissan investigated the possibility of production in the USA by forming a project team in 1974. The team examined potential models, production capacity, profitability and labour relations. As a result, it decided to construct a pick-up truck manufacturing plant in 1980, thus taking a prudent approach to the US market. There were two reasons for starting production with pick-up trucks: the first is that Nissan had already developed the truck market in the USA through sales of Datsun trucks, so it had a secure reputation in this segment; the other was that trucks are easier to manufacture than passenger cars, since they have fewer parts. The location of the plant was Smyrna, Tennessee, and construction was completed in 1982. The plant had integrated equipment, such as stamping, welding, painting and assembly. After the first vehicle rolled off the line in 1983, production capacity was expanded to include the manufacture of passenger cars. The plant had an annual capacity of 450,000 units and employed 6,312 people in 1998.

Nissan entered the European market through capital participation in Motor Iberica, S.A., a commercial vehicle maker in Spain, which was originally established as a subsidiary of Ford Motors in 1920. After Ford Motors withdrew from Spain in 1954, Motor Iberica became an independent, private company. When Nissan was invited to take a share in the company in 1979, it decided to invest to gain a foothold in Europe. At first, Nissan provided technical guidance based on a technical tie-up but gradually increased its ownership share to 99% at the time of writing. The company, whose name was changed to Nissan Motor Iberica, S.A. in 1987, has an annual capacity of 125,000 units and produces commercial vehicles and RVs.

Nissan implemented a feasibility study after announcing its intention to explore the possibility of passenger car production in the UK in 1981. The venture that resulted was accompanied by labour relation reforms initiated by Ishihara. The labour union objected to the venture, dispatching its own team to England to conduct a feasibility study and then making an alternative proposition to management. The union concluded that the UK venture would operate at a loss for an extended period of time, and that it would reduce exports from Japan. It also claimed that the company's primary mission was to restore its market share in Japan. The union even resorted to expressing its opinion at a press conference. It also rejected management's productivity improvement project, and labour–management negotiations became confrontational. As a result, management made concessions that led to an agreement regarding production in the UK that involved reducing the planned annual capacity from 200,000 units to 24,000. The company deferred the decision to raise the annual capacity to 100,000 units to a later stage.

Nissan chose Sunderland in north-east England as the site for its plant, and established Nissan Motor Manufacturing UK Ltd there in 1984. The first vehicles rolled off the line in 1986, and the plant has since expanded to an annual capacity of 300,000 units.

As mentioned above, Nissan Mexicana S.A. de C.V. started production in 1966, and before the move into Europe and the USA, was Nissan's only overseas production facility. Nissan committed itself heavily to its Mexican operations, enlarging capacity and constructing an engine plant between 1974 to 1979, in order to respond to government policy requiring a higher local content ratio as well as exports from Mexico. After finally showing a profit in 1979, Nissan embarked on a new enlargement plan, targeting a market share of 15%. This plan was drawn up in 1980 by the overseas operations department at the Japanese headquarters and involved the construction of a new plant and the addition of new products. At the time of writing, Nissan Mexicana has three plants producing passenger cars, pick-up trucks, engines and so on, with a total production capacity of 270,000 units.[2]

Regional headquarters and the global network

Nissan took the bold step of embarking on overseas production and making the strategic shift from exports to globalization in the 1980s. As Japanese automakers changed from exports to overseas production, the total volume of overseas production by all Japanese automakers first exceeded exports from Japan in 1994. In the case of Nissan, however, this stage was reached in 1992, while for Toyota it was not until 1995. Increasing overseas production requires the localization of R&D, and when sales, production and R&D are localized, then the headquarters in Japan is no longer able to control local business activities effectively, thus making it necessary at some point to establish a regional headquarters.

Nissan established regional headquarters to manage business activities and develop strategies in Europe in 1989 and North America in 1990. It devolved power successfully from the head office of the parent company in Japan to the regional headquarters. Toyota, on the other hand, was slow to establish regional headquarters. Although it established a European headquarters in 1993, it maintains separate headquarters for sales and for production in North America.

Nissan also established similar companies in Central and South America and in the Middle East. Nissan Mexicana S.A. de C.V. controls business activities in Central and South America, while Nissan Middle East FZE controls sales and marketing in the Middle East. Although the Japanese headquarters controls subsidiaries located elsewhere than those mentioned above, business offices have been established, such as the ASEAN office in Thailand, Beijing office in China, Jakarta office in Indonesia, and Johannesburg office in South Africa.

Nissan Europe N.V. is located in Amsterdam, the Netherlands. Nissan gradually expanded its activities in Europe from exports to local production in Spain and the UK. It also established an R&D centre and localized its basic functions. As unification of the European market appeared on the horizon in 1992, Nissan established a regional headquarters in 1989, from which it controls all its business functions in Europe other than R&D – namely, production, sales, marketing, finance, logistics, and its parts service.

Nissan Europe has even been given the authority to decided on the presidents of the manufacturing companies in this region. The manufacturing companies are considered as cost centres, and the sales companies as revenue centres. Nissan employs 15,000 people in Europe and sold 490,000 units in 1997. Though it posted losses in the early 1990s, it recovered profitability in the latter half of the 1990s.

Nissan North America, Inc. (NNA) was established in 1990, in California. Nissan's highest decision-making body in North America is its board of directors, consisting of five presidents of related companies including NNA and the senior vice-president of NNA. At the time of writing, NNA employs 2,400 people, including fifty Japanese expatriates, exceeding the number employed by Nissan in Europe. NNA has integrated sales and finance companies, which previously had been independent.

Overseas plant operation: hybridization by local managers

Nissan's hybridization pattern

The transfer of Japanese production systems to foreign countries has led to hybridized versions of the Japanese and local production systems (Abo, 1994; Boyer *et al.*, 1998). The hybridization patterns involved differ from company to company, and in the case of Nissan are characterized by the bold localization of management in developed countries. In Asia, Nissan Motor has entered into joint ventures with local partners without managerial authority. It has only attempted to implement its production system in response to requests by those local partners to dispatch engineers from Japan. Other Japanese automakers, such as Toyota and Honda, have taken a different approach to the localization of management. In these cases, Japanese managers initially assumed positions of responsibility (such as president and managers) and gradually transferred those positions to local managers after a period of time.

Nissan's localization strategy has resulted in the successful transfer of the production system and excellent productivity in the developed countries, where Nissan hired reliable managers and engineers. This strategy provided a chance for local managers and engineers to play decisive roles in plant management with the support of Japanese expatriate personnel. Local managers have the chance to exploit their experience fully in combination with Nissan's production system. This hybridization pattern in the developed countries resulted in successful plant operation, such as Nissan's American plant, which attained the highest productivity among all manufacturing plants in North America. According to the Harbour Report, Nissan attained the highest productivity measured in total labour hours per vehicle in 1995, 1996 and 1997. In 1997, Nissan scored 28.89 hours per vehicle, higher than any other maker (Honda 30.22; Toyota, 30.91; Ford, 35.62; Chrysler, 38.73; and General Motors 43.16). Nissan remains the most productive vehicle manufacturer in North America, with the lowest average labour cost per vehicle (Harbour Associates, 1998).

In the UK, Nissan's plant achieved the highest productivity in the whole of Europe. The Economist Intelligence Unit reported that the Nissan plant in Sunderland, England outpaced all other European plants in terms of productivity in 1997, at 98 vehicles per employee (EIU, 1998). According to its report, 'This is a major achievement since, for the first time, a plant in Europe has achieved world class standards of productivity at almost 100 cars per employee' (ibid.). Although Nissan succeeded in transferring the production system to local plants in developed countries, the situation is different in the developing countries. The transfer of Nissan's system to four plants, in the USA, the UK, Taiwan and Thailand, will be explained below.[3]

Hybridization by local managers

In contrast with other Japanese-affiliated auto plants in the USA, the plant of Nissan Motor Manufacturing Corp. is characterized by the fact that plant management has been handed over to the Americans. Japanese expatriates number approximately twenty, while in other Japanese plants the numbers range from fifty to 250.

Since the plant is 100% owned by Nissan, four of the five board member positions are securely held by Japanese staff, while one position, that of the president, is held by an American. Upper management is controlled by Americans, who comprise five of the six vice-presidents. The single Japanese vice-president acts in the capacity of adviser. Roles played by Japanese are therefore limited in comparison with other transplants. Unlike other Japanese transplants, Nissan's strategy of localizing management from the very beginning has resulted in American personnel heading up every section in the company. The first president, a former vice-president of Ford, implemented management methods he learned from visiting factories in Japan, and taking into consideration his own experience with American auto plants. The current system is a mixture of the slightly modified Japanese production elements he introduced and other elements of the Japanese system that have been implemented since he left the post. The current president is a person the first president brought with him when he left the Ford Motor Company.

The first president introduced a number of system innovations, including simplified job classifications, shared cafeterias for all personnel, company meetings in which all employees take part and so on. He implemented these features vigorously, with the benefit of his years of experience in the American auto industry.

In the case of simplified job classifications, instead of the large number of jobs that characterize traditional types of organization, there are only four classifications – namely, production technician, quality control technician, material handling technician, and maintenance technician. Moreover, employees in the first three of the job classifications receive the same amount of wages, while only the maintenance technicians receive a higher compensation. Wages are based on the job, but after 2.5 years' seniority, almost all employees receive extra pay for skill versatility, or in other words, the ability to perform five or six different jobs. In addition, all employees receive a bonus. The combined wage and bonus income is comparable to the wage levels that existed for members of the UAW.

Other innovations concerned, for example, the path to promotion. While other Japanese transplants either follow the seniority method or a combination of ability and seniority, the Nissan plant opted for a unique approach involving the recommendation of fellow workers. This path for advancement from technician (production worker) to group leader is based on the principle of internal promotion. First, a worker applies for a vacant position, then the other workers in that group must supply their recommendations, and finally, the manager must accept or reject those recommendations.

Industrial engineering experts determine standard time, but the manufacturing division decides work standards for individual workers. This is the same method that the parent company in Japan uses. The employees turned down a full-scale attempt by the UAW to unionize the plant, based on the issues of line speed and occupational accidents. Apparently, management produced counter-arguments by presenting certain facts.

As mentioned above, Nissan experienced severe internal friction before finally making its decision to construct a plant in the UK (Nissan Motor Manufacturing Ltd). The British government was pinning its hopes on Nissan's decision to go ahead with those plans, and in 1984 an agreement was finally reached with the government. The Amalgamated Engineering Union agreed to a single labour union in 1985, and production began the following year. Annual capacity was 24,000 units in the first phase, after which it gradually expanded. At the time of writing, the plant has an annual capacity of 300,000 units, and 4,100 employees. Since 1992, its production has concentrated on two models, the Primera and the Micra.

Nissan adopted a revised approach to management localization for this plant. In the first stage, Japanese managers held the positions of president, and divisional directors of engineering, manufacturing engineer, and quality control. Japanese managers began the initial stage of operation based on the Nissan style, especially in the areas of engineering and quality control. Later, these positions of responsibility were gradually shifted to British managers. The second president was British, and under him, Japanese personnel held the posts of a single vice-president and a director of the accounting division. Other Japanese expatriates are advisers in the areas of engineering, quality control, purchasing, production control and office administration.

This plant has implemented a single-status policy for all employees in each area. All employees are subject to the same wage and salary pay system, including a merit system. Supervisors evaluate and describe performance as 'outstanding', 'average', or 'below expectation'. Wage increases consist of two parts: a general increase and a merit increase. The latter is determined by the performance evaluation and is not included among the items negotiated with the trade union. Occupational classifications, which are limited to jobs that may be carried out by union members, consist of eight categories, including supervisors. Each classification has separate wage zones. Cafeterias, parking lots and uniforms are common to all employees.

At its UK plant, Nissan has obtained a unique agreement with the trade union, whereby the 'company council' is in charge of all negotiations concerning wages and work conditions. This company council replaces the traditional trade union. Of course, managers expect workers to be multifunctional and they implement OJT (on-the-job training) and off-line training.

Yue Long Motor was established in 1953 by Chinese capitalists fleeing from mainland China. In 1958, the company entered into a technical tie-up with Nissan, forming Nissan's first overseas KD plant. Yue Long Motor is Taiwan's oldest automobile company, and has enjoyed a monopoly in Taiwan for some time. When the government announced its intention to liberalize conditions for foreign firms in 1985, Yue Long Motor asked Nissan for a capital injection to strengthen itself against expected competition from imported vehicles and domestic producers. As a result, Nissan now holds a 25% share, while the local owners retain management control. Some fourteen Japanese expatriates are employed at this company, one in the position of vice-president, another as a senior manager, and the others as advisers to Taiwanese managers. The top decision-making group is a management board composed of the president, vice-president and senior managers, including two Japanese expatriates. As the Japanese occupy only two seats on the board, management control is in the hands of the local partners. In 1989, the company formed a rationalization section to improve productivity in the face of the fierce competition expected after economic deregulation. The board also asked Nissan to dispatch engineers from Japan to improve product quality and productivity on the shop floor.

Yue Long Motor introduced the Japanese production system in 1989. Japanese advisers initiated the '5S' movement to improve quality in manufacturing and to develop multi-skilled workers. In quality control, Yue Long Motor originally applied the American system, in which products were checked at the final inspection stage and any faults were put right by skilled workers. The Japanese techniques, based on improving quality throughout the entire factory, replaced the American QC system with an approach that combined quality checks in an audit room together with a feedback process that integrated the results of these checks back into the manufacturing process. All operators maintain personal quality sheets at their workplaces, and when a defect is discovered it is noted in a quality guide sheet and a result check-sheet, in an effort to build quality into the manufacturing process. When Yue Long Motor introduced this approach there was a remarkable improvement in quality. Defects in the audit room dropped from between twenty and thirty a day to less than ten. While the initiative for introducing the system came from the local managers, who recognized the need for it, the system itself was implemented directly by Nissan engineers from Japan. However, the Taiwanese and Japanese sides failed to agree over the long-term implementation of this system and Japanese expatriate managers expressed their dissatisfaction when the rationalization section was absorbed into another division as a result of organizational reforms.

In 1952, a group of overseas Chinese industrialists established an automobile company to import and market Nissan cars in Thailand. This was Nissan's earliest overseas sales company. Then, in 1962, Nissan established a KD plant to assemble automobiles in Thailand. In 1973, when the government announced a policy to support Thai domestic assembly in preference to imports, Nissan constructed another assembly plant, this time for both passenger cars and trucks. While the company initially increased sales under an aggressive local manager dubbed 'the Automobile King of Thailand', the company's market share dipped because of severe competition with domestic assemblers. Pressed by its creditors, the cash-strapped local partner, which suffered a financial crisis in the late 1980s, invited Nissan to inject some capital into the venture: Siam Nissan Automobile of Thailand. In line with its strong commitment to the enterprise, Nissan sought a 40% share in the business. Its partner, however, intended to remain Thailand's only indigenous automaker and therefore restricted Nissan to 25%. In 1991, Nissan injected more capital, becoming much more than merely a technical partner. It led the move to replace family-style management when it set up a management board as the top decision-taking body of Siam Nissan and dispatched eleven Japanese staff to serve in the company. The management board consists of an honorary chairman, a chairman, a president, and four vice-presidents. One of the vice-presidents comes from Nissan in Japan. He attends board meetings, and while this one individual cannot really affect management decisions, Nissan has succeeded in setting up a modern managerial framework to run the company. Nissan also began to introduce the Japanese production system. Of the expatriates, six serve at the plant, and one assists the local plant manager in the business of plant reform. Whereas, previously, division and section managers had their own separate offices and secretaries, section managers and below now work together in an open-style office and the company is modifying its management system from a 'top-down' to a committee-style, participatory approach. On the shop floor, the company is establishing precise work standards, implementing the '5Ss' movement, and strengthening small-group and quality control activities. Staff strive to improve the results of '5Ss' activities, which are announced at each plant. However, the plant still has a long way to go in its efforts to improve quality and productivity. For example, it is still looking at pre- and post-repair defects in the audit room, and wondering how to feed these results back into manufacturing processes.

Financial crisis and strategic alliance with Renault: 1999–?

Financial crisis in the 1990s

Nissan's aggressive globalization strategy also produced a financial crisis. Globalized operations require appropriate financial resources that enable the company to focus its efforts on strategically important areas. While engaging in the overseas market, Nissan also competed with Toyota in the domestic market, and maintained a full line-up of products. When the market suddenly turned down and there was a change in consumers' tastes, Nissan was unable to react appropriately (Hanada, 1998). Nissan should also have developed new vehicles specifically for the foreign market during the 1990s. However, it was unable to construct an effective organization for the development of new products and for the promotion of sales, thus revealing weaknesses in product development and marketing. The sales division resorted to selling at low prices, production costs mounted because of low sales, and Nissan drifted into a vicious circle.

Nissan was consistently in the red during the first half of the 1990s. Its consolidated financial statements showed net losses after taxes from 1992 to 1998. The only year in which it was in the black was 1996. Its losses were mainly caused by decreased domestic sales, which fell from 1,378,329 units in 1990 to 1,067,130 units in 1993, and 861,411 units in 1998. Its share of the domestic market fell from 17.7% in 1990 to 14.7% in 1998. Nissan's domestic production also dropped sharply in the 1990s. After peaking at 2,379,634 units in 1990, it fell each year, dropping as low as 1,528,461 units in 1998. After the bubble economy burst, vehicle demand decreased drastically and customers opted increasingly for cheaper cars. Customers also shifted away from 4-door sedans to SUVs and RVs. Nissan did not respond effectively to these market changes. For example, the new Sunny, which was delivered in 1994, earned a good reputation for technology but failed to sell well because it was more expensive than competitor cars. Nissan also lagged in the development of SUVs and RVs.

Nissan also suffered losses on its foreign operations during the 1990s. Its operations in both Spain and Mexico went into the red in the mid-1990s, and its North American business posted losses in 1987. In general, Japanese automakers consider North America to be the most profitable market in the world, and while Nissan had transferred its production system successfully into its local North American plant, it made mistakes in its product development and marketing strategies. The first mistake was the change in brand name from Datsun to Nissan. Datsun was a very familiar brand to American customers in the late 1980s, and the company had to strive to achieve similar brand recognition among US consumers for 'Nissan'. Second, Nissan's model choice was inappropriate and the automaker eventually resorted to a strategy of cheap prices and lease sales. As Nissan gradually lost market share, it switched to sales methods such as three-year leasing, which only resulted in plummeting resale prices when the leased cars were returned. The 80 billion yen losses that Nissan North America recorded in 1997 was one factor behind Nissan Motor's financial crisis.

During the 1990s, Nissan announced several restructuring plans to cope with the severe conditions it faced. The first plan was announced in 1993, and included the closing of Nissan's Zama plant. A second plan was announced in 1995 but later abandoned after the situation deteriorated further. Conditions had been complicated by sizeable losses in the North American operation in 1997, ending expectations that North American profits might compensate for any domestic losses. A third plan, announced in May 1998, acknowledged the possibility that an alliance with a foreign firm might be necessary to enable Nissan to keep its global operations intact in the midst of severe financial conditions. This was the plan that led to Nissan's alliance with Renault.

Strategic alliance with Renault

After announcing its third restructuring plan, Nissan entered into negotiations to form an alliance with Renault. Negotiations started in June 1998 and both sides signed a tie-up agreement on 27 March 1999. Under the terms of the agreement, which was not a merger but an international capital alliance, Nissan retains its president and remains an independent manufacturer. Renault takes a 36.8% stake in Nissan and has decision-making authority within Nissan management. It is said that Yoshikazu Hanawa, the president of Nissan, asked Renault to send Carlos Ghosn to Japan. Ghosn has since been appointed Nissan's chief operating officer.

There are three important problems that Nissan must tackle. The first is the urgent need to reduce net loss and high costs, as Nissan has become a high-cost operation because of over-extending its production capacity. The second is an apparent weakness in Nissan's product R&D and marketing strategy, as reflected in the company's falling share of the domestic market. The goal must be to gain flexibility in both product design and marketing strategy that is more attuned to consumer trends. The third problem Nissan faces is its apparently overly bureaucratic and poorly integrated operations. It must restructure its organization in such a way as to foster efficient inter-departmental co-ordination. Nissan and Renault created a governing body for the alliance named the 'global alliance committee' in which the chairman and CEO from both companies participate. This committee determines joint strategy and decides on how to implement co-operation.

To reduce its losses and cut costs, Nissan on 18 October 1999 revealed a drastic 'revival' plan, that includes shutting down five factories and cutting 21,000 jobs. This 'Nissan Revival Plan', consists of three parts, the first of which is cost reduction. This part of the plan contains concrete proposals for action and mentions actual figures. The second part concerns product development and sales growth, and includes a mention of certain innovations in R&D, while the third relates to company reorganization and decision-making. In fact, the plan mentions something about organizational changes, but it is vague on the details.

Specifically, the cost reduction scheme entails bringing costs down by 1 trillion yen and the net debt down from 1.4 trillion yen to less than 700 billion yen by fiscal year 2002. Thanks to the disposal of assets and capital injection by Renault, Nissan reduced its net debt of 2.6 trillion yen in 1998 to 1.4 trillion yen in 1999. The additional reduction in net debt will be achieved by the disposal of land, securities and non-core assets. The immediate targets of cost reduction are to return to profitability in fiscal year 2000 and to achieve operating profits greater than 4.5% of sales by fiscal year 2002. Although the plan targets cost reduction in the areas of purchasing, manufacturing, and sales, I shall focus only upon the manufacturing part of the formula.

Nissan closed three auto assembly in 2001 and two powertrain plants in 2002. The number of assembly plants was reduced from seven to four. The company estimates that its current vehicle assembly capacity is an annual 2.4 million units. The closure of these three assembly plants reduced capacity to 1.65 million vehicles. Nissan operated at a 53% level of capacity for fiscal year 1999, producing 1.28 million vehicles. If it produces at the fiscal 1999 level under the new scheme, it will be operating at above 70%.

Nissan also plans to reduce the number of platforms by drastically changing its vehicle assembly configuration. It produced 24 platforms at seven assembly plants, but under the new scheme it had fifteen platforms at four plants in 2002 and it will have twelve platforms at four plants in 2004. As a result of consolidation, the average production per platform per site will increase from 50,000 today, to 100,000 in 2004. In 2004, its Oppama plant will have two platforms, the Tochigi plant three platforms, and the Kyushu plant only one platform. The Shonan plant will have eight platforms.

The plan also calls for a 14%, or 21,000-person, reduction in its group workforce from the current 148,000 employees in the Nissan group to 127,000 by the year 2002. This is to be achieved through natural attrition, increases in part-time and flex-time schedules, spin-offs and early retirement programmes. Nissan has announced that it will not resort to outright lay-offs. Management has already started negotiations with the labour union on employees' transfer from plant to plant.

Concluding remarks: the 'Nissan paradox'

The 'Nissan paradox' might be an appropriate description for globalization and its effects. Although Nissan shaped a global network successfully and achieved the highest productivity in developed countries, it fell into financial crisis in the 1990s. Nissan did not have a firm strategy for meeting environmental change in the 1990s. Since it could not develop a coherent strategy and organization as a global maker, it could not fully exploit its global network. Conversely, globalization imposed a heavy burden on the company's financial situation. Global operations require the appropriate allocation of resources within the company. The absence of integrated resource allocation was reflected in Nissan's weakness in product development and marketing that reappeared in the 1990s.

Nissan has accumulated superior engineering and manufacturing technology, and its overseas plants have a record of superior productivity in the developed countries. Nissan should bank on its accumulated advantages to survive as a global automaker. Renault is capable of innovative product styling and has experience in comprehensive organizational restructuring. Nissan's survival depends on whether it can change its traditional path with the help of Renault. Nissan's survival will be the test of the alliance.

Statistical appendix, Nissan

Table A6.1 Statistical data, Nissan, 1965–2000 (000s.)

Year	Domestic Production	Domestic Sales	Exports Total	Asia	North America	Europe	South America	Oceania	Africa	Middle East	Overseas Production	America	England	Employees
1965	352,514	264,576	73,157	19,316	24,585	6,678	6,384	7,423	7,929	842				20,917
1966	548,580	451,161	98,219	21,994	40,440	5,623	9,925	7,973	10,713	1,551				22,642
1967	781,207	614,337	132,507	30,064	45,331	9,533	14,225	14,636	16,517	2,201				34,063
1968	1,026,112	748,002	206,657	39,592	91,745	14,576	19,624	22,073	15,194	3,853				40,014
1969	1,209,620	882,472	300,292	40,628	145,183	26,702	31,155	23,194	26,317	7,113				43,820
1970	1,421,142	931,119	395,301	39,056	216,518	36,627	39,077	27,054	29,011	7,958				45,930
1971	1,666,124	995,017	631,205	44,513	355,335	77,208	52,602	41,426	49,161	10,960				47,570
1972	1,903,414	1,222,099	715,770	50,763	352,400	140,178	59,718	41,524	43,632	27,555				51,972
1973	1,996,427	1,159,723	710,623	54,484	288,425	163,102	59,585	58,231	50,331	36,465				53,508
1974	1,851,271	1,034,021	863,986	56,402	366,248	167,652	65,463	79,497	74,490	54,234				52,819
1975	2,111,957	1,139,304	884,861	59,063	326,812	194,408	64,687	65,854	83,216	90,821				51,612
1976	2,301,444	1,097,131	1,142,967	70,562	454,790	221,090	80,846	96,670	100,495	121,514				51,454
1977	2,353,729	1,064,504	1,216,986	91,629	528,088	217,816	99,509	73,211	94,365	112,368				52,577
1978	2,374,023	1,192,362	1,218,986	117,923	533,376	204,319	92,659	74,049	98,554	98,106				54,411
1979	2,412,069	1,228,941	1,134,191	72,066	511,814	287,969	49,295	31,293	69,125	112,629				55,747
1980	2,648,674	1,153,294	1,465,827	92,368	652,903	336,975	79,860	48,585	103,325	151,811				56,702
1981	2,575,110	1,161,445	1,436,995	75,064	663,550	302,919	74,053	56,377	157,579	104,273				56,284
1982	2,406,169	1,112,387	1,342,196	74,561	588,772	307,177	53,699	53,139	89,219	172,967				57,800
1983	2,518,491	1,114,928	1,359,724	90,991	621,426	327,111	43,758	40,995	49,935	183,202		44,442		58,962
1984	2,473,191	1,071,645	1,375,075	124,840	668,046	321,030	47,227	47,881	36,899	129,152	325,643	107,210		59,615
1985	2,438,520	1,028,249	1,408,024	75,477	758,998	357,646	54,920	29,095	30,450	101,438	369,032	160,045		58,925
1986	2,275,098	1,006,587	1,293,892	33,378	719,845	419,590	31,856	19,497	28,764	40,962	414,785	191,178	9,534	57,612

Table A6.1 continued

Year	Domestic		Exports								Production			Employees
	Production	Sales	Total	Asia	North America	Europe	South America	Oceania	Africa	Middle East	Overseas	America	England	
1987	2,159,748	1,054,765	1,138,069	46,257	573,495	389,150	24,402	19,303	33,833	51,629	515,375	217,883	36,023	54,573
1988	2,239,280	1,173,736	1,084,746	88,291	460,516	379,140	15,537	36,079	55,328	49,855	569,886	214,678	65,725	51,237
1989	2,371,769	1,385,187	987,614	70,573	404,317	385,290	16,066	41,577	13,080	56,711	645,802	242,926	71,321	52,808
1990	2,379,634	1,378,329	959,120	78,364	380,980	358,186	24,618	32,968	14,214	69,790	683,430	237,279	91,448	55,326
1991	2,323,720	1,318,111	964,139	72,997	357,800	363,256	35,132	24,554	16,585	93,815	761,131	266,492	131,723	56,873
1992	2,036,664	1,179,002	900,463	101,183	313,805	304,696	35,047	30,506	15,744	99,482	926,618	331,749	211,814	55,566
1993	1,749,814	1,067,130	629,990	85,345	260,480	156,590	21,870	35,156	12,313	58,236	993,484	401,576	214,662	53,071
1994	1,589,393	1,080,793	611,215	62,907	314,713	129,949	22,211	32,335	7,910	41,190	1,090,376	452,800	228,205	51,398
1995	1,676,947	1,125,333	593,597	64,077	294,129	146,950	14,462	26,477	8,050	39,452	1,054,114	446,674	209,687	49,177
1996	1,662,776	1,131,331	598,244	72,237	284,253	122,036	16,334	30,417	8,523	64,444	1,079,864	409,958	248,026	44,782
1997	1,671,510	967,169	711,392	82,463	295,023	144,972	29,779	43,889	16,219	99,047	1,083,088	369,887	277,509	41,256
1998	1,528,461	861,411	710,845	39,394	247,053	197,705	28,724	57,406	19,520	121,043	937,402	279,392	275,993	39,969
1999	1,336,918	760,139	611,990	61,874	293,884	117,450	26,924	48,966	7,769	55,123	1,067,732	348,214	286,865	32,707
2000	1,313,527	732,582	604,866	84,345	284,342	86,313	23,441	51,822	7,020	67,583	1,300,421	352,927	332,532	30,747

Note: 'Employees': in Japan.

Source: Nissan Motor Co., Ltd.

Notes

1   All the data derive from Nissan Motor annual reports and company histories.
2   There were other trials, which were soon cancelled. Nissan was asked by Italian Alfa Romeo to help restructure the company in 1979, and signed a joint venture contract the following year, considering it a chance to gain its first production base in Europe as well as to develop technical relations with a European maker. They constructed a new plant and started production in 1983. But the joint venture was cancelled after Fiat took over Alfa Romeo. Nissan entered into an agreement with VW to collaborate in production in 1981. Although the production of VW's Santana started at the Zama plant in 1982, this collaboration was also cancelled.
3   Hybridization pattern analysis is based on field research.

References

Abo, T. (ed.) (1994) *Hybrid Factory: The Japanese Production System in the United States*, Oxford/New York: Oxford University Press.

Boyer, R., Charron, E., Jürgens, U. and Tolliday, S. (eds) (1998) *Between Imitation and Innovation: The Transfer and Hybridization of Productive Models in the International Automobile Industry*, Oxford/New York: Oxford University Press.

Cusumano, M. A. (1985) *The Japanese Automobile Industry: Technology and Management at Nissan and Toyota*, Cambridge, Mass.: Harvard University Press.

EIU (Economic Intelligence Unit) (1998) *The West European Motor Industry Worldwide*, 3rd quarter.

Freyssenet, M. (1998) 'Intersecting Trajectories and Model Changes', in M. Freyssenet, A. Mair, K. Shimizu and G. Volpato (eds) (1998) *One Best Way? Trajectories and Industrial Models of the World's Automobile Producers*, Oxford/New York: Oxford University Press.

Garrahan, P. and Stewart, P. (1992) *The Nissan Enigma: Flexibility at Work in a Local Economy*, London: Mansell.

Ghosn, C. and Nakagawa, H. trs. (2001) *Runesansu: Saisei heno Chosen* (Renaissance: challenge for rebirth), Tokyo: Diamond Sha.

Hanada, M. (1998) 'Nissan: Restructuring to Regain Competitiveness', in M. Freyssenet, A. Mair, K. Shimizu and G. Volpato (eds) (1998) *One Best Way? Trajectories and Industrial Models of the World's Automobile Producers*, Oxford/New York: Oxford University Press.

Harbour Associates (1998) *The Harbour Report 1998*, North America: Harbour Associates Inc.

Itagaki, H. (ed.) (1997) *The Japanese Production System: Hybrid Factories in East Asia*, London: Macmillan.

Kamii, Y. (1994) *Rodo Kumiai no Shokuba Kisei: Nihon Jidosha Sangyo no Jirei Kenkyu* (The activities of the enterprise union on the shopfloor: a case study of the automobile industry in Japan), Tokyo: Daigaku Shuppankai.

Nissan Motor (ed.) (1965) *Nissan Jidosha Sanjyu-nenshi: Showa 8 nen–38 nen* (Nissan Motor's Thirty Years: 1933–1963), Nissan Motor Co. Ltd.

Nissan Motor (ed.) (1975) *Nissan Jidosha-shi: Showa 39 nen–48 nen* (History of Nissan Motor: 1964–1973), Nissan Motor Co. Ltd.

Nissan Motor (ed.) (1983) *21 Seiki heno Michi: Nissan Jidosha 50 nenshi* (Road to the 21st Century: 50 Years of Nissan Motor), Nissan Motor Co. Ltd.

Nissan Motor (ed.) (1985) *Nissan Jidosha-shi: 1974–1983* (History of Nissan Motor: 1974–1983), Nissan Motor Co. Ltd.

Nissan Motor (ed.) (1999) *Fact File: 1999*, Nissan Motor.

Saga, I. and Hanada, M. (1999) 'Nissan: Recent Evolution of Industrial Relations and Work Organization', in J. P. Durand, P. Stewart and J. J. Castillo (eds), *Teamwork in the Automobile Industry: Radical Change or Passing Fashion?*, London: Macmillan.

Shimokawa, K. (1994) *The Japanese Automobile Industry: A Business History*, London: The Athlone Press.

Wickens, P. (1987) *The Road to Nissan: Flexibility, Quality, Teamwork*, London: Macmillan.

7
Honda, an Independent Global Automobile Company, Out of the 'Four Million Units Club'

Koichi Shimokawa

Introduction

The Honda Motor Company Ltd is unique even among Japanese automobile manufacturers. The uniqueness originates mainly in Soichiro Honda, the founder of Honda Motor, who pursued technology ceaselessly and had a fearless entrepreneurial spirit. Thus, in the company, Soichiro's successors inherited his spirit to reject imitation, preconceived ideas, preceding examples and even hierarchical structures.

However, Honda's culture will not, by itself, help to understand why and how Honda succeeded, how its strategic developments changed, and what problems it has. Having become such a world-famous and large corporate, Honda needs to build new strategies to grow to a global enterprise representing Japan in the twenty-first century.

In the twenty-first century, the automobile industry will not be allowed to stand on the ground of the mass production, mass sales, and mass consumption that characterized the twentieth century. We are meeting challenges so significant in the history of civilization, such as environmental problems, in particular, reduction of CO_2 emission on the global level and the end of fossil energy. Furthermore, automobiles are about to be integrated in a transportation system. Honda, with awareness towards such challenges, set out on building strategies that are suitable for the globalization era.

With globalization of economy and because of the structural recession of Japanese economy in the 1990s, the wave of mergers and alliances also swept the Japanese automobile industry. While many Japanese automakers with European and American automakers start capital relationships, Toyota and Honda are the only remaining independent automobile manufacturers. Honda is determined to stay self-reliant and clearly away from global restructuring in the future. However, in order to comprehend under what conditions this will be possible, it is necessary to first understand the historical trajectory of Honda and its strategies. It will be clear what kind of strategic problems Honda carries in the era of global restructuring, by discussing the strategic changes and total quality management (TQM) focused reforms took place in the time of Kawamoto, the president who held a significant meaning in forming Honda's corporate nature and management system into what they are today.

An historical overview of Honda's world-wide business strategies

Looking back on the history of Honda Motor Company Ltd, there were some recognizable moments in its development as a corporation. Some of them were stepping stones for its brilliant growth and others were crises even while it was rapidly developing.

The first remarkable point was its success as a motorcycle manufacturer by developing and selling inexpensive, practical, small size motorcycles rather than those high class vehicles available from Harley-Davidson or BMW. Honda improved their performance step by step while even creating a mass market for them. Honda Motor achieved to establish a world market of small- and medium-sized motorcycles. What symbolized Honda Motor's success and helped quickly spread its name was the 1960 Isle of Man TT races, the internationally renowned motorcycle races on the British island. Honda riders swept the first five places in both in the 125cc and 250cc classes.

While the victories in these races gave the name of Honda Motor world-wide recognition and heightened its corporate image, the company had already become the world's number one of the producers of motor-cycles, leading the pack of four top Japanese manufacturers (including Suzuki, Yamaha, and Kawasaki). Honda Motor's success owed, in the best part of it, to the founder Soichiro Honda thanks to his knowledge of engine technology, and his vitality as an industrialist. He gained them through first starting business as a garage-man and then running and inventing various items for his company which produced piston rings for Toyota Motor Corporation during the Second World War. Soichiro's distinguished ability as an engineer and an industrialist who feared no risk was recognized by and received backing from the Yaesu Branch Manager of Mitsubishi Bank and many other bankers of the time. His rather weak areas of management, namely sales, finance and strategic planning, were strengthened by Takeo Fujisawa, a man of rare talent as a corporate manager.

Ever since Fujisawa joined Honda Motor in 1949, he fully recognized and appreciated Soichiro's expertise as an engineer and an industrialist. So on the one hand he allowed Soichiro to purchase state-of-the-art machinery from West Germany without considering the company's cash flow status and the Japanese Ministry of Trade and Industry's (MITI) allowance of foreign currency spending around 1953, and to produce sports car engines made of aluminum embodying the best of the forefront technology but disregarding the manufacturing cost in the early 1960s. But on the other hand, Fujisawa controlled him from running wild or cleaned up after him whenever he did go wild.

However there were several management crises. One example was the 1953 stock surplus of Super Cubs resulting from the largely increased production of the small sized motorcycles in response to the rapid growth of export to the US market. The lawsuit related to the problem of defective units and the following recall of N360, the successful minicar for Honda when the company went into the automotive industry very late, was another example. An even more peculiar case occurred when, Soichiro, single-mindedly persisted in his idea of air-cooling system for the engines, and young engineers at Honda R&D Co. Ltd insisted on a water-cooling system that would provide less constraining counter-measures against the governmental regulation over exhaust gas emission effected in 1960s. Fujisawa, with his managerial expertise and strategic ability, led the company out of all these critical situations.

However, one-sidedly emphasizing Fujisawa's managerial expertise as above may lead to an underestimate of the founder Soichiro Honda's role. The dynamic and original technology of Honda Motor came from the founder, Soichiro. And it was Fujisawa who fully understood the expertise and energy of Soichiro and tried desperately to let them come out. Fujisawa could do what he did because of Soichiro in the first place and not vice versa. However, it should very well stand true that Honda could not be what it is today without Fujisawa.

After Honda Motor had established a world brand in the field of motorcycle as explained above, Soichiro himself designed a sports car though in those days, sports cars were rare to find. The car was a result of pursuing dreams of an engineer all the way and paying no attention to cost–profit calculations. It never passed the break-even point therefore its product life was short. It was only so good as to demonstrate that Honda was ready to enter the automobile market.

To do that the first strategy for Honda was to launch a minicar, the N360, sold at 300,000 yen or less because of the low tax rate which was a spin-off of the national car project conceived by the government. The national car project promoted by MITI then was such that one model of vehicle would be selected from all models developed by automobile manufacturers in a competition and afterwards the selected model would be produced by all manufacturers. However, this idea was not implemented as exactly planned because of the rejection by the industry for being against the principle of free competition. Immediately after, Japan's MITI drew up a bill to selectively promote specific industries which would have affected the automobile industry by concentrating all manufacturers into three groups. This bill, had it been passed, was about to close out Honda from the automobile industry because of not having any actual business. Faced with the immediately approaching liberalization of capital flows at the time, what this bill aimed at was to avoid foreign capitals, the US Big Three in particular, from taking over Japanese automakers. However, it was not approved by the legislature because of opposition by the industry and Honda was still able to enter the market.

Finally the discussions lead to a special tax privilege for minicars, which became the driving force in expansion of the mass market. Honda increases rapidly sales of its minicar N360. Other players entered the minicar market one after another including: Suzuki out of Hamamatsu, the town where Honda also started, Daihatsu which originally started as a three-wheel vehicle manufacturer, Mazda, Fuji Heavy Industries which was a scooter manufacturer (originally an aircraft manufacturer) before entering the automobile market, and Mitsubishi Motors which turned to automobiles from aircraft manufacturing (at the time called West Japan Heavy Industries Ltd, which was separated from Mitsubishi Heavy Industries Ltd). They shared the groundwork to broaden the mass market for automobiles.

Honda expanded its motorcycle business through exports and knocked down production, and caught the motorization wave of the time in Japan. However, the company experienced an unexpected defeat in so-called 'N360 defective car issue' in 1968. In those days automobile manufacturer's liability was still in a state of unclarity in Japan and this incident occurred right at the time when efforts were made to adopt a recall system like in the USA. The 'N360 defective car issue', which had been started with an accusation by a radical consumer organization, was blown up so big that it needed to be taken into court. Honda could not stop the rapid decline of sales of the N360 and its followers, the Honda Life and the Honda Z. This happened in the middle of a big boom in the automobile market and people's focus was quickly shifting from minicars to standard-sized cars with engine displacement of over 1000 cc. It was an urgent and significant problem for Honda to launch a standard-sized car on to the market. The answer to the problem was the Civic, a product of the company's original 'basic car' concept. It was a car for the masses with a simple but unique design featuring front-wheel drive and a monocoque body. The Civic basic car achieved a certain level of success in the 1000 cc class popular car market, where the Nissan Sunny and Toyota Corolla were the mainstream. It provided a beginning to solidify Honda's firm position as an automobile manufacturer.

What is most notable is that the Civic led Honda to full-scale exports to the USA, the world's largest automobile market, because consumer taste was shifting rapidly to small-sized cars after the first oil shock in 1973, and the quality levels of the automobiles produced by the US Big Three were declining. The CVCC engine developed by Honda engineers was to remove the blot of the 'N360 defective car issue' from its name and, with the company's destiny at stake, it passed the exhaust gas emission standard of Japan and contributed to regaining its good corporate image. When the Accord, a 1300 cc fully-fledged passenger car, entered the market trailing the success of the Civic by three years, Honda's two pillars of basic models in the automobile business were complete and it went on to succeed, rapidly increasing sales in the domestic market, and in particular, exports to the North American market.

Characteristics of Honda's business strategies and the evolution of its organization

After overcoming the crisis of the N360 defective car issue, Honda gradually withdrew from the minicar market and shifted operating resources to adding higher class models one by one that were based on the Civic and the Accord. It aimed for higher-class cars even though it still centred on small-sized cars. Of course, Honda kept the face of the world's number one motorcycle manufacturer, and furthermore it succeeded the multi-purpose engine business toward developing countries. The automobile business had become the main of these three business areas.

However, it is not to be forgotten that automobile-making by Honda, especially an engine technology, production engineering and overseas business development, reflected strongly the experiences in the motorcycle business. It is typically evident, in particular, in the design engineering of small-sized engines for cars, the production engineering that allows a quick change-over of models in large-variety, medium-volume productions, and the free flow line that allows adjustment of speeds and intervals between models of vehicles produced on the line. In overseas, Honda first exercised the principle, 'Produce where there is market demand', with the motorcycles and took the same path for the automobiles. The experiences in contacting local suppliers and raising them in localization of motorcycle production in developing countries was fully taken advantage of in the automobile business.

The simple and straightforward design of Honda's cars ever since the Civic first generation and the marketing orientation towards rather younger generations, result in the sporty feeling and mechanical designs that truly reflect the company. For example, Honda has been pursuing characteristics in the mechanical structure with its engines that rotate in the opposite direction to the other manufacturers engines and completely in-house made drive systems that go with the engines. So, it has been winning customers' hearts with the unique mechanisms and turning them into fans. Regarding Honda's strategy in production engineering, not only is it unique to be influenced by the motorcycle production system as already mentioned above, but also characterized by the ways to achieve flexibility in production, to implement concurrent productions, to organize productions according to the order of received orders, and to design production facilities.

Flexibility in production is characterized by a method to switch over models and versions on production lines and to set up production for a new model. For example, in the Sayama Factory, concurrent production of the main model Accord and other passenger cars in the same class was later joined by the crossover minivan Odyssey. In the Suzuka factory, the method adopted allows to counter-react to fluctuations between models. In the Takanezawa factory we produced by the completely craftsman type process for the luxury sports car NSX, whereas the medium volume of inexpensive sports cars and the limited volume of hybrid cars are produced on the same assembly line running with a relatively long 'tact time'. Honda's overseas factories are equipped with the production systems transferred from the corresponding mother factory or mother line in Japan. The factory in the UK, for example, runs mixed productions of the Civic and the Accord on the one production line. However, the multi-skill levels of the local workers and the conditions of parts procurement logistics are taken into consideration so that an adjustment of the production system to the local reality has been made. As for productions according to the order of received orders, Honda does not practise the kind of just-in-time production for each unit as used by Toyota, but rather runs on a method where productions are executed for expected medium volumes scheduled for each week which can be rearranged at any time as necessary. This approach can be considered unique to Honda.

Concerning production facility engineering, Honda has a 100% owned subsidiary, Honda Engineering. This subsidiary designs and produces specialized painting robots, welding robots, welding jig system, transfer presses and so on to the factories. Honda Engineering can be considered a unique organization by itself because not only does it develop and supply hardware of production facilities but also develop software of production engineering in unison with the factories, accumulate it, and use it in supporting production systems of all the Honda factories in the world.

The method of product development of Honda can also be considered unique. Honda's product developments are carried out by a separate organization called Honda R&D Co. Ltd, and Honda Motor pays 5% of its revenue to the R&D company. This arrangement allows the R&D company to perform research and development in a free atmosphere. Even though as an organization it is completely separated, there are frequent exchanges of personnel and many of the past presidents of Honda Motor were from the R&D company. In product planning, ideas are exchanged between the parent company and the R&D company at the basic concept stage, however, during design and development the daughter company takes the initiative. A chief engineer of development holds a full and enormous authority to manage a cross functional team of engineers. At Honda, persons who can demonstrate unique creativity are often given the opportunity to be such leaders without regard to hierarchical level or age. There is no fixed pattern to organize such a cross functional team of engineers, but rather a team is formed dynamically. This gives the team very high creativity and helps balance creativity and efficiency of development.

The sales and marketing strategy was mainly oriented to the North American market. This strategy took a firm shape during the time Fujisawa was the vice-president because, first and foremost, it was possible to quickly establish a dealer network in the US market, where demand for small vehicles was skyrocketing. There was also a very good reputation on Japanese cars; and multiple brands of cars could be sold in parallel by the same dealer. The strategy worked out so beautifully for Honda that, even at the time of writing, it receives two-thirds of its consolidated profit from the North American market.

In the domestic market, Honda could not escape the fact that it was very late and a newcomer and there was a considerable delay in setting up a dealer network. Initially, Honda cars were sold through small motor outlets in towns, which were selling motorcycles, and service work was provided by an organization called Honda SF founded in each prefecture by Honda's own investment. Honda did not have a single fully-fledged dealer that had its own service shop. In Japan there was a particularly strong tendency towards territory-based sales and manufacturer-affiliated sales channels. Large-scale dealer networks were completely seized by Toyota and Nissan who had taken early measures in this area. Therefore, in the 1980s, Honda established networks among directly owned dealers with service shops through its own investment to set up its own multiple sales channels under the names of Honda shops and Verno shops. Later the channels were joined by Creo shops of a small-scale dealer, which started from a motor shop.

Strategic transition and reform in the 1990s

Under the strategies as explained above, Honda made remarkable progress as literally a global corporation in the 1980s. When all other Japanese automakers were hesitating to take the big step because of the considerable risk, Honda decided to build a local factory in Ohio, USA, in 1978 to manufacture, at first, its luxury motorcycle. It was followed by the construction of the second production line in the factory to produce the Accord in 1981, which provided a significant opportunity to Honda to improve its brand image and to gain a firm foothold in North America. Since then and until the time of writing, it can be said that Honda has been earning most of its consolidated profit from North America. In the Japanese market, except the time when luxury models sold well because of the bubble economy, Honda was not able to gain large profit. First it is due to the excessive competition against the rival manufacturers like Toyota, Nissan, Mitsubishi and Mazda. Secondly, Honda, capturing young people and customers who like modern and sporty vehicles, has been a niche manufacturer in essence. What seems closely related to this is that Honda is the most enthusiastic about motor racing among auto-manufacturers. It is well known that, ever since Honda won the motorcycle race on the Isle of Man, it has been very enthusiastic about motor sports such as F1 races, and even owns a racetrack.

However, in the 1990s, competitions among automobile manufacturers in the world became global. While the European and American automakers took their steps towards restructuring themselves only to further intensify the competition, Honda also needed to change for the new era.

In 1985, the company's consolidated profit reached close to 150 billion yen. However, high yen exchange rate after the G-5 meeting caused the profit to lessen. While the consolidated revenue climbed from 3 trillion yen to 4.3 trillion, the consolidated profit dropped year after year. In 1993, even the consolidated revenue went down below 4 trillion yen and the consolidated profit slumped at 30 billion yen level, which was only a fifth of the peak time value (see Figure 7.1).

The man who took over the company's presidency in 1990 when the stagnant revenue growth and the declining pattern of profit became genuine was Nobuhiko Kawamoto, a former R&D engineer. He recognized that it was good for Honda to have been a niche manufacturer and to have been proud of its free company spirit. However, on the other hand, he deeply worried about Honda's company organization. Its unity was very much confused and its parts had become irrelevant with each other, individuals working in whatever ways they preferred. Having become a sanctuary-like existence, Honda R&D's tendency became noticeable that it went about developments of products or technology without paying attention to the costs. Other

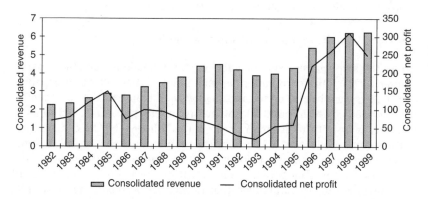

Figure 7.1   Transition in consolidated revenue and consolidated net profit and events for Honda, 1982–99

Note: For the years 1987 and before, the values were recalculated on a fiscal year basis because there was a change in the fiscal year period. Consolidated revenue: trillion yen; consolidated net profit: billion yen. 1999: forecast.

1982   Mass production of automobiles began in HAM in USA.
1983   Tadashi Kume became president.
1984   UK factory established.
1988   Takeo Fujisawa died.
1989   The third production line in Suzuka and the second factory of HAM started operations.
1990   Nobuhiko Kawamoto became president.
1991   Soichiro Honda died.
1992   Leave from F1 announced.
1994   RV Odyssey launched.
1997   Sales units of cars exceeded 800,000 in Japan in calendar year 1997.
1998   Hiroyuki Yoshino became president.
1999   Construction of the third factory in North America and Closure of Suzuka's first line announced.

Source: Nikkei Financial Data, Nikkei Business, 23 August 1999, p. 24.

noticeable problems included: development of products or technology intended to make a display of eccentricity as a result of over pursuit on niches, car race participation that fell into a rut, and situation where many people including directors spoke their minds in the '*wai gaya*' (whoever says whatever) management method but no one took responsibility for what was said and decided. Therefore, Kawamoto drastically proceeded to clarify the responsibility and the authority in the organization, to establish the process of decision making, and to reform the personnel management system. 'Forget the way you have been working' and 'Honda needs to be an ordinary automobile manufacturer' are the words Kawamoto spoke. He also said, 'We will keep what's good to keep but our attitude needs change or we won't survive. Now is the time we solidify the proof of reality as the foundation for dreams. But we will keep the youthfulness in our spirit as our heritage.'

Under the Kawamoto system, the management reform was carried out with the TQM reform at its core. The promptly developed products were based on market needs and the company's mission statement was reviewed in order to carry out this reform. The mission statement read, 'Provide moderately priced products with superior performance based on a global viewpoint', which was reviewed and revised to 'Provide high quality products at an appropriate price for the satisfaction of customers in the world'. This new value was established within the company as a Honda philosophy. This Honda's TQM went through four phases starting at the introduction phase, moving to the promotion phase in which they tried to establish the new philosophy, then moving into the development phase during which the total management system was established by acting on the new philosophy and finally the establishment phase in which the company system was shifted by establishing new methods as a Renaissance of car production. Through the process of TQM activities, Honda was able to implement the values that reflected the customers needs throughout the organization.

With the TQM promotion, they surveyed the true market needs and based on these findings, pursued various methods such as solving all issues in advance to avoid any adjustments, shorten the lead time on delivery for sales and execute simultaneous model changes for world production and development. The most emphasized point was the integration of development and production principles. A cross-functional CS (customer satisfaction) team was formed with personnel from each department including sales, production, development, and quality management and purchasing. They also tried to establish and propose product concepts in addition to pursuing the shorter lead-time as individual objectives for development. Due to this attempt, it has been said that Honda's shorter production preparation lead-time was emphasized.

The TQM activities changed Honda's conventional production of niche products drastically and pursued reforms step by step including the areas of reducing the gap of automobile performance and feeling, reducing design modifications, starting initial set-up at early stages, reducing rough evaluation procedures and simplifying the evaluation events and reducing the number of trials for moulds and equipment.

The reform carried forward under Kawamoto's leadership led Honda's business results to rapidly turn around to rise again since 1994 (see Figure 7.1).

Challenges for Honda in the global reorganization of the automotive industry

Reform under Kawamoto's leadership brought some good results in business growth in the forms such as: the big sales success of the RV Odyssey, the big sales success of the passenger car Accord locally developed by Honda R&D Americas, the success of the New Civic in 1998, and the product expansion in the North American luxury automobile sales channel. In 1997 the yearly unit sales exceeded 800,000 in the domestic sales in Japan, which were considered weak for Honda. Today, Honda is embarking on the construction of its third factory in North America in Alabama following the two older ones in Ohio and Canada. (See Figure 7.1 for Honda's transition in revenue and profit.)

In fiscal year 1999 Honda had 51.7 billion dollars of consolidated revenue and sales units of 2,270,000 world-wide. These figures in their apparent values are inferior to the world's Big Six automobile manufacturers after the global restructuring is completed (see Table 7.1). None the less, Honda is determined to stay independent ignoring such global restructuring. The main reason for this is that, backed by its original corporate culture, Honda has been practising unique product development system and methods of making unique and flexible production system and factory and thinks there is no merit in a merger with another auto-maker with totally different corporate culture. In particular, by taking advantage of the experiences gained by setting up factories for motorcycles, Honda aims to build factories that can earn profit even though they may be small in scale. For example, it is normally considered in the USA that an assembly factory, including those affiliated with Japanese companies, needs to produce 240,000 units a year to be profitable. However, Honda's break-even point is 120,000 units. It is said that the new Alabama factory will also be built on this concept. The factory set up in Turkey aimed to start up with 10,000 units per year and still break even. Simple economy of scale is not what they aim for but rather a production system that can break even with a limited volume production and allows variable variety, variable volume production to cope with switching over of models and changes, to some extent, of variations within a model. What is contributing to this are: Honda Engineering's development of jigs and tools that allow for variation, variable volume mass production while practising push style, make-to-stock production for medium-sized lots, and the skill level of the factory personnel to freely handle the jigs and the tools. However, it should not be forgotten that Honda takes a platform strategy where mass production effect per platform can be achieved by operating on global platforms. It produces between 600,000 and

Table 7.1 Honda compared with Big Six automobile manufacturers in the world

	General Motors (USA)	Ford Motor Co. (USA)	DaimlerChrysler (Germany)	Toyota Motor	Nissan Motor + Renault (France)	Volkswagen (Germany)	Honda Motor
Consolidated revenue	$173.3 billion	$174 billion	$154.6 billion	$110.8 billion	$97.1 billion	$74.9 billion	$51.7 billion
World-wide unit sales	9,800 thousand vehicles	8,220 thousand vehicles	4,500 thousand vehicles	5,170 thousand vehicles	4,750 thousand vehicles	4,740 thousand vehicles	2,270 thousand vehicles
Main companies in Group	Isuzu Automobile, Opel (Germany), Suzuki	Mazda, Volvo (Sweden)		Daihatsu Industries, Hino Automobile Industries		Audi (Germany), Rolls-Royce (UK)	
Funds at hand	$10.9 billion	$4.8 billion	$7.4 billion	$16.7 billion	$8.5 billion	$14.9 billion	$3.1 billion

Note: Figures for Japanese companies are based on the financial year ending March 1999, and for others December 1998. For Nissan and Renault, individual figures are simply added. Conversion made at 1 US$ = 115yen.

Source: Nikkei Business (see Figure 7.1 for details).

800,000 (sometimes more) units of the company's main model on the same platform at its sites in the world. By taking a strategy to maintain mass production effect and cost competitiveness per basic model on the whole but to mix limited volume productions and variable variety, variable volume productions at each production base, Honda thinks it can stay fully competitive on the global level and meet the challenges of the global competitions without joining the so-called 'four million units club'.

While Honda maintains its original and individual course even in the age of global restructuring, the company still has many problems that need to be solved. The first problem is how the company will survive as a global enterprise while adjusting its product strategy and brand strategy that it has taken. After declaring that it would be an ordinary automobile manufacturer under the lead of Kawamoto, the company has already been making course corrections in this regard. A product strategy is already under way based on segmentation and differentiation between mass-production models and derivative models centring on platforms of a basic mass-production models. It does not necessarily mean that Honda is completely throwing away its niche approach but rather the niche markets will be mainly addressed with derivative models. More than twenty new models of cars or full model changes have been planned between 2000 and 2003. More than two-thirds will be SUV. While these steps were taken to break away from being a niche manufacturer, a brand promotion office was installed to work towards reinforcement of Honda's world brand and to fix the common and global grand slogan 'The Power of Dreams'. Regarding brand image, compared to what it is in the USA, Honda's brand power in Japan or other countries is not so strong. Overcoming this problem has been a big challenge.

Honda aims to achieve a consolidated revenue of 7 trillion and unit production of 3 million in 2003, which seems to be well within range. However, the world-wide profit structure is unbalanced between North America, which is currently where profit is largely concentrated, and the rest of the world (see Table 7.2). Two-thirds of Honda's current consolidated net profit relies on North America and the risk of being affected by its economic fluctuations is extremely high. As efforts were put into domestic sales in Japan, the annual unit sales goal of 800,000 was somehow reached. However the large costs incurred on sales promotions are not to be considered satisfactory. So it is necessary to turn the losing European business to the black and to establish corporate nature able to withstand the fluctuating currency exchange rates. Furthermore, it is necessary to gain more profit from the Asian business in the middle to long term. Even though prior investments have already been made in India and China, the two promising markets of the twenty-first century, and automobile business in ASEAN, being stimulated by the successful motorcycle business, it is a challenge to achieve results in the Asian business. Additionally, Central and South American business is worth attention for the profit even though still small scale.

Table 7.2 Comparison between Honda's domestic and US business (in millions of yen)

	Japanese market	US (North American) market
Revenue	3,450,969	3,398,867
Sales to outside customers after subtracting inter-regional sales	1,755,958	3,227,025
Operating profit	206,252	286,950
Assets	1,863,756	2,217,777

Note: Data relate to the financial year ending March 1999.

Source: Nikkei Business (see Figure 7.1).

Honda's ultimate global strategy is for each of the five division headquarters of the five regions worldwide to be independent in terms of profit and to implement and raise the level of mutual complement. Along this direction, procurement of parts begin to move to centralized sourcing of commonly sharable parts. While independence of the five divisions is the challenge that Honda is faced with, North American business must further increase its competitiveness and brand power and support the other four regions in their development. There exists an ironic situation that North America must first be reinforced in order to eliminate the unbalanced reliance on it.

It remains to be seen whether Honda's North American business, which has established a winning brand, and the Japanese headquarters, which need to maintain the tie among the five regional divisions, can build a co-operative structure in the development of global strategy. What needs to be done, in particular, includes: independence of each division in the five-region scheme and mutual complement in doing business, product development and operations based on global platforms, linking between global sourcing and local parts procurement harmonizing mutual complement of factory production systems and localization of Honda production system (into newly entered area), and mutual raising of levels of world brand and local brand. Honda's leap and challenge towards a global company requires support by a new personnel strategy. As a result of restructuring under Kawamoto's leadership, the average age of personnel in Honda's Japanese corporate bodies rose from 35.3 in March 1992 to 41.8 in 1999. Such trend of ageing in the corporate is unavoidable and will be so in the future. However, it must be noted that drastic move of young personnel into engineering staff and employment and training of human resource on a global level are the decisive key factors for Honda to leap forward as a global company while keeping the great inheritance from its founder: youthfulness, challenging spirit, and innovativeness that is free from preconceived ideas.

Conclusion

We saw the developmental stages of a small motorcycle manufacturer to a global automobile manufacturer. Honda's founder, Soichiro Honda, was a very exceptional technician with an entrepreneurial spirit. Soichiro Honda's youth and adventurous spirit to challenges without the fear of failure or preconceived conceptions reflect Honda's dynamic history of fifty-three years. However, he also experienced crisis and failures, which he managed to overcome and learned from these trials and tribulations. The team of Soichiro and Fujisawa established a global motorcycle manufacturer and this momentum encouraged the success of the automotive business. The guidance of president, Kawashima and his successor as president, Kume, were the first breakthrough phases as an international company with a main production facility in North America. During the 1980s the Japanese automotive industry was garnering international attention for its lean production method. The president, Kawamoto, took over this first breakthrough phase. He had to face the actual decline in business performance due to the collapse of the bubble economy and secondary increased value of the yen. Honda started management reform with TQM under the Kawamoto system. The management dedicates itself to customer satisfaction, and to disseminate the new values throughout the entire organization. They successfully made the shift to strategies as a global company that handles global products as well as niche products based on a global platform. They further improved the product planning ability by linking the development, purchasing and production departments as well as the sales and marketing department, and also improved the brand value. After this reform, Honda was able to launch new popular models that meet the market needs, and to develop a unique production system that allows them to change rapidly models and versions on the line. They are making progress for the world simultaneous model change between the five-regions, at least between Japan and America, for example, the simultaneous model changes for Accord and Civic.

The future of Honda is dependent on the restructuring of the European business, which is accumulating deficit and on the full development and independence of business in Asia including India and China in spite of the significant risk factors. In Asia, Honda had the advantage in the motorcycle business but competition emerged from China. It is essential to implement the global human resource strategy in order to challenge such issues. Furthermore, there is an issue of environment, especially the reduction of CO_2 emissions, which is not only for Honda but also for automotive manufacturers all over the world. For the time being they will try to get by with engines with good fuel efficiency. However, Honda needs to pursue Honda's uniqueness in fuel batteries and other environmental strategies in the future.

Statistical appendix, Honda

Table A7.1 Historical trend of Honda business, 1967–2000

Year	World-wide vehicle sales	Production in Japan	Exports from Japan	Production North America/ Europe	Net sales plus operating revenue	Proportion of turnover abroad	Profits	Profits/ turnover	Employees Japan	Employees world-wide
1967	–	150	–	0	–	–	–	–	–	–
1968	–	319	–	0	–	–	–	–	–	–
1969	–	365	–	0	–	–	–	–	–	–
1970	–	393	23	0	–	–	–	–	17,500	–
1971	–	309	34	0	–	–	–	–	18,100	–
1972	–	331	38	0	–	–	–	–	18,300	–
1973	–	355	74	0	–	–	–	–	18,300	–
1974	–	429	120	0	–	–	–	–	18,500	–
1975	–	414	201	0	–	–	–	–	18,500	–
1976	–	560	307	0	–	–	–	–	19,100	–
1977	–	665	445	0	–	–	–	–	20,000	–
1978	–	743	496	0	–	–	–	–	21,000	–
1979	–	802	547	0	–	–	–	–	20,800	–
1980	–	957	659	0	–	–	–	–	22,900	–
1981	–	1,009	668	0	–	–	–	–	25,000	–
1982	–	1,015	613	–	–	–	–	–	26,900	–
1983	–	1,031	613	–	–	–	–	–	28,000	–
1984	–	989	633	–	–	–	–	–	26,900	–
1985	1,283	1,120	668	145	2,740	73	129	4.7	28,100	55,700
1986	1,365	1,236	708	238	3,009	70	146	4.9	30,700	59,000

Table A7.1 continued

Year	World-wide vehicle sales	Production in Japan	Exports from Japan	Production North America/ Europe	Net sales plus operating revenue	Proportion of turnover abroad	Profits	Profits/ turnover	Employees Japan	Employees world-wide
1987	1,585	1,241	695	341	2,961	68	84	2.8	29,700	63,000
1988	1,727	1,293	681	416	3,229	64	99	3.1	30,000	65,500
1989	1,903	1,363	685	446	3,489	63	97	2.8	31,200	71,200
1990	1,936	1,384	715	540	3,853	66	82	2.1	31,600	79,200
1991	1,915	1,358	662	550	4,302	68	76	1.8	31,500	85,500
1992	1,961	1,200	589	563	4,392	67	60	1.4	31,100	90,500
1993	1,793	1,151	571	537	4,132	67	37	0.9	31,000	90,900
1994	1,753	993	510	645	3,863	67	24	0.6	30,600	91,300
1995	1,794	967	434	765	3,996	67	62	1.6	–	92,800
1996	1,887	1,092	371	884	4,252	64	70	1.7	–	96,800
1997	2,184	1,307	544	921	5,293	65	221	4.2	n.a.	101,100
1998	2,343	1,243	531	993	6,000	71	260	4.3	n.a.	109,400
1999	2,333	1,220	532	1,086	6,231	75	305	4.9	n.a.	112,200
2000	2,473	1,223	477	1,097	6,099	74	262	4.3	n.a.	112,400

Notes: Vehicle refers to all passenger cars and commercial vehicles production, sales and exports are 1,000 units. Production abroad excludes production for Honda by Rover. Net sales, operating revenue and profits are in billion yen. They refer to Honda as a whole (including motorcycles and power products). Figures for employment refer to Honda as whole.

Sources: 1967–97: Andrew Mair, 'The Globalization of Honda's Product-led Flexible Mass Production System', in M. Freyssenet *et al.*, *One Best Way?*, Oxford University Press, 1998; 1998–2000: *Honda Fact Book*.

Table A7.2 Transitional financial summary of Honda Motor Company Ltd, 1976–2000

Fiscal year ended	Production (units)		Export (units, sets)		Net sales (millions of yen)	Net income (millions of yen)	Employees
	Total	Passenger cars	Finished cars	KD sets			
1976.2	430,260	351,289	214,582	–	563,805	11,954	185
1981.2	977,995	859,237	690,176	7,400	1,344,892	30,137	229
1986.2	1,160,821	986,708	677,195	241,980	2,245,743	45,232	281
1995.3	982,124	820,852	493,951	758,250	2,469,150	21,616	306
1998.3	1,324,661	1,212,826	557,649	1,026,840	3,077,427	127,988	281
1999.3	1,218,535	1,135,787	536,047	1,051,920	2,962,170	135,944	287
2000.3	1,214,645	1,140,451	502,776	1,126,040	2,919,840	135,322	288

Note: Figures for production and finished car export for the year 1976 and earlier include KD sets. Production and export include automobiles only.

Source: Nikkan Jidosha Shinbun, *Jidoshasangyo Handbook 2001* (Handbook of the Automobile Industry).

Table A7.3 Honda 2000 Forecast and 2001 Plan for domestic and overseas production and sales

		1998	% change	1999	% change	2000 forecast	% change	2001 plan	% change
World-wide	Production	2,351,468	2.8	2,423,000	3.0	2,494,000	2.9	2,650,000	6.3
	Sales	2,273,814	2.0	2,393,317	5.3	2,540,000	6.1	2,690,000	5.9
Japan	Production	1,243,468	4.8	1,220,955	1.8	1,225,000	0.3	1,250,000	2.0
	Sales	691,225	14.6	705,843	2.1	760,000	7.7	810,000	6.6
	Exports	530,717	2.5	531,866	0.2	475,000	10.7	440,000	7.4
	(Export/ production)	42.7%	+1.0 points	43.6%	+0.9 points	38.8%	−4.8 points	35.2%	−3.6 points
Overseas	Production	1,108,000	0.4	1,202,045	8.5	1,286,000	7.0	1,430,000	11.2
	(Share of world-wide)	47.1%	+1.1 points	49.6%	+2.5 points	51.6%	+2.0 points	54.0%	+2.4 points
	Sales	1,582,589	4.8	1,687,474	6.6	1,780,000	5.5	1,880,000	5.6
	(Share of world-wide)	69.6%	+4.5 points	70.5%	+0.9 points	70.1%	−0.4 points	69.9%	−0.2 points

Note: Data is for calendar years; in units and percentages.

Source: Public relations material by Honda Motor Company Ltd; FOURIN's Monthly Report on the Domestic Automotive Industry, no. 22, January 2001.

Table A7.4 Honda actual and planned figures for geographical production and sales (units)

		1996	1997	1998	1999	2000 forecast	2001 plan	2003 goal*
Japan	Total	761,784	809,283	691,225	705,843	760,000	810,000	900,000
	Cars	597,269	593,050	469,338	416,436	460,000	510,000	570,000
	Mini-vehicles	164,515	216,233	221,887	289,407	300,000	300,000	320,000
Americas	Total	928,536	1,071,198	1,173,068	1,258,226	1,392,700	1,455,000	1,535,000
	North America	919,643	1,053,444	1,140,261	1,227,487	1,323,000	1,374,000	1,450,000
	USA	843,928	940,386	1,009,600	1,076,893	1,160,000	1,200,000	–
	South America**	8,893	17,754	32,807	30,739	69,700	81,000	85,000
Europe		233,629	274,074	294,338	279,763	204,000	210,000	350,000
Asia–Oceania		185,990	170,118	132,040	149,485	183,300	215,000	215,000
World-wide total		2,109,939	2,324,673	2,290,671	2,393,317	2,540,000	2,690,000	3,000,000

Notes: * Figures based on fiscal year 2003. Years until 2001 are calendar years; ** South America figures are Americas minus North America. 300,000 units are the goal for the fiscal year 2003 for South America and Asia–Oceania combined. Domestic sales includes Jeep sales (2 units in 1999, the highest was 11,098 units in 1995).

Source: Public relations material from Honda Motor Company Ltd; FOURIN's Monthly Report on the Domestic Automotive Industry, no. 22, January 2001.

Table A7.5 Honda management strategy

Planned figures as goals for the Medium Term Plan

Result	Fiscal Year 2000 Forecast Consolidated Net Sales: 6.2 Trillion yen
	Fiscal Year 2003 Consolidated Net Sales: Exceed 7 Trillion yen
	Net Income: 220 Billion yen, Exceed the best income on record
	(Fiscal Year 1998 Net Income: 305 billion yen)
Unit sales	Fiscal Year 1999: 2,473,000; FY 2000: 2,600,000; FY 2003: 3 Million.
Motorcycle sales	FY 1999: 4,436,000; FY 2000: 4,830,000; FY 2003: 7 Million

Main policies

Unconsolidated volume increase: challenges will be faced in Japan and Europe

Japan	• Increase product strength
	Launch new models of cars: plan to introduce more than 20 new models or full model changes in financial years 2000–3. Two-thirds of them to be RVs
	Seven models in 2001 (new models of Integra, Stepwagon, and CR-V; new small car; Civic Felio HEV)
	Strengthen brand equity: use the global brand slogan, 'The Power of Dream', world-wide starting from 2001
	• Increase sales efficiency and ability
	Reinforcement of sales staff at the sales subsidiaries, deployment of mobile terminals, reinforcement of used car business (sales and trade-ins), increase in available cars for online sales quote and so on
Overseas	• In North America, enhance local production capacity (up to 1.16 million units in second half of 2001); expand and substantiate small truck products
	• Sales promotion of new small cars in Europe, Asia and South America. Establish South American headquarters April 2000
	• Aim to increase share in ASEAN to 10% in 2003 (70 K units in 2000 → 146 K units). In some nations, integrate facilities to streamline the system from production to sales
	• In Europe, minimizing influences of exchange rates is the biggest challenge. Concurrently prepare a sales system to achieve 350 K unit goal
	• Accomplish world-wide deployment of the new model of the Civic as early as possible. Start sales in Japan in September, 2000, extend to Europe and Thailand in October

All-out effort to pursue low-cost operation

Production	Mid-term goal is doubling the resource efficiency for areas of in-house manufacturing within the Honda Group; horizontal and vertical expansion of general purpose line and synchronized production method.
	→ A trial calculation indicates a cost reduction of 100 billion yen in 2003 compared to 1999 (approx. 20% reduction in production-related costs: 70 billion yen in body area, 30 billion yen in powertrain area)
	Actions are completed for Suzuka Line No. 1. More action taken for Suzuka Line No. 3, Sayama Works, East Liberty factory in North America, Canada factory, and UK factory by end of 2000

Table A7.5 continued

Procurement	Currently optimized procurement within each region of the world-wide five-region scheme → Move to centralized sourcing for common parts; convergence of sources according to parts
Pursuit of technological advantage	
Mid-term Plan	• First step: achieve higher efficiency with gasoline engines. • Second step: hybrid system – a Civic-based hybrid model in to be released for sale in 2001 • Third step: fuel-cell car – plan is to launch a fuel-cell car on to market by 2003. The third-generation fuel-cell car was announced in September 2000
Joint efforts	Co-operation with GM in the fields of environment and car-mounted communications (start one by one from 2001) Joint research with NTT through subsidiaries towards sophisticated car-mounted information system will start. Demo system targeted for construction in 2001 (November 2000)

Table A7.6   Co-operation with GM in environment and communications fields

Field	Time frame	Overview
Low emission engine	Agreement reached in December 1999. Contract signed in July 2000 for supply in the USA	• American Honda→GM: V6 gasoline engine (complies with ULEV) and AT • Five years starting autumn 2003. 90,000 pieces per year, for high-class GM cars. • Isuzu→Honda: diesel engine (Isuzu Poland→Honda UK) • November 2000, Mr Munekuni, Chairman, announced Honda is seriously considering sourcing diesel engines from Isuzu (in Poland). Planned to start in 2001
Car-mounted communication service	Agreement reached in May 2000. To start in 2001	• Acura RL which will be launched in 2001 in the USA is planned to be the first to adopt the OnStar car-mounted communications service from GM. Agreement also reached to co-operate with OnStar and XM Satellite Radio towards the development of future car-mounted communications service, technology and applications.

Source: FOURIN's Monthly Report on the Domestic Automotive Industry, no. 22, January 2001.

References

Fujisawa, T. (1974) *Taimatsu wa jibunnotede* (Light our way with a pine-torch by ourselves), Tokyo: Sangyonoritsu-tandai Shuppanbu.

Ginsburg, D. H. and Abernathy, W. J. (eds) (1979) *Government, Techonology, and the Future of the Automobile*, McGraw-Hill.

Honda, S. (1962) *Watashi no Rirekisho* (My life and career), Tokyo.

Honda Motors (1974, 1984) *Honda no Ayumi* (A brief history of Honda), Tokyo.

Honda Motors *Kataritsugitaikoto – Challenge no 50 nen* (What we want to succeed for our next generation – our 50-year challenge) 50 year' Honda History.

Ide, K. (1999) *Honda Den* (The bibliography of Honda), Tokyo: Wac Shuppan.

Mair, A. (1994a) *Honda's Global Local Corporation*, London: Macmillan.

Mair, A. (1994b) 'Honda's Global Flexifactory Network', *International Journal of Operations and Production Management*, vol. 14, no. 3.

Mair, A. (1996) 'Honda Motors: A Paradoxical Approach to Growth', in C. Baden-Fuller and M. Pitt (eds), *Strategic Innovation: An International Casebook*, London.

Mair, A. (1997) 'Strategic Localization: The Myth of the Post-National Enterprise', in K. R. Cox (ed.), *Putting Space in its Place: Globalization and its Politics*, New York.

Mair, A. (1998) *The Honda Production System*, manuscript.

Mair, A. Florida, R. and Kenney, M. (1988) 'The New Geography of Automobile Production: Japanese Automobile Transplants in North America', *Economic Geography*, vol. 64.

Mito, S. (1990) *The Honda Book of Management*, London: Athlone Press.

Nonaka, I. (1991) 'The Knowledge-Creating Company', *Harvard Business Review*, November–December.

Pascale, R. T. (1984) 'Perspectives on Strategy: The Real Story behind Honda's Success', *California Management Review*, vol. 26, no. 3.

Pascale, R. T. (1990) *Managing on the Edge*, Harmondsworth: Penguin.

Sakiya, T. (1987) *Honda Motor: The Men, the Management, the Machines*, Tokyo: Kodansha International.

Shimokawa, K. (1980) 'Honda Soichiro', *Nihon no Kigyoka* (Japanese Entrepreneur), vol. 4. Yuhikaku.

Shook, R. L. (1988) *Honda: An American Success Story*, New York: Prentice-Hall.

Yamamoto, O. (1978) 'Hondano genten' (The origin of Honda), *Jidosha Journal*, Tokyo.

Nikkei Business (Nikkei Business Journal) Nikkei Publisher, 1999 Aug. 2.

Jidoshakogyo Handbook 2001 (Handbook of the automobile industry), Nikkan jidosya Shinbun.

8
The Chance for a Peripheral Market Player: The Internationalization Strategies of the Korean Automobile Industry

Myeong-Kee Chung

Introduction

The pattern of globalization followed by the major automakers can so far be split into three stages. The first stage is exporting. At this stage the goal is to create a car that fits into a world-wide automobile category. The second stage of globalization comes after the expansion of exporting. This is the setting up of transplants in major market regions. The final stage of globalization is the complete localization of transplants on the one hand and the establishment of a global business network on the other.

This chapter first investigates the historical and ongoing development of internationalization in the Korean automobile industry. Then it explores the transition of the globalization strategy from exporting in the core market to the setting up of KD production sites in peripheral regions between 1985 and 1998. There was a clear change in the Korean automakers' globalization strategy at the end of the 1990s that was primarily built up by market leaders' strategies in the peripheral markets. The concluding reflections deal with the multi-regional strategy of Korean automakers. Finally, based on this observation, we briefly analyse the new trend of individual firms' multinational activities in the financial turmoil since late 1997.

Strategies for export: the alliances of the Korean automobile industry

The growth in the Korean automobile industry has been remarkable. Korea emerged in the 1980s as a significant world producer. Automobile output increased by almost thirty-six-times between 1978 and 2000 – from 85,693 units to 3,098,761. Exports are the engine of the contemporary Korean automobile industry's success. Korea emerged in 1995 as a significant world producer in which five leading countries produced 2.6 million units.

The Korean automobile industry's capacity reached 4,332,000 units in 2000, and in the same year, Korean automakers exported about 1.544 million units.[1] In the 1980s, Korean automakers began to explore strategies to increase access to the overseas market. From an examination of the present trend, there seem to be three strategies that Korean automakers could follow in terms of export-orientated growth: a technological and financial link between a domestic corporation and multinational automakers; a joint venture between a domestic corporation and a multinational vehicle corporation whose production strategies were partially influenced by the concept of a world car; the export promotion policies by the government accelerated in substance the internationalization of the Korean automobile industry. That is, wage control, a protected home market and government subsidies have helped in the creation of this dynamic new industry.[2]

The successful private conglomerates from the Third World to organize and benefit from technological links with multinational automakers are undoubtedly Korean firms. Hyundai, the largest Korean automobile company, was founded in 1967. Hyundai first assembled American models on a CKD (complete knocked down) basis, with the technical assistance of Ford, but the number was extremely small. At this stage, Hyundai began to assemble the Ford models Cortina and Taunus. After seven years of CKD and SKD (semi-knocked down) production, Hyundai succeeded in developing Korea's first independently designed and manufactured model, the 'Pony'. After the rupture of negotiations for joint ventures with Ford, Hyundai declared the development of an export-orientated market strategy through the development of their own model.

For this project, Hyundai began technical co-operation with Mitsubishi. They obtained chassis components and other parts that were difficult to manufacture, such as gears and engines, directly from Mitsubishi, but fabricated the cylinder heads and blocks, housings and transmission cases in-house. Because of the small size of the domestic market, Hyundai has had to export in order to achieve economies of scale. In the early 1980s, the company constructed a new plant for the first front-wheel drive automobile in Korea that needed Japanese technology and capital. Hyundai and Mitsubishi set up a strategic alliance in 1982. Mitsubishi owns 12% of Hyundai. Hyundai created the 'Excel Phenomenon' in 1985 and entered the market in the United States successfully in 1986.

The penetrations into the world market by Daewoo and Kia followed a different route from Hyundai. At least two corporations have forged technological and financial links with the two major proponents of the world car concept, GM and Ford. Daewoo was in a 50/50 joint venture with GM up to 1994. Daewoo produced the world car Pontiac Le Mans, in order to sell in North America. The design is derived from the Opel Kadett produced by GM's German subsidiary, with technological improvements provided by GM's Japanese affiliate, Isuzu.

In 1983, Mazda paid a 10% shareholding to Kia in order to avoid a financial crisis caused by the second oil crisis. Three years later, Ford invested US$30 million in Kia and now owns 10% of the company. With Ford's new capital input, and technological assistance from Mazda, Kia has produced export models since 1987. The VRA (voluntary restriction agreement) and the overvaluation of the yen in 1980s stimulated the strategic alliance of Ford and Mazda with Kia.

Although Daewoo and Kia both have major capital participation from GM and Ford, these auto assemblers have incorporated Japanese partners to adopt process technology and organizational methods. However, they had considerably less marketing success in the all-important US market than did Hyundai during 1980s. To drive to a more aggressive export oriented marketing, Daewoo decided to end its joint venture with GM in 1992.

In the 1980s, the Korean automobile industry learned how to produce competitive cars within their worldwide car category.

The trend towards internationalization by the Korean automobile industry in the early 1990s

The early-1990s features of the Korean automobile industry were: maturity of the domestic market; diversification of the international market because of the gradual loss of the market in North America and the effect on strengthening internationalization; and sharply increased competition in the domestic market for foreign-made cars.

Internationalization and globalization presented an alternative way out of this market situation. Because of the problems of product quality, worker productivity, overseas delivery and marketing, and the overvaluation of the Korean won (the Korean currency) until the financial turmoil in late 1997, the Korean automakers lost their important overseas export markets, particularly in the United States. In view of the recession in the US market, the obvious strategy for the industry was to seek overseas export markets. In this context, Korean automobile manufacturers saw the need to expand into the European market.

The United States remained the largest overseas market for Korea until 1995 in spite of the decline of its share of Korean auto exports. Korean auto exports to North America decreased by 14%, from 234,904 vehicles in 1994 to 202,786 in 1995. Shipments to North America accounted for 20.7% of the total, down from 33.9%. Exports to North America fell by 19.4% of the total shipment in 1997, while export units rose by 1.3% to 211,614 units, because of the rise in exports of new models by Hyundai. Korean automobile exports to Western Europe were 331,935 vehicles in 1997, up almost 150% from 132,876 in 1994. In 1997, European countries were the largest markets for Korean auto assemblers. Since 1999, Korean automakers have concentrated their marketing on SUVs and expanded warranty services in the USA.

The international competitiveness of Korean cars is acknowledged widely, as 78.8% of Korean-made automobiles were exported to North America and Europe in 2001, where world-renowned makers are located, and these brands are staging fierce competition to expand their market share (see Appendix Table A8.1).

The direct investments by Korean firms in overseas market concerned first the commercial network, after the manufacturing and lastly R&D facilities. This sequence (sales—manufacturing—R&D) is essentially the same as the one observed in the internationalization of the Japanese automobile industry, although the timing is somewhat different; the internationalization of the Japanese car industry was apparently carried out sequentially but the stages of manufacturing and R&D in internationalization by Korean firms moved forward simultaneously. The design of right products play a particularly important role in order to penetrate into the mature markets.

Hyundai operates eight research institutes in Korea and overseas. In Los Angeles, they set up a design centre, and established a technical centre in Ann Arbor, Michigan, in 1986 to supply the parent company with the latest technology and to develop cars that satisfy diverse needs of local customers. In 1997 a research institute was created in Yokohama (Japan) for mutual exchanges of R&D with the existing institutes, development of new cars and electronics systems, and the analysis/assessment of advanced cars. Hyundai's domestic research institutes are as follows: Mabookri Central Research Centre, Ulsan Passenger Car Institute No.1, Namyang Passenger Car Institute No.2, Chunju Commercial Vehicle Institute, and Namyang Design Centre. Hyundai spent 3,826 million won or 3.3% of their total turnover on R&D projects in 1997 (see Appendix Table A8.2).

Hyundai is creating an overseas distribution network. There are two agencies in North America, thirty-seven in Europe, forty in South America, forty-four in the Middle East/Africa, and twenty-nine in Asia/Pacific. Hyundai Motor America is responsible for sales in North America. Parallel with the extension of the network of overseas dealers from 2,968 to 3,200, they also will extend the 3,700 after-sales service chains worldwide. In 1996, Hyundai invested a total of around US$30 million constructing one of the most modern parts logistic centres in Lummen City, Belgium. The service and supply of auto parts and components from this centre will cover the whole of Europe. Before the establishment of this centre, car components and parts were supplied from Ulsan at the European distributor's request. Hyundai will be able to shorten the delivery time from fifty-six days to a mere eight days in the case of general orders. For emergency orders, the delivery time is reduced from ten days to two days. Hyundai also operates parts centres in the North American region. Additionally, America's Caterpillar Logistic Service Inc. has been hired to take charge of parts and components warehouse operations, the transportation of parts and components, customs clearance, and stock management. Hyundai has set up a world-wide maintenance training network system in seven major regions. The network maintenance centre facilities cover seven regions and nine countries: North America (USA and Canada), Central/South America (Chile), Western Europe (Germany), Eastern Europe (Slovenia), East Asia (China and Thailand), Middle East (UAE), and Africa (South Africa).

The internationalization of Kia was based orginally on OEM export for Ford. Then the automaker set up manufacturing facilities with a joint venture in a peripheral area of the world auto market. Kia is also spending huge amounts of funds on the creation of a global network in the field of R&D such as Kia engineering in California and Kia R&D in Tokyo, while trying to enhance the status of Korean automakers in the world market. Kia also established a joint venture firm – Motor Systems & Technology Co. Ltd – in co-operation with Bosch of Germany. It has helped the firm to strengthen its international competitiveness in the world automobile market. Kia spent 852 million won, or 1.3% of its total turnover, on R&D in 1996, while it fell 0.1 percent in 1997 due to the financial problems of the company (see Appendix tables). Finally, they have been exporting their own models into the US market since 1992. Kia puts top priority on consolidating its production systems for international competitiveness and strengthening its marketing activities. It is building a network of more than 1,200 dealers in a total of twenty-two countries with a view to exporting its own model, the Sephia. Kia has also built an independent marketing and after-sales services network with fifty dealers in the United States to export the Sephia and Sportage models developed by its own technical team through its subsidiary, Kia Motors America Inc. in Los Angeles, which has solid links to the Toronto branch office in Canada.

Daewoo became more aggressive in globalization after the dissolution of shared ownership with GM in 1992. Daewoo had to wait two years more to be free to undertake globalization as GM restricted its marketing areas to Eastern Europe, Asia and South America until the end of 1994. Daewoo has been bolstering its overseas sales promotion activities in Western European countries, including Germany and Britain. As an initial step to survive the fierce competition in the world automobile market, Daewoo took over the research centre of International Automobile Design (IAD) in Worthing, Britain, a world-renowned auto design and engineering company, in 1994. Daewoo also set up a new technical centre in Munich in 1995, where it has been conducting development of new engine systems. Daewoo spent 1.7% of its total turnover on R&D in 1995 (see Appendix Table A8.1).

A new globalization strategy: a peripheral market player

The new trend of internationalization by Korean automakers is the expansion of knock-down kits and/or joint venture investments in the less developed countries of the automobile industry to avoid intensifying trade friction. Two parallel patterns of Korean activities are likely to continue. On the one hand, they will continue to be heterogeneous forms of enterprise, namely project-based collaborations, licensed manufacturing or joint ventures. But on the other, Korean automakers founded transplants through the acquisition of local existing car assemblers. Korean automobile manufacturers started mainly with South Asia and Eastern Europe operations (see Table 8.1).

After their initial success in entering the world market through exporting, Hyundai created in 1989 a plant (100,000 unit annual capacity) in Bromont (Canada). This project was the first investment by an automaker from an NIE (newly industrializing economy) into an advanced country in order to become a true vehicle multinational with a productive base in North America. However, the Bromont plant failed in 1991, and was closed.

Many of the reasons given to explain this decision are still a hot issue among management. The major reason for the closing of the first Hyundai transplant was the rather poor performance of the plant in terms of quality and productivity. The total production of this plant in 1990 and 1991 was 27,409 and 28,201 units, respectively. This was far below capacity and expectation. At that time, the plant had a workforce of 1,200. This plant was not involved in the process of the establishment of a new production system, with increased flexibility and participation in the concept of a lean production system. Nevertheless, the Fordist manufacturing system also characterized the production system of this plant, which meant that the production line only had limited conversion flexibility. There were no attempts at using new concepts to achieve increased efficiency and quality in production. After a promising start in the mid-1980s, Hyundai sales have been sluggish in the USA because of problems with after-sales service, and poor quality and design. Since 1987, labour disputes in the main plant in Korea have been rising year on year. This has brought about lockouts and caused the loss of cost-reducing opportunities. Consequently, Hyundai did not supply assembly parts to the Bromont plant, which created an obstacle to increased productivity and capacity utilization. No Korean component suppliers invested in Bromont because they did not want to take a risk on the limited demand in that transplant. Another reason was the intention to use the low-cost production basis in new emerging markets such as South Asia. At the end of 1996, the machinery and equipment at the Bromont plant was shipped to India, where Hyundai set up India's first fully foreign-owned automobile factory.

The new strategy by Hyundai is access to emerging markets that might include the need to overcome tariff and/or non-tariff barriers. Since 1990, Hyundai has moved from a world-wide export strategy to a multi-domestic structure based on manufacturing sites in different regions. In the second half of the 1990s, the international structure of production appeared to be based on an axis between two regional poles: one new pole of integrated activities in South East Asia, extended to China, Europe and Africa; and one new pole in South America based in Venezuela.

Table 8.1 Korean automobile makers' local production and operations overseas

Firm	Country	Partner	Model	Capacity	Start of production
Daewoo	Ukraine	Avtozac	Lanos, Leganza	72,000	1998
	Egypt	AFE Group	Lanos, Leganza	20,000	1998
	Morocco	Dawoo Maghreb	Lanos, Nubira, Polone	100,000	1996
	China	FAW	Auto Parts	300,000	1996
	China	n.a.	Bus	5,000	1996
	India	DCM-Daewoo	Cielo	60,000	1995
	Indonesia	Stars Auto	Espero, Cielo	20,000	1995
	Romania	Rodae	Cielo	100,000	1996
	Poland	FSO	Cielo, Tico	125,00	1996
	Vietnam	VIDAMCO	Bus, Car	22,000	1996
	Uzbekistan	UZ-Daewoo	Cielo, Tico	100,000	1996
	Philippines	Trans-Daewoo	Espero, Cielo	20,000	1996
Hyundai	China	Grand Motor Co.	Minibus	60,000	1996
	Taiwan	Jack Wang	Excent Avante	20,000	1997
	Egypt	Ghabbour	Excell	20,000	1995
	Botswana	Sabot	Excell, Elantra	60,000	1993
	Vietnam	990 Co.,	Excell, Minibus	20,000	1996
	Turkey	Hyundai-Assan	Excell, Minivan	50,000	1996
	India	100%	Excent	100,000	1998
	Zimbabwe	n.a.	Excell	10,000	1994
	Thailand	United Auto Sales	Excent	20,000	1993
	Philippines	Italcar	Excell	2,000	1995
	Malaysia	Bimantara	Minivan	10,000	1995
	Indonesia	Sobieslaw	Elantra	10,000	1995
	Romania	Automobile Dacia S.A.	Excent	50,000	1998
	Poland	Zasada Centrum	n.a.	4,000	1998
	Venezuela	Manufacturas Automotriz	Excell	30,000	1996
Kia	China	n.a.	Minivan	6,000	1995
	China	n.a.	Mini truck	6,000	n.a.
	Taiwan	FLH	Festiva	30,000	1993
	Iran	SAIPA	Festiva	30,000	1993
	Pakistan	NDM	Ceres, Festiva	15,000	1994
	Germany	KMN	Sportage	30,000	1995
	Indonesia	Kia-Timor	Sephia, Sportage	50,000	1996
	Vietnam	n.a.	Ceres, Festiva	1,000	1993

Source: Various publications.

Therefore, the internationalization of automobile manufacturing by Hyundai started mostly in peripheral regions. Hyundai's CKD plant in Botswana is the only assembly plant of foreign automakers in Botswana, with an annual capacity of 40,000 units. In 1996, Hyundai was producing about 15,000 units on an SKD basis, with South Africa absorbing 95% of the output. The company has scheduled the Accent, New Elantra/Lantra and Sonata for assembly at the plant. Manufacturas Automotriz Venezuela S.A.,

Hyundai's local partner, is the sole investor in the plant. This brings Hyundai one step closer to the South American markets. The CKD plant assembles the Excel at an annual rate of 10,000 units. HMC provides core parts, such as engines and transmissions to this assembler, while tyres, batteries and door trims (accounting for 30% of content) are supplied locally. The Turkish plant produces (50,000 units annual capacity) the Accent and the H-100 (Minibus). In the early stages of production, Hyundai will concentrate on the Turkish domestic market, but will eventually start exporting its vehicles to neighbouring countries. Hyundai will provide the joint venture company with key parts such as moulds, jigs, machinery and other production facilities, along with core parts such as engines and transmission. Turkish suppliers will provide tyres, batteries and other parts in an effort to obtain a 30% local content rate from the outset. By 1999, a press plant was added to increase the domestic content rate to 50% and by 2002 the rate will increase to 60%. Also, it has produced commercial vehicles jointly with Renault of France in Malaysia since 1997.

In this phase, the internationalization strategy of Hyundai is characterized by a peripheral market strategy. This means that overseas production sites are limited to the peripheral area, where there is no hard competition from advanced automakers. Therefore, KD export by Korean manufacturers as an internationalization strategy has been freed from the import quota system of auto-importing countries. They have been able to increase Hyundai's overall market penetration despite increased import barriers or the raising of dumping charges against foreign-made cars. This strategy involved the decision to integrate South East Asian operations in terms of products and manufacturing. Ultimately, Hyundai created a single vehicle, launched in India in 1998 and the following year in Indonesia and Thailand. An organizational structure is emerging based on three world regions: Asia, North and South America, and Europe. Hyundai has made significant regional advances as far as its Asia-Pacific operations are concerned, as it has attempted to co-ordinate the activities of its various subsidiaries spread out among the ASEAN countries, creating a regional division of labour, and linking the factories in India and Indonesia into a network of global sourcing of components and parts. Hyundai continues to expand in markets it has already entered and influenced through its exports, with the internationalization of its sales, and the after-sales service network as a basis upon which to make investments in production.

In South East Asia, the company was to start production and sales of a specific vehicle destined for these markets (Asian Car) on the basis of a platform shared with Korean products (Accent and Atos Model).[3] This led Hyundai to utilize its components and platforms to the maximum. On the other hand, this platform strategy permits the accelerated pace of product replacement in the home market. Since late 1996, Hyundai has begun the construction of its largest manufacturing plant outside Korea, in Chennai, India. Hyundai have invested approximately US$1.1billion in the Chennai plant by the year 2001. The Indian project has a two-phase construction plan: 1998 completed the first stage of this construction project with an annual production capacity of 120,000 units. In this phase, Hyundai manufactured 1300 cc and 1500 cc Accents and 800 cc Atos. The second phase will be complete in 2002, when Hyundai plans to manufacture additional models in India. Hyundai's Chennai plant will consist of shops for engines, transmissions, press, body, paint, assembly and plastic injection moulding. Also in the plan is an R&D centre, a proving ground and a vehicle performance test centre will be built in the plant. These facilities will enable the Chennai plant to become a self-sufficient manufacturing and production site for developing automobiles that meet the needs of its local market. Hyundai is in tune with the global trend of offshore expansion and is setting a precedent in the world's auto industry. In particular, sixteen Korean parts and components suppliers to Hyundai will be setting up their facilities jointly with their local Indian partner near the Chennai plant.

Ultimately, Hyundai created a single vehicle, launched in an Indian transplant in 1998. Hyundai spent more than two years developing its first overseas model, the Santro. With Atos as the base model, the newly developed Santro is a low-roof model, made to fit the conditions of the Indian market. Characteristic of the Santro is its newly developed suspension and air conditioning system, which prevents condensation being formed under local conditions of rough roads and hot, humid weather.[4] Hyundai's overseas production capacity was around 382,000 (including KD and transplant) in 1997. Hyundai's KD exports decreased by 30% to 41,500 units in 2001 over the previous year.[5]

After the ending of the equal ownership with GM, Daewoo adopted two different strategies. One is a marketing strategy. The other is a take-over of the East European automakers in order to export in all Europe.

Daewoo has been bolstering its overseas sales promotion activities in Western European countries, including Germany and Britain. For example, the company has been advertising its vehicles on TV and in newspapers aggressively since 1995. The direct investment of Daewoo in setting-up overseas car production plants was obviously concentrated on Eastern Europe. The first European facility – Rodae Automobile S.A. in Romania – now has an annual production capacity of 100,000 units. They also started up a joint venture with FSO Co., a state-owned automaker in Poland. The export of KD kits increased by 20.8% to 111,804 units in 2001 over the previous year, even though the firm is experiencing financial problems (see Table 8.2).

The globalization strategy of Daewoo consists of two parts. One is to R&D in the advanced countries such as Britain or Germany. The other is to build up a CKD plant in low-wage countries and closed markets such as those in Eastern Europe. Daewoo is trying to link more strategically the three areas of R&D, production and marketing at globalization level. Evidence suggests that the firm's activities in Europe are moving in that direction, which is consistent with globalization models, although whether they will become a

Table 8.2 KD exports by Korean automobile makers, 1991–2001

Companies	1991	1992	1993	1994	1995	1996	1997	1998	1999	2000	2001
Total	47,990	38,447	63,778	45,820	104,589	202,143	193,196	220,722	277,733	245,249	276,429
Hyundai	25,020	14,220	12,510	3,900	17,758	15,980	3,606	52,500	35,760	58,980	41,500
Kia	22,970	23,677	50,868	41,620	70,443	70,182	61,490	71,560	101,130	93,090	119,832
Daewoo	0	0	0	0	15,986	115,383	94,187	57,736	135,880	92,573	111,804
Ssangyong	0	550	300	300	402	598	913	n.a.	n.a.	n.a.	n.a.

Source: KAMA, monthly automobile statistics.

Table 8.3 Production capability of Korean automobile makers, 2000 (units)

Companies	Domestic production capability	Overseas production capability
Hyundai	1,500,000	496,000
Kia	1,030,000	243,000
Daewoo	1,070,000	920,000

full-scale development remains to be seen.[6] At the time of writing, Daewoo has a total overseas production capacity of 920,000 (see Table 8.3).

Kia has been pushing ahead aggressively with the following projects: to expand export markets, carry out KD projects and set up overseas corporations. Under this globalization, the automaker has mapped out five major strategic objectives:

(i) to build an expanded, internationally competitive production base, and to make its Asan Bay plant an overseas production base;
(ii) to bring about technical self-reliance through expansion in investment and technical manpower;
(iii) to establish a global managerial system through world-wide sales and after-sales service networks;
(iv) to strengthen international competitiveness through the specialization of vendors; and
(v) to seek a harmonious relationship between labour and management through expansion in welfare and education programmes for employees.

Kia puts top priority on consolidating its production systems with international competitiveness, and strengthening its marketing activities. It also places an equal emphasis on continuing its efforts for globalization and localization through joint venture projects with foreign partners. Kia embarked on overseas assembly in Taiwan for the first time in 1989, and the company has set up CKD plants in the nine following countries: the Philippines, Taiwan, Germany,[7] Indonesia, Iran,[8] Vietnam, Venezuela, Pakistan and Namibia. The export of KD kits rose to 70,443 units in 1996, an increase of 69.3% over the previous year. In 1997, Kia exported 61,690 KD kits, down 12.4%, with exports to South East Asian countries falling off because of the Asian crisis (see Table 8.4). By 1997, Kia had overseas production bases in twelve countries, with a production capacity of 320,000 units. Export of KD kits rose to 119,831 units in 2001, an increase of 28.7% over the previous year, in contrast to the decrease in Hyundai.[9]

Notably, Kia opened a joint venture auto plant in Indonesia. PT Timor, chosen as Indonesia's first 'national car' project, is permitted to sell imported sedans from Kia for less than half the price of competing models – that is, about US$15,000 compared to US$30,500 for a Toyota Corolla. Under the

Table 8.4 Korean automobile makers' KD exports by region, 1991–7

Region	Company	1991	1992	1993	1994	1995	1996	1997
Germany	Kia	0	0	0	30	4,080	9,880	12,240
Netherlands	Hyundai	0	0	0	0	208	140	0
Canada	Hyundai	25,020	14,190	10,860	0	0	0	0
Poland	Daewoo	0	0	0	0	0	0	13,248
Romania	Daewoo	0	0	0	0	768	39,720	10,992
Czech Republic	Hyundai	0	0	0	0	0	360	150
Uzbekistan	Daewoo	0	0	0	0	445	42,904	66,204
Botswana	Hyundai	0	0	0	0	0	0	90
Zimbabwe	Hyundai	0	0	0	600	540	530	1,530
Bangladesh	Daewoo	0	0	0	0	0	10	0
China	Hyundai	0	0	0	0	0	480	720
	Kia	0	0	0	0	0	0	1,120
	Daewoo	0	0	0	0	0	290	240
	Ssangyong	0	0	400	0	0	0	0
Indonesia	Hyundai	0	0	0	0	2,490	2,340	3,720
	Kia	0	0	0	0	0	0	2,240
	Daewoo	0	0	0	0	1,080	96	504
	Ssangyong	0	0	0	0	0	36	0
India	Daewoo	0	0	0	0	12,192	28,008	648
Pakistan	Kia	0	0	0	0	3,912	2,630	0
Malaysia	Kia	0	0	0	0	0	550	950
	Daewoo	0	0	0	0	0	230	40
	Ssangyong	0	0	0	0	0	18	72
Philippines	Hyundai	0	0	0	60	1,350	840	0
	Kia	5,324	1,141	3,582	6,814	8,731	6,178	5,680
	Daewoo	0	0	0	0	259	265	35
Taiwan	Hyundai	0	0	0	0	0	0	1,020
	Kia	17,616	21,432	31,800	18,096	25,260	24,800	12,040
Thailand	Hyundai	0	30	1,650	2,160	2,100	0	0
Vietnam	Kia	0	0	270	120	1,624	1,080	420
	Daewoo	0	0	0	0	1,194	1,292	448
	Ssangyong	0	550	0	300	402	544	841
Egypt	Hyundai	0	0	0	1,080	11,070	8,140	8,820
Iran	Kia	0	0	10,728	10,992	21,768	21,960	23,160
	Daewoo	0	0	0	0	48	2,568	1,824
Turkey	Hyundai	0	0	0	0	0	0	16,386
Venezuela	Hyundai	0	0	0	0	0	3,150	4,170
	Kia	0	1,104	4,488	5,568	4,968	3,104	3,640
Brazil	Daewoo	0	0	0	0	0	0	4

Source: KAMA, monthly automobile statistics.

agreement, Kia shipped its four-door Sephia saloon to Indonesia without paying import duty or luxury tax.

Kia's overseas production is concentrated on the Asian regions and on a smaller scale. Its stakes in joint ventures are lower than those of Hyundai and Daewoo. Kia's global strategy to expand its overseas production operations has been concentrated on KD kit assembly rather than large-scale investment in overseas markets in order to minimize operation risks in global business.

The ever-increasing internationalization in the automobile industry has crucially important implications for component suppliers. Suppliers also face pressure to contain or reduce costs in order to reduce the costs of assemblers. These conditions have inter-related implications for structural change in the components industry. There is an increasing emphasis on international organization and operations. The supplier industries move forward to relocate their production sites in areas with low wage costs, such as China and South East Asian countries. By 1996, approximately 178 Korean parts suppliers had constructed plants in overseas countries, of which 55.6% are in China and 33.7% in South East Asian countries, with 16.8% of the overseas investment suppliers exceeding US$1 million in investment (see Table 8.5). The investment strategy of suppliers is initially of a follow-the-client type, which is encouraged by assemblers, aiming at the diversification of world clients. Obviously, this parallel overseas penetration of suppliers and assemblers has improved economies of scale. This strategy will help to establish the global sourcing that is becoming a leitmotiv of Korean automakers. For example, Hyundai Motor India plans to export cars and key parts, such as engines and transmissions, to the KD plants and neighbouring South East Asian countries. More recently, Korean parts suppliers have established facilities on their own initiative in order to reduce production costs. As a consequence of increased global sourcing of components by assemblers, the internationalization of suppliers is increasing.

The strategy of internationalization of Korean car manufacturers is characterized by a peripheral market strategy to avoid competition with advanced automakers. Otherwise, KD exports by Korean manufacturers as an internationalization strategy has arisen from the import quota system of auto-importing countries. Manufacturers have been able to increase their overall market penetration despite increased import barriers or raised dumping charges against foreign-made cars in Western Europe and South America, and a fluctuation in the Korean currency.

Table 8.5 Overseas investment by Korean component industries (1996)

Region	Companies		Investment (unit: $1,000)		
	Number	Percentage	Amount	No. of companies	Percentage
China	99	55.6	0–99	43	24.2
South Asia	60	33.7	100–499	78	43.8
North America	9	5.1	500–999	27	15.2
Europe	9	5.1	1000–49,999	25	14.0
Pacific	1	0.5	Over 50,000	5	2.8
Total	178	100	Total	178	100

Source: Korea Auto Industries Co-operation Association (1997).

The logical target for transplants via KD kits is throughout Asia and Eastern Europe, but that means hard competition between Korean automakers in peripheral areas and stimulation to develop local automotive industries. The markets of many Asia Pacific countries are already dominated by Japanese automakers. The Korean automakers also face hard competition in the European market – the largest market for Korean manufacturers. However, it is not expected that European countries will have a surge in demand for cheap Korean cars because several European companies already make similar cars, therefore that market is also more difficult to penetrate.

Strategic alliance restructuring and globalization among economic turmoil

Since late 1997 the Korean automobile industry has been embroiled in an unprecedented controversy over industrial restructuring coupled with an oversupply problem and a trade dispute with the USA on further auto market openings in the wake of the International Monetary Fund (IMF) bailout package. The natural solution to the dilemmas in the Korean automobile industry would be a merger and acquisition based on restructuring.

Hyundai carried out large-scale organizational restructuring with extensive lay-offs affecting about 30% of its officials. According to Hyundai, it streamlined its organization from fourteen divisions with 404 teams, to seven divisions with 340 teams. About thirty-six officials were dismissed or made redundant. After the executive level lay-offs, the company dismissed about 4,830 employees by 1998. In addition, the country's largest automaker encouraged 1,936 workers to retire voluntarily, after having implemented voluntary early retirement programmes. The year's total number of employees leaving Hyundai Motor was 9,239. The lay-off still leaves 6,642 redundant employees, but they will remain employed through the expedient of slashing the company's overhead expenditures by 21.6%.[10] Kia also fired ten executive officers from fifty officials and plans mass lay-offs of white-collar workers, despite laying off 4,000 workers in 1998.[11] All the auto manufacturers also limited production to eight hours a day, because of flagging demand in the domestic market.

Mergers and acquisitions are one of the hot issues in the Korean automobile industry sector: Renault took over the ailing Samsung Motor; and in November 2000, Daewoo Motor filed for bankruptcy protection and applied for court receivership. Finally the Korean government and creditor banks sold Daewoo Motor off to GM in 2002.

The Hyundai Motor emerged as the winner of the third round of auctions for the bankrupt Kia Motors and its sister commercial vehicle maker, Asia Motor Co., in December 1998.[12] According to the company's new management guidelines, the Hyundai Group's auto division was restructured into two units – Hyundai Motor and Kia Motors – and each unit will maintain its own brands for a long period. Hyundai Precision Industries which produces four-wheel drive (4WD) vehicles and vans, and Hyundai Motor Service Co. Ltd was merged into Hyundai Motors.

As a result of the acquisition of Kia, the productive internationalization of Hyundai was strengthened by Kia's overseas plants.[13] Kia's overseas production is concentrated in the Asian regions but on a smaller scale. Its stakes in joint ventures are lower than those of Hyundai and Daewoo. Kia's global strategy to expand its overseas production operations has concentrated on the KD kit assembly method rather than on large-scale investment into overseas markets, in order to minimize operation risks in global business. Therefore, Hyundai expects its synergic effect with Kia's internationalization strategy could lead to it becoming a strong market player in the peripheral regions.

Hyundai has concentrated on re-establishing its business operations – especially overseas – and has seen a positive response. An increase in global competitiveness is one of the preconditions for survival. In this context, Hyundai will also continue to push for strategic tie-ups with major foreign automakers to introduce advanced technology and jointly advance into world markets. In September 2000, Hyundai sold a 9% stake (20.618 million shares) to DaimlerChrysler for about 430.9 billion won (US\$389.9 million) – or 20,900 won per share. The stake sale came as part of a broad strategic alliance signed between Hyundai and the German–US company on 26 June 2000. Under the alliance, Hyundai agreed to hand a 10% stake over to DaimlerChrysler and engage in technological co-operation and the joint development of a world car.[14]

Together with Mitsubishi, DaimlerChrysler and Hyundai will develop and produce a range of high-quality small cars to compete in all key global markets including Asia, the NAFTA, South America and Europe. According to Hyundai the envisioned car will be less than 3.8 metres in length, and will be equipped with a 1.0 to 1.5 litre engine. Compared with the Verna, one of Hyundai's sub-compact models, the new car will be 40 cm shorter, 20–30% higher in fuel efficiency, and more environment-friendly. The three car makers will begin this 'world car' mass production from 2002 and jointly sell 4 to 5 million units during the following five years to meet a target of 45 trillion won (US\$40.5 billion) in sales and 2.5 trillion won (or 5.1% of the sales revenue) in profits. Specifically, Hyundai will produce 300,000 to 350,000 units domestically and 100,000 to 150,000 units in China from 2002; Mitsubishi will produce 100,000 to 200,000 units in Japan from the second half of 2002; and DaimlerChrysler will roll out 250,000 to 300,000 units in Europe from 2003. In total, the three companies will produce 750,000 to 1 million units a year world-wide. As Hyundai President Lee said at a press conference:

We have agreed to share the platform and make such core parts as the engine and transmission interchangeable. The strategic partnership clearly demonstrates that Hyundai's capabilities in development and production of small cars have reached world-class levels. It will improve the global recognition of the domestic auto industry's technological prowess and competitiveness.[15]

The two companies will also jointly explore other opportunities, including research and development, and supply chain management. Other areas under investigation for joint ventures include financial services and common component production and application. Hyundai has already used the sales networks of their new alliance partner. Hyundai Motors has been selling the 'Atoz' minicar in Mexico through its strategic alliance partner DaimlerChrysler's sales networks in that country. Under the agreement with DaimlerChrysler's affiliated company in Mexico, Hyundai aims to sell about 35,000 Atoz cars annually. The 1,000 cc-engine Atoz minicar bound for Mexico will carry the DaimlerChrysler brand 'Dodge'. The domestic Atoz model will be manufactured with 800 cc engines. This pending agreement is the first tangible development from the recently forged strategic tie-up between Hyundai and DaimlerChrysler. The Mexican auto market is estimated at 1.65 million units per year, with DaimlerChrysler taking the lead in market share with 23%. Besides DaimlerChrysler, Volkswagen, GM, Ford Motors and Nissan are operating assembly plants in Mexico. Only foreign automakers with production lines installed in Mexico are allowed to bring in finished cars into the country. Because of these rigorous entry regulations, Hyundai and other Korean automakers have not been able to enter the Mexican market. However, Hyundai will now be able to overcome the regulations, thanks to its tie-up with DaimlerChrysler.

Hyundai will also be concentrating more on the Chinese market. Hyundai and Kia already have assembly operations in China. Together they will become the largest manufacturer in this country. The opening of a regional head office will enable Hyundai and Kia to build full sales and service support for the potentially huge Chinese market as the development continues. It will then spearhead Hyundai–Kia efforts for the development of the Chinese and regional market including small and medium-sized passenger cars, RVs, buses and trucks.

Hyundai and the Brazilian government have also agreed to extend the deadline for the construction of a Kia Motors plant in Brazil to 2003 originally planned for 2001. The agreement has provided a breathing space for Hyundai from the US$210 million in fines the Brazilian government was to impose on Kia in the event of a failure to meet the 2001 construction deadline. In 1997, the now-defunct Asia Motors, then an affiliate of Kia Motors, suddenly suspended its US$300-million commercial-vehicle plant project in Brazil after being implicated in a fraud scandal, prompting the Brazilian government to impose a US$210 million fine for violating the investment contract. At the beginning of the project in 1996, the Brazilian government promised a 50% reduction on customs tax for Asia, on the condition that it completed the car plant by 2001. Kia's bankruptcy in 1997 completely halted the project, and Brazil has since stated that Kia's resumption of the Brazilian project would come only after full payment of the fine. Kia had received tariff waivers totalling US$72 million on its exported finished cars, dependent on the completion of the plant. Now Hyundai have asked the Brazilian government for customs incentives in connection with Kia's plan to build a 30,000-unit per year van assembly plant at an investment of US$150 million in Brazil's north-east state of Bahia.

Hyundai are also interested in further penetration into the European market. The expansion of Hyundai's Turkish plant has given firm access to the EU market. Hyundai Motors unveiled ambitious expansion plans for its auto assembly plant there, under a long-term bid to use Turkey as a bridgehead to a bigger share of the European market. Hyundai has selected the Turkish plant as a strategic point for Europe. It is a key pillar of the company's global production system, along with assembly lines in India and China. Further to its expansion plans, Hyundai's local joint venture plant, Hyundai Assan Otomotiv Sanayi (HAOS), will soon double its annual output capacity to 120,000 units, aiming to seize a third of the Turkish car market. To this end, the compact Avante XD and 3.5-ton truck models will be assembled by the HAOS. The company will also consider localizing the production of engines for the Accent model, in an effort to cut costs.

Changes in the market and finance environment have given rise to different strategies on the part of firms. The strategies of firms, how they change, and whether they are successful, appear to depend on the managerial resources that can be mobilized. Because of the financial crisis, the country's auto manufacturers are over-extended and lack liquidity. To solve these problems, they urgently need to increase strategic alliances and take-overs with foreign automakers. Daewoo can be expected to invite foreign participation increasingly. Daewoo launched three new models simultaneously and a costly debt-financed project of acquisitions in Eastern Europe. Daewoo will finance this project through its strategic alliance with GM.

Daewoo has become the most globally ambitious Korean automaker, embarking on a costly debt-financed programme of new projects and acquisitions, especially in Eastern Europe. To carry out this project, Daewoo must find a new financial source and has signed a memorandum of understanding with GM. Daewoo will produce and sell GM models on the Korean market, co-operate in the joint development of small, low-priced automobile models and manufacture GM cars at Daewoo's plants in Poland, Romania, the Ukraine and India. GM's purchase of Daewoo stakes – now under review – is estimated at about 50% of the Korean automaker's total equity, which is valued at about 500 billion won (US$330 million), with Daewoo Motor having managerial control. GM owned 50% of Daewoo Motor from 1978 to 1992.

These two big automakers will be able to boost their joint expansion thrust into the world car market through their alliance. GM can take advantage of

Daewoo Motor's spread of production strongholds in Asia, Eastern Europe and India, while the Korean automaker will be able to acquire the advanced technology and funds needed to push its marketing in the United States and to enhance its brand value in Asia. Daewoo Motor and GM severed their co-operative ties in 1992, but have since sought to reunite while expanding their operations separately.

Because of the effect of the Asian economic downturn on the global auto industry, Korean car manufacturers are expected to boost their exports overseas, especially to keep the market share in the European and US markets, which absorb about 78 per cent of its overseas exports, improving quality and strengthening marketing in the USA and Western European countries are necessary conditions. Attempting to increase exports has not been an alternative way for the ailing automobile industry. An aggressive export drive might give rise to trade conflicts with Europe and the USA, which have threatened to invoke an anti-dumping lawsuit against the Korean industry.

Conclusion

At the time of writing, the Korean automakers' trajectory is characterized by a transition from a world-wide export strategy to a multi-domestic strategy based on manufacturing sites in the differential regions, because they cannot continue to depend on the domestic market for sustained growth and lose out on a vast potential market. The Korean automotive industry has adopted two ways of making this transition.

Korean companies have continuously extended production sites with KD manufacturing based in peripheral areas. Through this periphery-targeting strategy, the companies have been able to increase market penetration despite increased import barriers or raised dumping charges. More recently, they became interested in the construction of overseas transplants in spite of Korea's domestic economic crisis. For example, Korean firms will develop the 'Asian Car' based on a transplant in Asia. For the core markets, they will maintain their direct export strategy.

The logical target for transplants using KD kits are throughout Asia, but that means hard competition between Korean automobile manufacturers in the periphery. Otherwise, in emerging markets such as South East Asia and Eastern Europe, competition is expanding rapidly from domestic manufacturing, frequently as a part of a joint venture between a local company and a global leader. It may be that Korean automakers' access to these regions may need important strategic challengers. In response to the growth of the emerging markets, they must be equipped with modern technology and operate under modern management concepts in their overseas plants in these regions.

In spite of the pressures globalization creates, the strategy of global sourcing and localization is in its infancy. Obviously, the major task is to stimulate the organization of an international suppliers' network. It may be that Korean automakers need this to be secured through Korean sourcing from suppliers in South East Asia and Eastern Europe.

To survive fierce sales competition in core markets, Korean automakers must exert their best efforts to improve technology and quality. High quality and advanced technology are preconditions for survival. They must also improve their own brand image, which has a reputation for poor quality cars in the main export market. They can succeed in improving quality with the application of appropriate human resource development.

In summary, Korean automakers, as major cost-based exporters, will find themselves under significant pressure during globalization. In their adjustment to these situations, a number of systemic impediments such as higher finance costs, lack of labour flexibility and downsizing also hamper Korean players. Recently, they have been more effective in responding to challenges. But it is hard to survive global competition, therefore the future trajectory of Korean automakers is hard to predict. They are now at a critically important crossroads in the globalization process.

Statistical appendix: Korean automobile manufacturers

Table A8.1 Korean automakers, export volumes by region, 1992–2001

	1992	1993	1994	1995	1996	1997	1998	1999	2000	2001
Total	431,451	609,929	704,202	911,731	1,008,929	1,092,838	1,228,144	1,390,072	1,544,473	1,397,315
Hyundai	283,513	349,603	393,959	472,696	478,611	494,989	439,419	555,354	756,895	752,400
Kia	105,023	158,417	210,469	201,577	181,509	184,455	205,983	358,494	393,580	420,793
Daewoo	42,915	101,909	99,774	237,458	298,073	332,515	142,213	178,499	146,869	104,419
North America	142,432	140,477	234,904	202,786	208,988	211,614	254,828	450,704	658,097	694,907
Hyundai	102,314	118,261	148,239	126,638	138,505	146,411	110,380	240,390	349,205	401,634
Kia	40,118	22,216	86,665	76,148	70,483	65,170	105,839	151,563	222,919	257,819
Daewoo	–	–	–	–	–	33	38,609	58,751	85,973	35,454
West Europe	109,363	127,996	132,876	267,058	272,775	331,935	355,308	469,661	460,942	406,668
Hyundai	103,207	99,858	96,251	130,576	139,717	160,656	184,291	193,235	237,352	221,265
Kia	6,106	20,313	24,615	32,681	37,192	33,337	26,665	94,615	73,472	78,758
Daewoo	50	7,825	12,010	103,801	95,866	137,942	144,352	181,811	150,118	106,645
East Europe	9,068	19,371	17,691	67,854	135,863	177,642	97,728	155,664	54,896	27,349
Hyundai	7,687	7,388	6,962	15,141	21,790	13,362	11,411	13,507	17,405	11,626
Kia	56	1,059	1,728	5,245	6,737	11,052	15,032	27,717	9,830	8,558
Daewoo	1,325	10,924	9,001	47,468	107,336	153,228	71,285	114,440	27,661	7,165
Africa	11,345	10,834	16,279	37,982	80,150	38,721	53,828	55,104	44,947	25,301
Hyundai	5,001	5,649	10,508	24,926	22,637	24,577	15,282	11,873	10,995	7,322
Kia	1,718	1,669	1,624	3,979	1,197	1,354	1,903	5,948	9,297	6,848
Daewoo	4,626	3,516	4,147	9,077	56,316	12,790	36,643	37,283	24,655	11,131

Asia	50,925	1,00,063	55,322	37,160	42,274	36,627	5,702	23,594	44,939	34,242
Hyundai	12,188	31,196	12,323	12,555	11,028	6,985	2,899	5,452	17,863	17,495
Kia	26,505	39,797	28,941	10,601	21,393	25,136	1,052	16,445	23,115	14,271
Daewoo	12,232	29,070	14,058	14,004	9,853	4,506	1,751	1,697	3,961	2,476
Middle Asia	40,934	96,481	90,969	84,676	53,142	54,931	48,073	59,314	65,627	58,090
Hyundai	16,118	30,025	41,700	54,043	29,952	28,412	20,249	25,132	42,412	26,315
Kia	8,563	42,400	25,820	18,126	8,392	12,514	13,302	17,266	14,951	20,865
Daewoo	16,253	24,056	23,449	12,507	14,798	14,005	14,522	16,916	8,264	10,910
Pacific	20,114	30,142	45,564	74,752	103,700	108,393	85,447	116,506	88,006	55,594
Hyundai	15,111	19,974	7,901	45,670	67,191	64,703	59,067	59,067	46,680	36,004
Kia	4,961	9,722	9,754	16,575	15,413	19,207	24,629	24,629	19,813	11,326
Daewoo	42	446	7,750	12.507	21,096	24,483	1,751	32,810	21,513	8,264
Latin America	42,270	84,565	110,756	139,463	112,037	132,975	114,473	64,121	102,223	87,179
Hyundai	21,887	37,252	50,075	63,147	47,791	49,883	35,840	17,229	37,183	30,739
Kia	16,996	21,241	31,322	38,222	20,792	16,685	17,561	19,445	20,183	22,348
Daewoo	8,387	26,072	29,359	38,094	43,544	66,407	61,072	27,447	44,857	34,092

Source: KAMA, monthly automobile statistics, various issues.

Table A8.2 Korean automobile manufacturers, 1991–2000

Firms	Data	1991	1992	1993	1994	1995	1996	1997	1998	1999	2000
Hyundai	Gross sales[a]	56,052	60,790	71,812	90,523	103,392	114,898	116,620	86,980	142,445	182,309
	Profit[a]	538	416	582	1,368	1,567	868	465	−331	4,143	6,677
	Investment[a]	5,023	3,622	5,556	6,683	10,591	13,046	11,293	9,178	7,112	6,678
	R&D[a]	1,045	1,183	1,532	2,129	2,616	3,491	3,826	7,686	8,169	9,108
	Employment	40,649	41,195	41,409	44,083	45,297	47,098	46,196	37,752	50,984	49,023
	Production[b]	767,090	859,250	960,057	1,134,611	1,213,694	1,281,762	1,239,032	812,078	1,269,542	1,582,545
	Domestic sales[b]	512,932	563,130	617,597	722,912	746,067	740,341	645,597	30,859	80,929	104,681
	Exports[b]	254,555	282,511	349,580	392,959	472,813	551,274	565,235	56,121	61,516	77,628
Kia	Gross sales	27,448	32,823	41,129	47,308	56,885	66,071	63,815	45,107	79,306	108,060
	Profit	158	150	187	−696	115	70	−3,829	−2,798	3,307	1,357
	Investment	4,663	4,865	6,264	5,419	4,369	3,768	3,790	n.a.	n.a.	n.a.
	R&D	314	202	318	425	620	852	70	n.a.	2,434	6,958
	Employment	22,103	23,549	26,139	28,948	29,525	29,619	18,098	17,652	29,937	29,857
	Production	425,296	502,227	599,904	619,875	631,644	703,116	613,920	439,485	782,483	905,004
	Domestic sales	350,190	396,333	441,855	412,294	441,532	458,400	354,016	n.a.	37,340	60,496
	Exports	80,020	103,023	158,419	210,469	200,477	252,244	281,501	n.a.	41,966	47,564
Daewoo	Gross sales	15,956	17,067	21,594	27,859	34,700	43,543	57,977	51,191	61,248	57,852
	Profit	−1,467	−956	−847	−91	105	229	2,512	176	−46,402	n.a.
	Investment	n.a.	n.a.	n.a.	n.a.	n.a.	n.a.	n.a.	n.a.	n.a.	n.a.
	R&D	186	252	316	435	612	n.a.	n.a.	1,552	n.a.	n.a.
	Employment	17,383	16,041	13,675	15,113	15,928	17,194	17,500	18,599	18,059	17,235
	Production	203,792	179,020	300,094	340,707	454,353	447,581	607,559	606,261	758,583	624,534
	Domestic sales	151,394	141,539	206,020	249,444	198,917	179,452	293,592	183,286	257,609	242,123
	Exports	52,253	54,653	102,133	99,774	247,510	298,236	333,004	422,975	468,911	383,693

Note: (a) Units: 100 million won; (b) Including CV.

Source: Hyundai Motor Company (2002); Hyundai, Annual Report, various years; Kia, Annual Report, various years; Daewoo, Annual Report, various years.

Notes

1 KIA Economic Research Institute (1998), p. 44; and KAMA, February 2002.
2 Until the late 1980s, the Korean automobile industry benefited from a well-educated and disciplined workforce, which co-operated closely with management and accepted low wages. See Chung (1998).
3 This 'Asian Car' strategy, especially orientated towards emerging markets may expect a major new stage in the Hyundai globalization process. Hyundai will be producing a total of 500,000 units from its auto plants in South East Asia by 2005. See the *Korea Herald*, 22 January 1997.
4 Hyundai imported this model for domestic sale in second quarter of 1999.
5 KAMA, February 2002.
6 Daewoo will develop the Asian Car in the India transplant based on their subcompact car.
7 Under a contract with Wilhelm Karmann GmbH, the firm embarked on production in Germany in early 1995 for 30,000 units of Sportage on an OEM basis. It will be conducive to increasing Kia's exports to Europe. To this end, it established a subsidiary named Kia Motors Europe GmbH. In 1995, exports to Western Europe grew by 32.8%, from 24,615 units to 32,681.
8 Kia scheduled to ship to Iran 320,000 units of its compact passenger model 'Pride', worth US$2 billion, in components for local assembly until 2000; *Korea Economic Weekly*, 13 April 1998.
9 KAMA, February 2002.
10 *Korea Economic Weekly*, 6 July 1998.
11 The *Dong-A Ilbo*, 3 April 1998.
12 Kia Motors became bankrupt and the Korean exchange market collapsed in late 1997. In fact, Kia Motors bankruptcy was rooted in Kia Group's excessive investment in its steel and construction industries rather than the automotive industry.
13 Hyundai's overseas production capacity expanded by around 700,000 units after the acquisition of Kia.
14 *Korea Herald*, 8 May 2000.
15 *Korea Herald*, 27 June 2000.

References

Chung, M.-K. (1993) *Transformation of the Subcontracting System in the Automobile Industry: A Case Study in Korea*; Boston: MIT, International Motor Vehicle Program.

Chung, M.-K. (1994a) 'Transforming the Subcontracting System and Changes of Industrial Organization in the Korean Automobile Industry', in M. Boyer and M. Freyssenet (eds), *From Firms' Trajectories to Industrial Models*, Proceedings of Second GERPISA International Colloquium, Paris.

Chung, M.-K. (1994b) 'Production System in the Korean Automobile Industry', *Korean Economic Studies*, vol. 3.

Chung, M.-K. (1996) 'Internationalization Strategies of Korean Motor Vehicle Industries', *Actes du GERPISA*, no. 18.

Chung, M.-K. (1998a) 'Globalization Strategies of Korean Motor Vehicle Industries: A Case Study of Hyundai', *Actes du GERPISA*, no. 22.

Chung, M.-K. (1998b) 'Hyundai Tries Two Industrial Models to Penetrate Global Markets', in M. Freyssenet, A. Mair, K. Shimizu and G. Volpato (eds), *One Best Way?*

Trajectories and Industrial Models of the World's Automobile Producers, Oxford/New York: Oxford University Press.

Chung, M.-K. (2001) 'The Expanding Buyer–Supplier Partnership for Product and Process Technology Development in the Korean Automobile Industry', *International Journal of Automotive Technology and Management*, no. 2/3.

Cohen, S. and Boyd, G. (2000) *Corporate Governance and Globalization: Long Range Planning Issues*, Edward Elgar.

Daewoo Motor Co. (various years) *Annual Report* (in Korean), Seoul.

Hiraoka, L. S. (2001) *Global Alliances in the Motor Vehicle Industry*, Quorum Books.

Humphrey, J., Lecler, Y. and Salerno, M. (eds) (2000) *Global Strategies and Local Realities: The Auto Industry in Emerging Markets*, London: Macmillan.

Hyundai Motor Co. (1992) *The History of Hyundai* (in Korean), Seoul.

Hyundai Motor Co. (1994) *Hyundai Internal Report* (in Korean), Seoul.

Hyundai Motor Co. (1997) *Hyundai Internal Reports* (in Korean), Seoul.

Hyundai Motor Co. (1998) *The Direction of the Korean Auto Industry* (in Korean), Seoul.

Hyundai Motor Co. (2002) *Korean Automobile Industry* (in Korean), Seoul.

Hyundai Motor Co. (various years) *Annual Report* (in Korean), Seoul.

Hyundai Motors Workers Union (1994) *Report of Activities* (in Korean), Ulsan.

Hyundai Motors Workers Union (1997) *Report of Activities* (in Korean), Ulsan.

KAMA (Korea Automobile Manufacturers Association) (various years) *The Korean Automobile Industry* (in Korean), Seoul.

KAMA (Korea Automobile Manufacturers Association) (various years) *Monthly Automobile Statistics* (in Korean), Seoul.

Kia Motor Co. (various years) *Annual Report* (in Korean), Seoul.

Kia Research Institute (1994) *The Korean Automobile Industry* (in Korean), Seoul.

Kia Research Institute (1998) *The Korean Automobile Industry* (in Korean), Seoul.

Korea Auto Industries Co-operation Association (1997) *Overseas Investments of Korean Component Industries* (in Korean), Seoul.

Korean Institute for Industrial Economics and Trade (1994) *Development Tendencies towards the Twenty-first Century of the Korean Automobile Industry* (in Korean), Seoul.

Lee, Y.-H. (1994) *Fordism and Post-Fordism: Hyundai, Toyota, Volvo* (in Korean), Seoul.

Michie, J. and Grieve Smith, J. (1998) *Globalization, Growth, and Governance: Creating an Innovative Economy*, Oxford: Oxford University Press.

Yang, X. (1995) *Globalization of the Automobile Industry: The United States, Japan, and the People's Republic of China*, Praeger.

Newspapers

Chosun Ilbo, 27 March 1998.

Dong-A Ilbo, 18 March 1998 and 3 April 1998.

Korea Economic Weekly, 13 April 1998; 22 June 1998 and 6 July 1998.

Korea Herald, 22 January 1977; 2 April 1998; 8 May 2000 and 27 June 2000.

9
Conclusion: Regionalization of the American and Asian Automobile Industry, More Than Globalization

Michel Freyssenet, Koichi Shimizu and Giuseppe Volpato

The automobile sector is often presented as the archetypal global industry. In this view, the auto business is one of the main drivers behind the homogenization of the world, both because of firms' internationalization strategies (mergers/acquisitions, the establishment of facilities in emerging countries, world cars, international division of labour and so on) and as a result of the social practices such firms enact via their organization of work and at the lifestyle (automobile civilization) level.

This chapter is an attempt to deconstruct a representation that neglects, as we have seen in the previous chapters of this book, the heterogeneity of firms and spaces; the great diversity of the strategies being pursued; and the inherent contradictions of the competitive process. We shall use and test the analytical approach of productive and geographical trajectories of the automobile industry firms that we have expanded from the first and second international programmes of GERPISA (Boyer and Freyssenet, 2000b, 2002; Freyssenet and Lung, 2000).[1]

Growth modes, profit strategies and productive models

An analysis of automakers' trajectories and performances over the course of the twentieth century has allowed us to renew our understanding of the two essential conditions that are a prerequisite for profitability. The first is the relevancy of the 'profit strategy' to the 'growth mode' that typifies the countries in which the firm is deploying its activities. The second is the 'company government compromise' that exists between a firm's principal protagonists, a meeting of the minds that enables players to implement means that are coherent with the profit strategy being pursued – in other words, to invent or adopt a 'productive model' (Freyssenet *et al.*, 1998; Boyer and Freyssenet, 2000b, 2002).

Profit strategies are combinations of profit sources in compatible proportions. Basically, there are six sources of profit: economies of scale, diverse offerings, quality, innovation, productive flexibility, and permanent cost reduction. Until now, there have been no examples of firms exploiting all these profit sources simultaneously and with the same level of intensity. This is because of the contradictory nature of the sources' preconditions and means of implementation. For this reason, firms must choose from among possible combinations of profit sources, unless they can invent ways of overcoming contradictions, as General Motors (GM) was able to do during the inter-war period, when it created compatibility between volume and diversity. At the time of writing five different profit strategies can be observed in the automobile sector. These are 'volume', 'volume and diversity', 'quality', 'permanent cost reduction', and 'innovation and flexibility'.

Profit strategies do not all possess the same degree of relevancy in time and space. Their appropriateness depends on the market and labour factor structures that characterize the different national modes of growth. These growth modes are not infinite in number, and several countries may at any point in time be applying a similar mode (Boyer and Saillard, 1995, 2001). These are divided into three main categories: growth modes with a national income distribution that is 'nationally co-ordinated and moderately hierarchized'; those with a 'competitive' type of distribution; and those with an 'inegalitarian' type of distribution. These categories are sub-divided subsequently according to the main driver of the growth: investment, consumption or export. The success of an internationalization policy is therefore predicated first and foremost on the relevancy of the firm's profit strategy to the growth mode(s) of the new countries it is entering (Boyer and Freyssenet, 1999; Freyssenet and Lung, 2000).

Profit strategies cannot be implemented with just any available means. Each has certain requirements that the firm's players must satisfy through a product policy, productive organization and employment relationship that are coherent and acceptable to them. The creation of an acceptable type of coherency between these various means infers the building of a 'company government compromise' between the firm's main players (executives, shareholders, banks, employees, labour unions, suppliers and so on). The means used to implement one and the same profit strategy can therefore differ from one company to another if this is needed to satisfy the requirements mentioned above. As such, the firm's protagonists do possess some room for manoeuvre during the development of their own compromise. In the case of an internationalized company, it is possible to have a variety of compromises, depending on the host country. Nevertheless, the firm's subsidiaries must each be in control and in charge of their own production systems and markets. This is not the case when they are part of one and the same regional or global industrial complex, and deliver their output to markets that change depending on the current economic situation.

The liberalization of international capital movements and the deregulation of the labour market

The two main changes at the turning point of the 1990s were the liberalization of international capital movements and the deregulation of the labour market in some countries.

The liberalization of the movement of capital was one of the key elements of American economic growth during the 1990s, and was the origin of the destabilization of the previously best performing countries (Japan, Germany and Sweden) and of the sudden temporary increase among the so-called emerging countries. This American economic growth enabled American automakers to become profitable once again. The destabilizing of the countries characterized by a 'co-ordinated and export-orientated' growth mode (Japan, Germany and Sweden) made their automobile firms less competitive, and the sudden increase from the emerging countries created the hope of a new development in the world car market. The free movement of capital also engendered two speculative bubbles: the first concerning precisely the emerging countries, and the second the so-called 'new economy', mainly in the USA. The bursting of the bubbles of the emerging countries in 1997, and of the new economy in 2000, stopped world growth and revealed weaknesses in some Korean, Japanese and European automakers. This situation caused a new wave of mergers and alliances in the car industry.

With the deregulation of the labour market, the second main change mentioned above, national income distribution became more 'competitive'. But this type of distribution was not developed to the same degree and the same extent in all the countries of the Triad. 'Competitive' distribution of income, through the economic and social disparities it engendered also gave birth to a second automobile market for pickup trucks, minivans, recreational vehicles and other conceptually innovative means of transport. This second market has become just as large as the market for saloon cars in the USA.

It is against this background that the rearrangement began of a world space that had been split into several facets: the generalization of trade liberalization; the constitution of regional areas; and the affirmation or reaffirmation of nations, whether 'emerging' or not.

None of the scenarios of global space reshaping will be exclusive of the others, except through an accident of history. In order to avoid economic and political instability, generalized free trade pre-supposes world-wide rules and means to make them respected. However, it could be thought that these rules would require many years of operation before being considered part of a sufficient and satisfactory agreement for all parties. Nor are there sufficient countries powerful enough to impose them on others in the foreseeable future.

This is why the countries who already maintain major trade exchanges seek (directly or by default) to make up free trade zones, the rules of which are less difficult to work out and the immediate benefits easier to spread on a limited territorial scale. In this case, either a satellitization of emerging countries by powerful industrialized countries will be seen, as is already the case in NAFTA, or accords between emerging countries who dispense with some of their autonomy, as the Mercosur countries are attempting to do. These free trade zones will either be steps to world-wide free trade, or if the latter is revealed to be utopian or impossible, towards the formation of regional economic and political poles. The scenario of a multi-polar world made up of countries grouped together according to regions whose economic growth would once again be self-centred and regulated would also only be partially possible in the best of cases. The formation of such political and economic poles is a long and winding path with many potholes, as the experience of European Union (EU) construction has shown. In the medium term, one or two of these poles are possible.

Ultimately the trends discussed above will not alter the fact that independent nations survive and expand either because they make up regions by themselves, or continents through the size of their population and natural resources; or because of their very independence they fill the role in the international economic system that other countries do not wish to see disappear.

Under these conditions, what are the chances for different profit strategies possible for automobile firms?

A utopian globalization at the core of the volume strategy

The 'volume' strategy emphasizes a single source of profit: economies of scale (that is, mass production for as long as possible in constantly growing markets, with a reduced number of models that are specific to each major market segment). It can only be durably relevant under two conditions: the market must be in an extension mode (either because it is in an initial equipment phase or because it is homogenizing) and comprised of two or three homogenous segments; the labour factor must be copious and capable of being mobilized for repetitive production.

These conditions presuppose a growth mode that is consumption-based as well as a type of income distribution that is either nationally co-ordinated and highly egalitarian or else clearly stratified into two or three stable and numerically equivalent sections. As one can see, these conditions are very restrictive. No growth mode that has ever been seen in a capitalist economy has ever satisfied them durably. For these reasons, up to now the volume strategy has only been profitable during relatively short-lived initial automobile equipment phases – that is, before the demand has diversified. This was the case for Henry Ford with the Model T during the the 1910s, and for Volkswagen with the Beetle.

The policy of world cars, one per major market sector, each having its own platform, would regain pertinence in a world where the parties are converging towards similar forms of competition and a similar mode of income redistribution. This being improbable, as can be seen above, does it necessarily mean that it is totally unthinkable? It can be viable under two conditions. The first is sufficient freedom of exchange between main countries so that customs duties and exchange rate variations do not prevent world-wide concentration and specialization of production sites, an essential element of a strategy for economies of scale. The second is that a fraction of the customers on the main markets looks for low price cars and accepts an average quality.

From the mid-1980s, Ford tried once again to implement a 'volume' strategy with its world cars policy, but this was not successful. The Korean automakers' highly ambitious internationalization drives of the early 1990s also aimed at this strategy. This involved one or two entry-level vehicles targeting both emerging and industrialized countries (in the latter, the cars were marketed to low-income households as bottom-of-range models) – two markets where a low price could offset comparatively low quality. Korean prices for new cars are often equivalent to the price of a top-quality second-hand car. This low price is obtained by using a strategy that is primarily volume-orientated, and thus geared towards expansion into new markets (see Chung, ch. 8 in this volume). The sudden rise in the Korean automobile firms' production capacities during the 1990s also helped to bring about their decline – no independent Korean automakers have survived now that Renault has taken over Samsung, DaimlerChrysler Hyundai and GM Daewoo.

The 'volume and diversity' strategy: a global commonalization of platforms and a regional differentiation of models, under certain conditions

Six automobile firms – three European (Freyssenet *et al.*, 2003), two American and one Japanese (GM, Ford and Nissan) – are pursuing the profit strategy we called 'volume and diversity'. Internationalization and commonalization are the two indispensable conditions for the volume and diversity strategy, when the market increases slightly. But internationalization can concern only the countries where commonalization is commercially acceptable. The current change in the structure of several markets limits this acceptability.

Characteristics, conditions and requirements

This strategy combines two sources of profit that would at first glance appear to be contradictory – volume and diversity. What GM invented during the inter-war period was a way of overcoming this contradiction by designing different marques of car model on the basis of a single platform (at that time, the chassis), and by setting up a productive organization and employment relationship that made it possible to manage ostensible diversity (body, internal fittings and equipment) in an economic manner. During the 1940s, GM succeeded in defining a productive model, the Sloanian model, that became for many managers the 'one best way' until the 1970s. The volume and diversity strategy thus precludes specific models as well as models that are conceptually innovative, and that are not compatible with many parts being commonalized with models from the traditional product range.

This requires a growing and moderately hierarchized market as well as a copious, polyvalent and promotable workforce. In fact, if potential clienteles are to accept this superficial differentiation and deep-seated commonalization, there cannot be any excessive economic and social differentiation between the various social categories, and social and professional mobility must have attained a certain level. Growth modes featuring a national income distribution that is 'nationally co-ordinated and moderately hierarchized' are the ones that best fulfil such conditions, so a volume and diversity strategy was the most pervasive (albeit not the only) strategy during the post-war boom years. It ran into difficulties when the market entered a product renewal phase in the countries where firms were pursuing this strategy. Indispensable economies of scale could no longer be obtained because of an extension of the market.

However, they could be achieved by penetrating those markets that found themselves in an initial equipment phase, or through mergers and alliances with other firms. Still, certain preconditions had to be fulfilled for this to occur. Internationalization, for example, had to involve moving into countries that possessed the same types of growth mode, and designing local models that shared identical platforms to those that could be found in the country of origin. The 'volume and diversity' strategy would thus be fully pertinent in the framework of a world where automobile owners would globally have basically common expectations and would only differentiate regionally on secondary aspects. Mergers and alliances had to quickly lead to a commonalization of the relevant marques' platforms. Automakers who had developed a volume and diversity strategy during the post-war boom years, found it difficult to make this change (Freyssenet *et al.*, 1998).

Volkswagen was the only automaker to succeed in finding a profitable way to implement durably the 'volume and diversity' strategy after 1974, and to implement the Sloanian model under these new conditions, GM, Ford and Nissan failed to do it, as did Fiat in Europe. In the 1990s, they tried, without success, to commonalize their platforms at a global level and to differentiate them at a regional level.

Ford: an unsuccessful transregionalization

From the mid-1980s onwards, Ford pursued a strategy based on the concept of centres of excellence, delegating and dividing the responsibility for the renewal of its models and main mechanical systems between three poles, according to the set of competencies each had acquired: Ford North America for large-cylinder vehicles (V6 and V8 engines), automatic transmissions and electronic components; Ford Europe for small and medium-sized vehicles, for four-cylinder engines, and for manual transmissions. Mazda, in which Ford has a 25% stake, and with which the company had started up a production of small sub-compact cars for the North American market (with the Escort being renovated to approximate the 323). In addition, the Japanese partner was central to Ford's Asia-Pacific activities, where most of the cars being sold under Ford's blue badge were in fact superficially changed Mazdas: the 121, the 323 and the 626 (see Bordenave and Lung, ch. 3 in this volume).

The structuring of Ford's space had been based directly on K. Ohmae's Triad concept. In the Southern Hemisphere countries (markets that had not as yet 'emerged'), Ford arranged local collaborations, most particularly with VW in the Autolatina joint venture that grouped the American and German companies' activities in Argentina and Brazil. Again, the idea was to benefit from projected regional integration (Mercosur) by rationalizing all of the two automakers' activities.

These initiatives were subsequently altered or abandoned en route. The Ford 2000 project, first announced in 1993, was an attempt to overcome Ford's regional structures (Ford Europe in Europe and NAAO in North America) through a global integration of activities. It is true that the initial results of the global platforms concept that had been developed as an extension of the poles of responsibility strategy have been unsatisfactory, certainly in relation to the small-car market. The Escort (Lynx in North America), developed on the Mazda 323's platform, has not achieved the results that had been hoped for; and Europe has assumed responsibility for the development of the platform of the Focus that replaced the Escort on both sides of the Atlantic. In the lower mid-range, the first transatlantic (global) platform to be designed in Europe has given birth to the Mondeo, and to its equivalent(s) in North America (the Contour/Mystique) – where it has not been as successful as expected. Finally, the upscale model that was supposed to be developed in North America to replace the Scorpio, or at least its design, has turned out to be stillborn. The Ford Scorpio will not be replaced by a top-of-the-range Ford Europe product: instead, a Lincoln, a Volvo or a top-of-the-range US Ford model will occupy this segment. In addition, Ford has not obtained the success it was hoping for in producing/ assembling its small European model, the Fiesta, in Brazil or in India. In South America, Autolatina's dissolution has meant that where hybrid Ford–Volkswagen models had previously been involved, each of the partners will now be refocusing on its own core product ranges. However, the two automakers have been unable to benefit from the opportunities that have been created by the Brazilian market's take-off, itself a result of the advent of the popular car. In India, Ford's products have also been too expensive, and the American automaker has eventually developed a model that is more basic, and targets the emerging markets specifically. As for Mazda, Ford has effectively taken control by raising its stake to 33.3% – however, the Japanese firm's recovery is taking place without any input from Ford, and it can even be said that the two companies are in the process of breaking off relations: witness the abandonment of the Ford US products that had been developed on a Japanese platform (the Pride/121, the Escort/323, and the Probe/626); the 121, supposedly derived from the European Ford Fiesta, and so on. The very idea of having Mazda run Ford's presence in Asia-Pacific has now been put in doubt. The role of a Japanese partner in Ford's global strategy, twenty-five years after the agreement was first signed, has still not been established clearly.

All in all, the outcome of Ford's internationalization strategy, as implemented over the 1990s, has been far from brilliant. Market share in Europe has slumped; Mazda has continued to decline in Japan and across the world; and its market-leader position has been lost in both the Australian and Brazilian markets. Far from generating additional profits, Ford's international activities have damaged the Group's profitability (see Jetin, ch. 2 and Bordenave and Lung, ch. 3, both in this volume).

Ford's record earnings are essentially due to two explanatory factors: the Group's financial activities, and its light truck sales in its domestic market (Froud *et al.*, 2000). In an environment such as the one that it is now facing, Ford's executives have had to take strong actions, recreating Ford Europe, and cutting costs dramatically. The race to globalize has been a failure, and regionalization is again becoming the core of the American firm's policy.

GM: a partial attempt to make world-wide platforms and regional models

This strategy presupposes, under the condition of similar automobile use, an income redistribution mode organized along a moderately hierarchical level in each of the areas, so that the limited differentiation between models will be accepted by buyers, and on the other hand that real income gaps between concerned countries will also be moderated. It would hence be necessary that the formation of regional poles according to growth and regulated redistribution modes prevails, and that these poles evolve economically and socially in a parallel manner. Yet, both between poles as well as within them, the difference in income is rising and cultural differences becoming deeper. Is it possible to invent a new form of commonization that would allow them to get over this difficulty? As observed at GM, the world-wide reorganization implied in this strategy provokes internal tension: regional subsidiaries, who designed and manufactured their range before that point refused to lose control of their product policy.

A certain cross-flow began to take place between the two sides of the Atlantic, and the newer platforms (first launched in 1996) have finally reached maturity. This should allow the group to devise specific models for its three market categories: North America, Europe and the emerging countries. The design of a platform to build a medium-sized car (the Epsilon) appears to have achieved the results that had been hoped for; a dozen or so models are going to be developed from this base. It should, however, be noted that at some point along the way, GM has abandoned its Delta global small car project platform, the group having decided to fall back on less ambitious local solutions (Bordenave and Lung, ch. 3 in this volume).

The increased number and intensity of GM's alliances has also created new problems. The American manufacturer's greater stake in Japanese automakers such as Suzuki, Fuji Heavy Industries and Subaru have provided it with access to South East Asia (in an approach reminiscent of Ford's with Mazda). In addition, this will help GM to broaden its portfolio of models (adding small city cars, for example), especially in the emerging markets. Cross-shareholdings between GM and Fiat should lead to a rationalization of Fiat's and Opel's activities in Europe, with mechanical systems (mostly engines), purchasing, and even platforms being shared in an effort to devise a range of specific models for the group's various marques. In the United States, GM is used to creating a range of models for its different marques (Buick, Cadillac, Oldsmobile and so on), and a question must be raised as to the reasons for this policy's lack of success in Europe. In any event, these alliances cast doubt over the role of GM's German subsidiary, Opel, which finds itself in direct competition with its Japanese cousins (where it had been market leader); and is now a rival of its Italian cousin (Fiat) in the European market (Volpato, 2000).

The Nissan failure

Since the 1970s, Nissan has tried to develop a volume and diversity strategy. But through historic management particularities, competition with Toyota and early international policy, Nissan has produced a very diverse classical model range, with mechanical perfection and reliability, but also with a rather bland style and, in particular, few shared parts. It privileged the costly path of flexible automation, and generalized and sophisticated computerization (unlike its competitor, Toyota), instead of truly involving its workers in these tasks (Hanada, 1998). These two orientations are grounded in the long-lasting power wielded by methods and concept engineers working at Nissan, and in social difficulties that have never really been solved. The ground that Nissan was progressively losing to Toyota and Honda in Japan was thus largely compensated by exports, until the time that their competitive advantage no longer sufficed, or disappeared (see Jetin, ch. 2, fig. 2.10 in this volume). The straw that broke the camel's back came with the prolonged recession in Japan and heavy debts of the group's banks (see Kumon, ch. 6 in this volume).

Explicitly, the alliance with Renault aims at commonalizing the platforms of the two firms. Apart from it being difficult to do that, this product policy appears to be contradictory to the 'innovation and flexibility' orientation of Renault (Freyssenet, 2002).

The dilemma for the 'volume and diversity' firms

The introduction of 'competitive' modalities of national income distribution has generated a second market. GM, Ford and Nissan, as the European automakers pursuing a similar 'volume and diversity' strategy (Fiat, PSA and Volkswagen), unsurprisingly copied the conceptually innovative models that Chrysler, Renault and Honda launched once they felt secure that these models would be a durable success. This copying has even allowed GM and Ford to become profitable again, in an environment of economic recovery.

But the 'volume and diversity' automakers are still faced with a dilemma. The models they have copied have become mundane, and will no longer offer the same kinds of profit margins in the future. Moreover, such models do not create economies of scale that are significant enough to compensate for the fact that their profit margins are lower than is usual with a novelty product – a consequence of firms' difficulty in commonalizing their platforms with the platforms of traditionally hierarchized cars.

Is it now the turn of the 'volume and diversity' automakers to take up the gauntlet of conceptual innovation, to benefit for a time from the considerable rent it offers? Some of these manufacturers seem to be interested in this possibility, and have been allocating the task to one of their marques. It remains that, since the birth of the automobile industry, no one has ever succeeded in carrying out two different profit strategies at the same time for a significant period of time. The requirements are far too contradictory.

We should still envisage the possibility that the current coexistence between the 'competitive and decentralized' distribution of income that tends to dominate in the private sector, and the 'co-ordinated and moderately hierarchized' distribution that is mainly preserved in the state sector, might last. Are automakers now facing the challenge of having to create compatibility between sources of profit that would on the surface appear to be incompatible (that is, 'volume and diversity' versus 'innovation and flexibility')? Has the time come for a major new strategic invention? Is it possible that modular vehicle design will enable economies of scale while allowing for the design of new vehicle types involving varying combinations of basic modules? The other path is to develop again a general 'co-ordinated and moderatly hierarchized' income distribution at regional level and to adopt consumption as the source of growth.

The 'quality' profit strategy: national-based production and globalized distribution

For a long time, one of the important characteristics of the European car industry was the presence of independent makers of top-of-the-range and luxury automobiles, known as 'specialist' manufacturers compared to 'generalist' manufacturers who target a wider market. Their profit strategy was the 'quality' strategy. They were located only in the country of origin and exported large numbers of cars. Since the end of 1990s, many of them, paradoxically, decided to be integrated into large automobile groups, in particular American, when the international market for top-of-the-range vehicles increased dramatically.

Characteristics, conditions and requirements

Here the word 'quality' means not only reliability and finish, but also and above all the social distinctiveness that the product's style, utilization of certain materials, emphasis on finishing and marque-related prestige offers in the opinion of a privileged clientele that looks for such factors, and which is in a position to pay for them. This strategy induces those firms that have adopted it to specialize in top-of-the-range automobiles, or in recent times in the upper part of each market segment. Earnings stem basically from the profit margins that the product and up-market customers allow – the high price also acting as a means of distinction and social tiering, above and beyond any material justification.

A quality strategy is the one that features the greatest relevancy in time and space. There are very few societies in which a small, wealthy section of the population is not ready to pay a high price to possess those products that can symbolize their economic and social position. For this reason, the top-of-the-range market has from the very outset been international in nature, and the specialist automakers the most commercially internationalized over a long period (Freyssenet *et al.*, 2002).

Futhermore, a 'quality' strategy infers the availability of a workforce that is for the most part highly skilled (and is reputed as such). Certain aspects of quality can, in fact, only be obtained by using the services of traditional professional workers (or inversely, of technicians and even engineers who are graduates of the top universities) to manufacture parts in small series on highly sophisticated machinery. The reputation of a top-of-the-range brand is often related to the renown of its country of origin, or of the region in which it is established, when this is famed for the personnel's seriousness and professionalism. In general, a 'quality' strategy is enhanced when the workforce is forced to maintain the national output's international specialization, notably so as to be able to continue benefiting from the high salary levels, social protection systems and stable employment perspectives that are supported by the production of unrivalled specialized products.

For these reasons, regarding the market or labour, the 'co-ordinated and specialized export-orientated' growth mode (Germany and Sweden) is the one that affords the greatest visibility to the 'quality' strategy.

In growth modes that feature a co-ordinated and moderately hierarchized national income distribution, the wealthy clientele is not totally cut off from other types of customers. So the specialist automakers have found it difficult since the Second World War to put together a 'productive model' that is durable – meaning one that can continually find the right balance between large series production methods and others that emphasize the product's 'hand finishing' and customized qualities (Ellegard, 1995; Freyssenet, 1998).

Competitive distribution modes do not stand in the way of this strategy. They allow many actors to seek their fortune, yet at the same time are less stable. They rely on the availability of workers who can be skilled but less attached to their firm. In the modes that feature a highly unequal type of distribution, wealthy clients are basically the only customers for new vehicles, and they are very devoted to the marque's international renown and to demonstrations of their own wealth.

A sea change in the international top-of-the-range market since the 1990s

With income distribution having become more 'competitive', the top-of-the-range segment tended to become more heterogeneous. Demand for the most luxurious saloon cars (which had become marginal products) rose again. Above all, demand from this section of society arose for small and medium-sized cars, and for recreational vehicles.

These developments have presented the 'specialist' manufacturers with a new situation. On the one hand, if they are to cover the new luxury sub-segments they must make substantial increases in their design-related spending, productive capacities and distribution network. And on the other, they must fight off ambitious 'generalists' who also want to benefit from the new situation. To cope, they have adopted a variety of different paths. Now their trajectories are diverging completely (Freyssenet *et al.*, 2002).

Some of them – Saab, Aston Martin, Jaguar, Volvo and Land Rover – ultimately opted to be integrated into an American automobile group pursuing a volume and diversity strategy: GM for the first, and Ford for the four last brands. By so doing, they hope to avail themselves of the resources they need. For these prestigious marques, which automobile groups are ready to spend considerable amounts of money on, the market remains a global one. In fact, it is precisely because of this homogeneity of the market, and of the brands' image, that firms feel they can justify the investments they have been making (the goodwill they have been paying). GM's global platform, with its code name Epsilon, should help with its development of one Saab model, two Opels, and several American models (ranging from Chevrolet to Saturn) that are entering the market. This development started in 2001. However, the logic of this 'volume and diversity' strategy that GM has been pursuing carries a risk that these luxury vehicles will lose their essential 'quality' – that is, their specificity (Bordenave and Lung, ch. 3 in this volume). Ford grouped, in a separate entity entitled Premier Automotive, all the marques involved in its corporate 'quality' strategy: Lincoln, Aston Martin, Jaguar, Volvo and Land Rover. The objectives are the rationalized purchasing of components; shared R&D investment (that is, Volvo's safety competency) and the 'commonalization' of a certain number of electronic or mechanical components, and even the sharing of platforms. Although the commonalization seems to be limited to top-range vehicles, the risk is not so different from the risk taken by GM. The consumers of top-range vehicles require very specific models, including, and even may be above all, platforms.

Industrial history is full of paradoxes. The paradox we are focusing on at present is that the main 'specialist' automakers have either been losing their independence or thinking they must change their strategy at the very moment that the international market for top-of-the-range products is most likely to launch them on to a new phase of expansion. But history is not finished yet. Some brands may become independent again.

The permanent cost reduction strategy and the Toyotian model: very restrictive conditions to succeed

Characteristics, conditions and requirements

In this strategy, costs are to be cut in all circumstances and at all times. To a certain extent, the other profit sources are no more than a complement, and even then only when they are feasible, useful and compatible. Cost reduction will always remain the prime objective when a firm envisages any situation, as no outcome is ever taken for granted. Strategy consists of lowering return costs by constant savings drives, both internally and by the suppliers. It requires that production is planned strictly, and that risks are avoided such as running into debt, or producing conceptually innovative products, entering volatile markets, mergers or acquisitions, productive internationalization and so on.

It is particularly well-suited when national growth is driven by the export of day-to-day products, and when the redistribution of competitiveness gains is done in a co-ordinated and moderately hierarchized manner. Employees are subject to external competitiveness constraints, and the volume and structure of national demand is sufficiently predictable to avoid any unforeseen and costly variations in production.

For the same reasons, this strategy, which Toyota has been pursuing since the 1950s, is not as robust as it would appear. This is because it is so demanding. The strategy struggles when sudden changes occur (related, for example, to shfits in demand levels or currency parities) – changes that can in one fell swoop destroy the patient and continual efforts required of employees and suppliers, who might then be inclined to curtail their participation in the cost-reduction drive, as was the case at Toyota in the early 1990s (Fujimoto, 1999; Shimizu, 1999).

Toyota, a unique company that invented a productive model to implement a permanent cost-reduction strategy

The Toyotian model is characterized first by the offer of well-equipped basic products in each market segment – products made without unnecessary novel features, to avoid costly diversity and/or the risks inherent in any innovation. In addition, and as far as possible, these products are turned out in increasing quantities (Lung *et al.*, 1999). A just-in-time productive organization reveals any problems that might prevent a continuous and regular work flow, since this would be a source of waste. The employment relationship and the sub-contractor network induce employees and suppliers to contribute to the cost-cutting effort, the former by a wage system in which pay is predicated on the realization of the targets that are set in this area, and the latter by a choice that revolves around their commitment to the application of the same production methods as the manufacturer itself. The company governance compromise in the Toyotian model focuses on the firm's longevity, job guarantees for employees and profit-sharing with sub-contractors.

The Toyotian company governance compromise can only survive under two conditions: employees must continue to accept a reduction in their standard times and an improvement in their performance while carrying out a parcellized type of work under severe time constraints (and working a great deal of overtime); and suppliers and sub-contractors must continue to lower their prices. The requirements of the strategy and the difficulty in building a productive model to satisfy them are so daunting that Toyota has always been extremely prudent in its internationalization efforts (Boyer *et al.*, 1998).

The constraint productive internationalization of Toyota

Toyota first faced the difficulty of reproducing its model in the United States when it was obliged to establish facilities in that country (an obligation imposed by the government on all Japanese automakers during the 1980s to enable them to continue to increase their sales in the American market). Toyota finally consented after a long period of hesitation, and after having taken a number of precautions (Shimizu, 1999). Its first step was to develop a joint venture with GM, called NUMMI, which took over a plant that GM had been preparing to shut down. Toyota used this experience to test whether it would be possible to come to an agreement with the UAW automobile workers' labour union. The UAW, which turned out to be more co-operative than Toyota had expected, accepted its work time and wastage reduction principles in exchange for the firm's commitment to avoid dismissals, maintain an equitable wage structure, and discuss its production plans, schedules and workforce allocations with the union. Nevertheless, Toyota was unable to transplant its wage, career development and scheduling systems to the USA. It also had to trim its assembly lines, in the sense that it had to introduce buffer stocks to loosen the constraints caused by just-in-time production. This system, born at NUMMI and copied in Toyota's other US transplants, did not feature the self-regulated and cumulative dynamics of the Toyotian model (Boyer *et al.*, 1998). Toyota was also very cautious in its product policy. It produced only two models in the compact car segment: the Corolla and the Camry.

The labour and market changes of the 1990s and the limits of the Toyotian model

It was back in Japan that the Toyotian model ran into the limits of its social acceptability. The company governance compromise that had spawned the model crumbled in the late 1980s. This took on the form of a work crisis in 1990, before the bursting of the 'speculative bubble' (Shimizu, 1998). Toyota's management team was forced to change its wage and promotion systems, eliminate overtime at the end of an eight-hour workday, and reintroduce buffer stocks along its manufacturing and assembly lines. Toyota could no longer rely on its operators to reduce their own standard times, and this task would henceforth be delegated to specialized teams. Average monthly wages would be slightly modulated to reflect the realization of materials and tools savings targets that the work teams would themselves devise. The two day shifts were to work one right after the other, making it impossible to extend the workday by overtime. Annual working hours dropped. Assembly lines were split into segments, separated by buffer stocks, to return a modicum of autonomy to the work teams (Shimizu, 1995, 1998, 1999; Fujimoto, 1999).

The structural changes in the automobile markets are also a big challenge for Toyota. The executives saw clearly that the traditional type of demand (hierarchized, stable and broken down into four major contiguous segments) was losing ground in all the Triad countries to a type of demand that was more heterogeneous and volatile in nature. They understood that this trend would create problems for the group's cautious and traditional product policy. Unsurprisingly, Toyota began to copy those conceptually innovative models that were most likely to be commercially durable. It launched with success a number of recreational vehicles and large pickups. In 1999, 40% of its sales in the United States were in the light truck market. But the executives know that copying is probably not enough. The rising demand for innovative products forces Toyota to take risks that are in contrast to its strategy. In the late 1990s, it launched the first hybrid motor vehicle, the Prius, as well as a vehicle that was specifically targeted at young urban residents. The question is, will it be able to assume the risks that are inherent in this type of innovation, without taking anything away from its previously satisfied priority a permanent reduction in costs? Honda's example demonstrates the extent to which an 'innovation and flexibility' strategy requires a specific utilization of a firm's financial, material and human resources. The challenge that it seems to want to meet is to create compatibility between cost-cutting and innovation, just as GM once overcame the contradiction between volume and diversity.

In Europe, Toyota encountered both labour and market difficulties. As in the United States in the 1980s, Japanese automakers were obliged to establish plants in Europe in the 1990s. Toyota chose Britain. But ever since the beginning, its English subsidiary did not succeed in being profitable because of insufficiently attractive products, labour instability and big exchange rate variation. With the opening of a new assembly plant in France in 2001 and the creation of a joint venture with PSA in the Czech Republic from 2005, Toyota is trying to offer products more adapted to, and to have the advantage of monetary stability in, the euro zone.

For the moment, Toyota maintains the same growth policy. Although it had the financial means and the opportunity, it did not try to buy or control any other automaker during the 1990s, as did Daimler, Ford, GM and Renault. It prefers internal growth with the help of a progressive internationalization in which a regional configuration (in Europe, North America and South East Asia) is articulated together with a locally adapted product range, even as it spills over into other regional markets. This organizes a division of labour at both intra- and inter-regional levels without weakening the central pole's authority.

Innovation and flexibility strategy: a necessary specific regional policy

Automakers who arrive late in the automobile sector and are trying to carve out a space for themselves among firms with already established market positions often choose to pursue an 'innovation and flexibility' strategy. This was the case of Honda in the 1960s. The relevance of the 'innovation and flexibility' strategy has been reinforced by certain countries' recent tendency to develop a 'competitive' distribution of national income.

Characteristics, conditions and requirements

This strategy consists of designing products that respond to new expectations and/or emerging demands; manufacturing them massively and immediately if actual orders match forecasts; or, conversely, abandoning them rapidly and for as low a cost as possible if they fail commercially. Profits stem from an innovation rent derived from commercial relevancy – as long as the innovation is not copied. The best way of delaying this outcome is to be able to satisfy the market segment that has been created in as a short a period of time as possible.

An innovation and flexibility strategy is reinforced when the needs or lifestyles of the social categories that are being targeted change periodically, or when new categories emerge, with people who are distinct at an economic and social level. This is generally what occurs in those growth modes that are marked by a 'competitive' type of national income distribution. It is the reason why this strategy, which became the bane of many automakers during the post-war boom years, has again become a winner, as witnessed by the good performances of Honda, Chrysler (before its merger with Daimler) and Renault (Boyer and Freyssenet, 2000b, 2002).

The firms pursuing this strategy must be financially independent. They must be entirely free to assume the risks that are inherent in conceptual innovation. They must also be free of any medium-/long-term commitment to their suppliers so as to be able to change production rapidly if need be. They must have at their disposal an easily convertible production tool and a workforce that enables innovativeness at both product and production process levels. Last, they must also possess an extremely in-depth knowledge of which customer expectations are unsatisfied and unexpressed, to be able to offer innovative vehicles that are commercially appropriate.

For this strategy to succeed, the regionalization and heterogenization of demand would have to prevail over globalization and homogenization. This hypothesis may suit the producers that remain concentrated on a single region, taking advantage of their detailed knowledge of their markets, just as producers who internationalize ensure that they have the means to understand consumer expectations in the regions in which they invest. In these cases, regional design offices do more than simply restyle base models – they modify them in response to local desires, and they may even design specific models. Regional subsidiaries have a broad autonomy because they have to detect emerging local requirements. To do so, they rely heavily on local managers, designers, engineers and distributors. The function of the company at the global level is to take responsibility for financial control, distribution of investments (particularly to new regions), and to ensure that knowledge drawn from experience is circulated.

The Hondian model

The Hondian model, mixed together inaccurately with the Toyotian model in the lean production concept, has best fulfilled the demands of an innovation and flexibility strategy. Honda was able to make great strides during the post-war boom years, despite the fact that this era was hardly favourable to a strategy of this nature. From the outset, Honda looked to the international marketplace for types of clientele that would be interested by what it was offering. It set up an internal system to detect and foster innovative personalities, and a design organization that gave them a chance to express themselves. Its production system, which had a very low level of automation, can quickly be converted, thanks primarily to a workforce whose responsiveness is enhanced by the firm's wage and career development systems. Honda has always refused to be a member of a *keiretsu* and to tie its own development to government policy, whatever that might be. The Hondian model is based on a company government compromise that stresses individual promotion, expertise and the quality of work life in exchange for the responsiveness and inventiveness from which arise the firm's performance (Mair, 1994; Freyssenet and Mair, 2000).

Honda: the regionalization of design and production

Honda's late entry into the passenger car market translates its attempt to base its growth on a significant North American presence (Shimokawa, ch. 7 in this volume). As the first Japanese automaker to have built an assembly plant in the United States, at the time of writing Honda owns a very well-balanced productive apparatus (a styling centre, product and process design activities, mechanical systems factories and assembly plants serving its production requirements, and a distribution network). In the mid-1990s, regional divisions were set up and allocated the task of co-ordinating all these activities in North America, Europe and Asia. These divisions were required to act in such a way as to support the local production of models that had been designed specifically for a regional market, but which shared platforms and other systems with models from other regions. This was a clearly affirmed regionalization initiative, and was translated by the famous neologism 'globalization', coined by Honda's chairman, along with another rather successful slogan: 'Think Globally, Act Locally'.

The productive model invented by Honda helped the company to cope with the various difficulties it faced in the early 1990s: tensions in the labour market, and the failure of several of its models. Although Honda, like the other Japanese automakers, was lacking in manpower during the late 1980s (as a result of the explosion in domestic demand that was one outcome of the speculative bubble), unlike in the case of Toyota, no doubts were raised about its production system. In part, this was certainly because of its better working and employment conditions; and to a mobility that was based primarily on employees' personal competency.

Honda's most severe difficulties were related to the failure of several of its models. The company had believed that the rapid enrichment of certain sections of the population (one result of the speculative bubble) would orientate demand durably towards sporty and/or luxury cars, and it therefore built up the number of models it offered in these categories. For as long as the speculative bubble lasted in the Triad countries, this appeared to be the right choice. In 1990, Honda's world-wide output was twice what it had been in 1979, reaching 1.94 million units. The company had become the world's eighth largest automaker, moving ahead of Chrysler and Renault. Half of its cars were sold in North America, 35% in Japan, 9% in Europe and 6% in the rest of the world. Half a million Hondas were being manufactured overseas.

However, once the speculative bubble burst and recession erupted in Japan, Honda's product policies were brutally invalidated. Realizing the errors it had made regarding qualitative changes in demand, Honda reacted without delay. While preparing to launch its own models, it began to market Land Rovers in Japan, as well as a restyled off-road Isuzu vehicle.[2] The successful launch of a recreational vehicle (the CR-V) in 1996, and of a minivan in 1997, contributed strongly to the resurgence in its sales. Its domestic output went back up to 1.31 million units in 1999, close to its historical peak of 1990 – despite the fact that its domestic market was still stagnating. That same year, Honda's global output reached 2.33 million vehicles.

Until now, Honda has kept well away from any acquisitions or mergers. To further its development, it would have to be able to pursue its strategy in each of the world's regions, meaning that it would have to design, with these regions in mind, models that satisfy the expectations of their new population sections. It might decide to do this on its own, or by arranging an alliance with a manufacturer that has shown itself capable of doing this; that is, who is already pursuing the same strategy. Honda has chosen to follow the first path, one with which it has already been successful in North America.

The regional future of the innovation and flexibility strategy

The most competitive redistribution of income in many countries today can favour the emergence of new strata or the modification of demand in existing categories. It must, however, not lead to social instability through excess competition, preventing truly new expectations from forming. The 'innovation and flexibility' strategy thus implies very fine attention to qualitative changes in different markets, but also markets vast enough so that new demand represents sufficient volume. The scenario of the making up of regional poles adopting a competitive mode of income redistribution is favourable to this profit strategy, as it offers both innovative demand and necessary volume. In this hypothesis, an automobile builder implementing the 'innovation and flexibility' strategy would not necessarily need to spread itself out on a world-wide basis and be perfectly profitable on a regional scale. This could be the case for Honda, Chrysler and Renault, each being the 'innovation and flexibility' firm in its own region of the world. A global firm pursuing this strategy is nevertheless conceivable. But it would be necessary for it to be able to design and produce innovative vehicles adapted to the new social strata that appear in the different spaces, as Honda was able to do in the USA in the 1970s and 1980s, and not be content to try to sell innovative models elsewhere that were designed in its home zone.

Conclusion

Although a logic of production (economies of scale) has induced automobile manufacturers to extend their area of commercialization on a global scale, it is in their articulation with a market, their synchronization with a demand, that they have incorporated the regional tier as a level at which they can achieve a certain coherence. Apart from the prestige automobiles, there are limits to the homogenization of global demand, and the failure of Ford's attempt to integrate its activities globally shows that automobile firms should be looking for more appropriate strategies – and, above all, for models or innovative forms of organization that are better adapted to a particular regional space. It is not at all certain that the real challenge is to be the first to globalize: mono-regional strategies (such as the one that PSA has pursued), biregional, multiregional, and even transregional, strategies can all be relevant at a certain time, and in a given area.

Notes

1 This chapter draws on the findings of the GERPISA's first and second research programmes (Boyer and Freyssenet, 2000b, 2002; Freyssenet and Lung, 2000), both of

which were co-directed by Michel Freyssenet, working together with Robert Boyer and Yannick Lung, respectively. The authors have benefited greatly from the discussions that have taken place within the GERPISA international network, but accept full responsibility for any errors that may have persisted in the present text.
2 Honda has been linked industrially and financially with Rover since its establishment in Britain. The surprise sale of Rover by British Aerospace to BMW in 1994 closed the possibility of developing four-wheel-drive vehicles.

References

Bordenave, G. (1998) 'Le premier demi-siècle de Ford en Europe: la résistance opiniâtre d'un espace à l'universalisme proclamé d'un modèle d'organization productive', *Le mouvement social*, no. 185.

Bordenave, G. (2000) 'La globalisation au coeur du changement organisationnel: crise et redressement de Ford Motor Company', in M. Freyssenet, A. Mair, K. Shimizu and G. Volpato (eds), *Quel modèle productif? Trajectoires et modèles industriels des constructeurs automobiles mondiaux*, Paris: La Découverte.

Bordenave, G. and Lung, Y. (2002) 'Concurrence oligopolistique et mimétisme des stratégies d'internationalisation dans l'industrie automobile: Ford et General Motors', in H. Bonin *et al.* (eds), *Transnational Companies*, Paris: PLAGE.

Bélis-Bergouignan, M. C., Bordenave, G. and Lung, Y. (2000) 'Global Strategies in the Automobile Industry', *Regional Studies*, vol. 34, no. 1.

Boyer, R. (1999) 'La politique à l'ère de la mondialisation et de la finance: le point sur quelques recherches régulationnistes', *L'année de la régulation*, vol. 3.

Boyer, R. and Freyssenet, M. (1999) 'L'avenir est à nouveau ouvert. Stratégies de profit, formes d'internationalisation et nouveaux espaces de l'industrie automobile', *Gérer et Comprendre, Annales des Mines*, June.

Boyer, R. and Freyssenet, M. (2000a) 'Fusions–acquisitions et stratégies de profit: une nouvelle approche', *Revue française de gestion*, no. 131, November–December.

Boyer, R. and Freyssenet, M. (2000b, 2002) *Les modèles productifs*, Paris: La Découverte, 2000; English revised edition: *The Productive Models: The Conditions of Profitability*, London/New York: Palgrave, 2002.

Boyer, R. and Freyssenet, M. (forthcoming), *The World that Changed the Machine*.

Boyer, R. and Saillard, Y. (eds) (1995, 2001) *Théorie de la régulation. Etats des savoirs*, Paris: La Découverte 1995; English edition: *Regulation Theory: The State of Art*, London: Routledge, 2001.

Boyer, R., Charron, E., Jürgens, U. and Tolliday, S. (eds) (1998) *Between Imitation and Innovation: The Transfer and Hybridization of Productive Models in the International Automobile Industry*, Oxford/New York: Oxford University Press.

Carrillo, J. and Hinojosa, R. (forthcoming) 'An Uncertain Trajectory in Regional Integration: The Future of Motor Vehicle Production in the NAFTA', in J. Carrillo, Y. Lung and R. van Tulder (eds), *Cars, Carriers of Regionalism*.

Carrillo, J., Lung, Y. and van Tulder, R. (eds) (forthcoming) *Cars, Carriers of Regionalism*.

Chanaron, J. J. and Lung, Y. (1995) *Economie de l'automobile*, Paris: La Découverte.

Ellegard, K. (1995) 'The Creation of a New Production System at the Volvo Automobile Assembly Plant in Uddevalla, Sweden', in A. Sandberg (ed.), *Enriching Production*, Aldershot: Avebury.

Freyssenet, M. (1998a) 'Reflective Production: An Alternative to Mass-production and to Lean Production?', *Economic and Industrial Democracy*, vol. 19, no. 1, February.

Freyssenet, M. (1998b) 'Intersecting Trajectoires and Model Change', in M. Freyssenet, A. Mair, K. Shimizu and G. Volpato (eds), *One Best Way? The Trajectories and Industrial Models of World Automobile Producers*, Oxford/New York: Oxford University Press.

Freyssenet, M. (2002) 'Renault: Globalization but for What Purpose?', in M. Freyssenet, K. Shimizu and G. Volpato (eds), *Globalization or Regionalization of the European Car Industry?*, London/New York: Palgrave.

Freyssenet, M. and Lung, Y. (2000) 'Between Regionalization and Globalization: What Future for the Automobile Industry?', in J. Humphrey, Y. Lecler and M. S. Salerno (eds), *Global Strategies and Local Realities: The Auto Industry in Emerging Markets*, London: Macmillan.

Freyssenet, M. and Mair, A. (2000) 'Le modèle industriel inventé par Honda', in M. Freyssenet, A. Mair, K. Shimizu and G. Volpato (eds), *Quel modèle productif? Trajectoires et modèles industriels des constructeurs automobiles mondiaux*, Paris: La Découverte.

Freyssenet, M., Mair, A., Shimizu, K. and Volpato, G. (eds) (1998) *One Best Way? The Trajectories and Industrial Models of World Automobile Producers*, Oxford/New York: Oxford University Press.

Freyssenet, M., Shimizu, K. and Volpato, G. (eds) (2003) *Globalization or Regionalization of the European Car Industry?*, London/New York: Palgrave.

Froud, J., Haslam, C., Johal, S. and Williams, K. (2000) 'Ford's New Policy: A Business Analysis of Financialisation', in M. Freyssenet and Y. Lung (eds), *The World that Changed the Machine: The Future of the Auto Industry for the 21st Century*, Proceedings of the Eighth GERPISA International Colloquium, Paris, June 8–10.

Fujimoto, T. (1999) *The Evolution of a Manufacturing System at Toyota*, Oxford/New York: Oxford University Press.

Guiheux, G. and Lecler, Y. (2000) 'Japanese Car Manufacturers and Component Makers in the ASEAN Region: A Case of Expatriation under Duress – or a Strategy of Regionally Integrated Production?', in J. Humphrey, Y. Lecler and M. S. Salerno (eds), *Global Strategies and Local Realities: The Auto Industry in Emerging Markets*, London: Macmillan.

Hanada, M. (1998) 'Restructuring to Regain Competitiveness', in M. Freyssenet, A. Mair, K. Shimizu and G. Volpato (eds), *One Best Way? The Trajectories and Industrial Models of World Automobile Producers*, Oxford/New York: Oxford University Press.

Humphrey, J., Lecler, Y. and Salerno, M. S. (eds), *Global Strategies and Local Realities: The Auto Industry in Emerging Markets*, London: Macmillan/New York: St. Martin's Press.

Jetin, B. (1999) 'The Historical Evolution of Supply Variety: An International Comparative Study', in Y. Lung, J. J. Chanaron, T. Fujimoto and D. Raff (eds), *Coping With Variety: Flexible Productive Systems for Product Variety in the Auto Industry*, Aldershot: Ashgate.

Lung, Y. (2000) 'Is the Rise of Emerging Countries as Automobile Producers an Irreversible Phenomenon?', in J. Humphrey, Y. Lecler and M. S. Salerno (eds), *Global Strategies and Local Realities: The Auto Industry in Emerging Markets*, London: Macmillan/New York: St. Martin's Press.

Lung, Y. (2001) 'The Coordination of Competencies and Knowledge: A Critical Issue for Regional Automotive Systems', *International Journal of Automotive Technology Management*, vol 1, no. 1.

Lung, Y., Chanaron J. J., Fujimoto, T. and Raff, D. (eds) (1999) *Coping with Variety: Flexible Productive Systems for Product Variety in the Auto Industry*, Aldershot: Ashgate.

Mair, A. (1994) *Honda's Global Local Corporation*, London: Macmillan.

Norberto, E. and Uri, D. (2000) 'La révolution des petites cylindrées Le marché nouveau des "voitures populaires" au Brésil', *Actes du GERPISA*, no. 29.

Shimizu, K. (1995) 'Humanization of the Production System and Work at Toyota', in Å. Sandberg (ed.), *Enriching Production*, London: Avebury.

Shimizu, K. (1998) 'A new Toyotaism?', in M. Freyssenet, A. Mair, K. Shimizu and G. Volpato (eds), *One Best Way? Trajectories and Industrial Models of the World's Automobile Producers*, Oxford/New York: Oxford University Press.

Shimizu, K. (1999) *Le Toyotisme*, Paris: La Découverte.

Volpato, G. (2000) 'La filière automobile italienne: vers la globalisation?', in F. Bost and G. Dupuy, *L'automobile et son monde*, Paris: Editions de l'Aube.

Womack, J. P., Jones, D. T. and Roos, D. (1990) *The Machine That Changed The World*, New York: Rawson Associates.

Appendix: The GERPISA International Network

The GERPISA (the Permanent Group for the Study of and Research into the Automobile Industry and its Employees) started out as a network of French economics, management, history and sociology researchers who were interested in the automobile industry. Founded by Michel Freyssenet (CNRS sociologist) and Patrick Fridenson (EHESS historian), it was transformed into an international network in 1992 in order to carry out a research programme called 'Emergence of new industrial models'.

With Robert Boyer (CEPREMAP, CNRS, EHESS economist) and Michel Freyssenet supervising its scientific orientations and under the management of an international committee, the programme (which lasted from 1993 to 1996) made it possible, thanks to its study of the automobile firms' (and their transplants') trajectories, productive organization and employment relationships, to demonstrate that lean production, which according to the authors of *The Machine that Changed the World* was to become the industrial model of the twenty-first century, was in fact an inaccurate amalgamation of two completely different productive models, the 'Toyotian' and the 'Hondian'. Moreover, it showed that there are, have always been, and probably always will be, several productive models that are capable of performing well at any one time. Shareholders, executives and employees are not only not obliged to adopt a *one best way*, they also have to devise a 'company governance compromise' covering the means that will allow them to implement one of the several profit strategies that are relevant to the economic and social environment in which they find themselves.

A second programme (running from 1997 to 1999) entitled 'The automobile industry, between globalization and regionalization', supervised by Michel Freyssenet and Yannick Lung (Bordeaux IV, economist), tested the analytical framework that had been developed during the first programme in an attempt to understand better the new wave of automobile manufacturer and component maker internationalization that had been observed over the previous decade. The outcome was that the viability of the choices being made depends primarily on the chosen profit strategies' compatibility with the growth modes in the areas in which investments are being made.

The third programme (2000–2) has been developed under Yannick Lung's supervision with the support of the European Union (COCKEAS project, thematic network, 5th Framework, Key Action 4: HPSE–CT–1999–00022). It focuses on the issues at stake in the 'Co-ordination of knowledge and competencies in the regional automotive systems'. Supplementing existing studies of forms of regionalization in the automobile industry, the programme analyses the sector's new contours as well as the development of new relational and co-operative modes among its actors.

In 2002, the GERPISA comprised 350 members from twenty-seven different countries. Affiliated with the Centre de Recherches Historiques (CRH) of the Ecole des Hautes Etudes en Sciences Sociales (EHESS), and acknowledged as a host structure by the French Ministry of National Education, its administrative offices are located in the Université d'Evry. It receives additional financial and material support from the French car companies, from their professional association (the CCFA), and from the European Union.

The international management committee comprises twenty-four members: Annie Beretti (Innovation Department, PSA); Robert Boyer (CNRS-EHESS, Paris); Juan José

Castillo (Universidad Complutense, Madrid); Jorge Carrillo (Colegio de la Frontera Norte, Mexico); Jean-Jacques Chanaron (CNRS, Lyon); Elsie Charron (CNRS, Paris); Jean-Pierre Durand (Université d'Evry); Michel Freyssenet (CNRS, Paris); Patrick Fridenson (EHESS, Paris); Takahiro Fujimoto (University of Tokyo); John Humphrey (University of Sussex); Bruno Jetin (Université Paris XIII); Ulrich Jürgens (WZB, Berlin); Yveline Lecler (MRASH/IAO, Lyon); Yannick Lung (Université de Bordeaux IV); Jean-Claude Monnet (Research Department, Renault); Mario Sergio Salerno (University of São Paolo); Koichi Shimizu (University of Okayama); Koichi Shimokawa (Hosei University, Tokyo); Paul Stewart (University of Bristol); Steve Tolliday (University of Leeds); Rob van Tulder (Erasmus University, Rotterdam); Giuseppe Volpato (Ca'Foscari University, Venice); and Karel Williams (Victoria University, Manchester).

GERPISA's publications

GERPISA edits in English and French a quarterly review entitled *Actes du GERPISA*, and a monthly newsletter called *La Lettre du GERPISA*. The review combines the writings that the network's members have presented on specific topics in various work meetings. The newsletter comments on news from the automotive world and provides up-to-date information on what is happening in the network. Findings from the first and second programmes have been published in a series of books:

Programme 'Emergence of new industrial models'

Boyer, R. and Freyssenet, M. (2002) *The Productive Models*, London/New York: Palgrave, 2002. First edition in French: *Les modèles productifs*, Paris: La Découverte, 2000.

Boyer, R. and Freyssenet, M. (forthcoming) *The World that Changed the Machine*.

Boyer, R., Charron, E., Jürgens, U. and Tolliday, S. (eds) (19918) *Between Imitation and Innovation. The Transfer and Hybridization of Productive Models in the International Automobile Industry*, Oxford/New York: Oxford University Press.

Durand, J. P., Stewart, P. and Castillo, J. J. (eds) (1999) *Teamwork in the Automobile Industry. Radical Change or Passing Fashion?*, London: Macmillan. First edition in French: *L'avenir du travail à la chaîne*. Paris: La Découverte, 1998.

Freyssenet, M., Mair, A., Shimizu, K. and Volpato, G. (eds) (1998) *One Best Way? Trajectories and Industrial Models of the World's Automobile Producers*, Oxford/New York: Oxford University Press. French translation: *Quel modèle productif? Trajectoires et modèles industriels des constructeurs automobiles mondiaux*, Paris: La Découverte, 2000.

Lung, Y., Chanaron, J. J., Fujimoto, T. and Raff, D. (eds) (1999) *Coping with Variety: Flexible Productive Systems for Product Variety in the Auto Industry*, Aldershot: Ashgate.

Shimizu, K. (1999) *Le Toyotisme*, Paris: La Découverte.

Programme 'The automobile industry between globalization and regionalization'

Carillo, J., Lung, Y. and van Tulder, R. (eds) (forthcoming). *Cars, Carriers of Regionalism.*

Charron, E. and Stewart, P. (eds) (2003) *Work and Employment Relations in the Automobile Industry*, London/New York: Palgrave.

Freyssenet, M., Shimizu, K. and Volpato, G. (eds) (2003) *Globalization or Regionalization of the American and Asian Car industry?*, London/New York: Palgrave.

Freyssenet, M., Shimizu, K. and Volpato, G. (eds) (2003) *Globalization or Regionalization of the European Car Industry?*, London/New York: Palgrave.

Humphrey, J., Lecler, Y. and Salerno, M. (eds) (2000) *Global Strategies and Local Realities: The Auto Industry in Emerging Markets*, London: Macmillan/New York: St. Martin's Press.

Programme 'Co-ordination of knowledge and competencies in the regional automotive systems'

Lung, Y. (ed) (2002) 'The Changing Geography of the Automobile Industry, Symposium', *International Journal of Urban and Regional Research*, no. 4.

Lung, Y. and Volpato, G. (eds) (2002) 'Reconfiguring the Auto Industry', *International Journal of Automotive Technology and Management*, vol. 2, no. 1.

Williams, K. (ed) (2002) 'The Tyranny of Finance? New Agendas for Auto Research', *Competition and Change*, vol. 6, double issue, no. 1/2.

Information on GERPISA's activities can be obtained by contacting GERPISA réseau international. Université d'Evry-Val d'Essonne.
rue du Facteur Cheval, 91025 Evry cedex, France.
Telephone: 33 (1) 69 47 78.95 – Fax 33 (1) 69.47.78.99
E-mail: contact@gerpisa.univ-evry.fr
Website: http//www.gerpisa.univ-evry.fr

Index